Contents

Section One — Language Frameworks — The Basics

Language Frameworks 2
Introduction to Grammar 4
Nouns and Adjectives 6
Verbs and Adverbs 8
Pronouns and Determiners 10
Prepositions and Conjunctions 11
Phrases and Clauses 12
Sentences 14
Morphology 16

Section Two — Language Frameworks — Meaning

Lexis 18
Semantics 20
Phonology 24
Non-verbal Communication 26
Cohesion 28
Pragmatics 30
Graphology 32
Register and Mode 34

Section Three — Varieties of English

Accent and Dialect 36
Standard English and RP 38
Sociolect and Idiolect 40
Slang 42
Sources and Exam Questions 44

Section Four — Language in Social Contexts

Language and Gender 46
Language and Power 50
Language and Technology 54
Language and the Media 56
Adverts 58
Language and Occupational Groups 60
Sources and Exam Questions 64

Section Five — Analysing Spoken Language

Spoken Language 68
Speech Features 70
Conversation and Turn-taking 72
Sources and Exam Questions 74

Section Six — Analysing Written Language

Purpose 76
Audience 78
Genre 80
Literary Texts 82
Ideology and Representation 84
Sources and Exam Questions 86

Section Seven — Language Development

Early Language Development 88
Phonological and Pragmatic Development 90
Lexis, Grammar and Semantics 92
More Grammar Acquisition 94
Theories of Language Development 96
Reading and Writing 98
Language for Children 100
Sources and Exam Questions 102

Section Eight — Do Well in the Exam

General Exam Advice 104
Commentaries 105
AQA A Exam 106
AQA A Coursework 107
AQA B Exam 108
AQA B Coursework 109
Edexcel Exam 110
Edexcel Coursework 111
OCR Exam 112
OCR Coursework 113
WJEC Exam 114
WJEC Coursework 115

Answers to Exam Questions 116

Glossary 121

Index 124

Language Frameworks

Section 1 is for you, whether you're studying AQA A, AQA B, Edexcel, OCR or WJEC — oh yes, all are welcome here.
On the next two pages are the essential tools you need for describing and analysing spoken or written language.

You should aim to **Analyse** all **Texts** in a **Similar** way

If you have to analyse a piece of language or discourse, there are several things to think about:

1) **Genre** — **what kind** of language it is. Written discourses could be **instruction booklets** or **adverts**, and spoken discourses could be **formal speeches** to an audience or **casual conversations** between friends.

2) **Register** — a type of language that's appropriate for a particular audience or situation, e.g. the language of a political party or the language of the justice system. Register also includes the level of **formality** in a discourse.

3) **Audience** — the **listener** or **reader**. When you're analysing language, think about how the audience is **addressed**. It might be **formal** or **informal**, **direct** or **indirect**. For example, in advertising the audience is often directly addressed as *you*.

4) **Subject** — what the discourse is **about**. This will be reflected in the **lexical choices**, e.g. a discussion about healthy eating may contain words like *low-fat*, *diet*, and *nutrition*.

5) **Purpose** — what the speaker or writer is trying to **achieve** through language (e.g. to persuade, instruct, etc.).

6) **Mode** — whether the language is **written or spoken**. You can also get **mixed modes** — e.g. in text messages, where the language is written, but contains many of the informal features of spoken language.

There are **Seven Main Language Frameworks**

This table is an **overview** of what makes up each language framework (also called **linguistic frameworks**, or **toolkits**, and how they can be used). There are more detailed explanations of each one throughout the rest of the book.

Lexis	• **Lexis** means the **vocabulary** of a language — the total stock of words. • When you're analysing spoken and written language you'll notice words that share a **similar topic** or **focus**. For example, in an advert for mobile phones you'd find words such as *SMS*, *text-messaging*, and *battery life*. Words that are linked together in this way are known as a **lexical field**.
Semantics	• **Semantics** is the study of how **meaning** is created through words and phrases. Sometimes this meaning is **explicit**, but sometimes it's **implicit**. A word will have a **literal** meaning but it can also be **associated** with other meanings. • For example, the word *red* refers to a **colour**, but it can also be associated with **danger**.
Grammar	• **Grammar** is the system of **rules** that governs how words and sentences are **constructed**. There are three parts to this: 1) A system that **groups** words into classes according to their **function** (e.g. nouns or verbs). 2) A system of **rules** about how these types of words function in relation to each other (**syntax**). 3) The individual units that make up whole words (**morphology**).
Phonology	• **Phonology** is the study of **sounds** in English — how they're **produced** and how they're **combined** to make words. • This framework includes **Non-Verbal Aspects of Speech** (NVAS) or **prosody** — features of spoken language such as pace, stress, rhythm and intonation.
Pragmatics	• **Pragmatics** is sometimes called **language in use**. It's about how social conventions, context, personality and relationships influence the **choices** people make about their language. • For example, how you address other people shows **levels of formality** and **social conventions** — a student might address a teacher as *Miss Rogers* or *Lizzie* depending on what the college or school expects, and what the teacher finds acceptable.
Graphology	• **Graphology** is the study of the **appearance** of the writing and the effect this has on a text. • When you discuss a text's graphology you describe and analyse features like the **typeface**, the **positioning** of text on a page and the relationships between **text** and **images**.
Discourse	• **Discourse** is an **extended** piece of spoken or written language, made up of more than one **utterance** (in spoken language), or more than one **sentence** (in written language).

Language Frameworks

Discourse has a **Structure**

The way language is organised is called its **discourse structure**. You need to look out for different features, depending on whether the discourse is written or spoken.

1) In **written discourse**, look at how a text is **put together**. It may have an **opening** section which leads the reader into the text. The following sections may develop a **theme or argument**. The final section may make some kind of **conclusion**.

2) In **spoken discourse** the structure can be less organised. For example, **conversations** are often **unpredictable** and speakers often **digress** (go off the subject). This is because conversations are usually **spontaneous**.

3) Even spontaneous conversation has some structure, though.

There'll often be an **opening sequence**, e.g.

> Speaker 1: *Hi, how you doing?*
> Speaker 2: *Fine thanks. How about you?*

This is often followed by **turn-taking** as the speakers talk about a topic (or topics). There's often a **closing sequence** too, e.g.

> Speaker 1: *Well, nice seeing you...*
> Speaker 2: *You too.*
> Speaker 1: *Catch you later.*

4) You can also look at how the discourse **fits together** — **cohesion**. There are **two types** of cohesion — **lexical** and **grammatical**. One example of grammatical cohesion is using **adverbs** like *furthermore* and *similarly* at the beginning of a sentence or paragraph to link it to the previous one. Lexical cohesion is when the words in the discourse **relate** to each other throughout, e.g.

> *There was no sign of **the car** — **her lift** was obviously stuck in **traffic**. Was it really worth it, just for a **ride** in a **Porsche**?*

There are **Three Main Steps** to discourse analysis

1) The **first step** in **discourse analysis** is to think about **what kind** of discourse you are looking at. To do this you need to think about genre, register, audience, subject, purpose and mode.

2) The **next step** is to look at how each of the **language frameworks** contribute to the discourse. You might not need to use all of the language frameworks, or you might need to give more emphasis to one than another. It depends on the discourse.

3) And finally, don't forget to discuss **discourse structure** (how the text has been organised) and **cohesion** (the devices used to knit the text together).

Keith tried to look busy but his approach had been spotted.

Practice Questions

Q1 Give two examples of written discourse.
Q2 What is the difference between lexis and semantics?
Q3 What is phonology the study of?
Q4 Define discourse.
Q5 What is grammatical cohesion?

Discourse is brilliant — way better than those Science and Maths ones...

Soooo... your first two pages of AS English Language. They weren't so bad, were they? Didn't think so — but they are vital for your exam. It's really important to get into the habit of applying these frameworks to texts that you have to analyse. Think of them as guidelines that are there to help you organise your work. Aww, see? That's nice.

Introduction to Grammar

Grammar is one of the most important language frameworks — it covers everything from bits of words to entire sentences.

Grammar controls how Language is Constructed

1) Grammar is the set of **structural rules** that controls the way language works.
2) There are **three aspects** of grammar that you need to focus on — word classes, syntax and morphology.
3) **Word classes** define the **roles** that each word can play in a sentence. **Syntax** is the set of **rules** that control where each word class can appear in a sentence. **Morphology** describes the **construction** of individual words.

There are Eight Main Word Classes

Words are **categorised** by the **function** they have in a sentence.
There are eight main **word classes** — also called **parts of speech**.

Word Class	Function	Example
Nouns	'naming' words	*London, book, romance*
Adjectives	describe nouns (and sometimes pronouns)	*large, sunny, featureless*
Verbs	'doing' words	*jump, read, return*
Adverbs	describe verbs (and sometimes adjectives and other adverbs too)	*steadily, incredibly, sadly*
Pronouns	take the place of nouns	*you, they, him, me, it*
Conjunctions	'connecting' words	*and, or, but, because*
Prepositions	define relationships between words in terms of time, space and direction	*before, underneath, through*
Determiners	give specific kinds of information about a noun (e.g. quantity or possession)	*a, the, two, his, few, those*

Word classes are Controlled by Rules

Word classes can take **different positions** in a sentence, but there are **grammatical rules** about how they work with each other (**syntax**). In the following sentence you can see all the word classes working together:

She	*saw*	*the*	*new*	*manager*	*and*	*his*	*assistant*
pronoun	**verb**	**determiner**	**adjective**	**noun**	**conjunction**	**determiner**	**noun**

at	*the*	*store*	*yesterday.*
preposition	**determiner**	**noun**	**adverb**

1) People **instinctively** know the rules for connecting words together. For example, you know that words in this order — *doctor she the yesterday saw* — are wrong, and you can **rearrange** them into something that makes sense straight away — *she saw the doctor yesterday.*
2) You also intuitively know **less obvious rules** about word order — you'd always say *the big brown bear* rather than *the brown big bear*, because you know that adjectives of size **come before** those of colour.
3) Sometimes there are **fewer restrictions** — some sentences mean the same thing wherever a word is placed, particularly with **adverbs**, e.g. *I completely disagree* or *I disagree completely.*
4) Sometimes the **meaning** of a sentence changes depending on the position of a word:
   He quickly told me to leave (he said it fast)   **or**   *He told me to leave quickly* (he wanted me to leave fast)

Grammatical rules Affect Word Formation

Grammar affects word formation (morphology) because extra bits have to be added to words to **change** things like number or tense. The extra bits are called **inflections**. Here are a couple of examples.

- *-s* is added to *cup* to change a **singular** noun into a **plural** — *cups* (p.6).
- *-ed* is added to *remember* to change the **present** tense verb into the **past** tense *remembered* (p.8).

Introduction to Grammar

Grammar choices can **Influence** the reader or listener

You can influence your **audience** in different ways by **changing** the **grammar** of a word or sentence.

Tense

1) Events that happened in the past are usually described in the past tense. Sometimes however, in both spoken and written discourse, past events are described using **present tense forms**.

- So she **went** up to the customer and **gave** him a good telling off. ⟵ past tense
- So she **goes** up to the customer and **gives** him a good telling off. ⟵ present tense

2) The first example sentence is in the past tense. There is a clear sense that some **time has passed** since the event actually happened. In the second, although the action happened in the past, the present tense creates a more **immediate** and **dramatic** impact. You'll see this technique used a lot in **newspaper headlines**:

> New evidence casts doubt on verdict

> Pop star admits to private hell

> Cop raid closes nightclub

Plurals

1) As well as telling you that there's more than one of something, plurals can **increase** the scale of a **scene**.

- There was a **mass** of fans outside the hotel. ⟵ singular
- There were **masses** of fans outside the hotel. ⟵ plural

2) Using the singular form *mass* creates the impression of a **specific** body of people. Adding the **-es inflection** to form the plural *masses* creates the image of a **big crowd** of people across a **wider area**.

Adjectives

1) Adjectives are a great way to **influence** your **audience** — compare the following two examples:

- If you're looking for the holiday of a lifetime, simply treat yourself to a **great** resort in Sri Lanka. Relax in **fine** accommodation. ⟵ simple adjectives
- Looking for the holiday of a lifetime? Simply treat yourself to the **greatest** resort in Sri Lanka. Relax in the **finest** accommodation. ⟵ superlative adjectives

2) These are similar **advertising discourses**, but the second example is much more **persuasive** than the first. The writer uses **superlative** adjectives (see p.7) (*greatest* and *finest*) rather than the simple adjectives in the first example (*great* and *fine*).

3) There are some **other grammatical features** that influence the reader in these examples.

- The second example begins with a **question**. This makes the reader feel **involved immediately**.
- The first example uses the **indefinite article** *a* before the adjective *great*, but the second uses the **definite article** *the* before *greatest* (see p. 10). This makes the reference very **specific** in the second example (it is **the** greatest resort), but the first could be referring to any one of **several** resorts.

Practice Questions

Q1 In the following sentence, identify each word according to word class:
> It was a cold winter and the Russian soldiers suffered terribly.

Q2 Define the term syntax.

Q3 Why does this sentence sound awkward?
> My blue old raincoat is now in tatters.

What rule about word order can you deduce from this?

If you don't take precautions, you could get a nasty inflection...

I know — grammar's got a reputation for being a bit stale and boring. But if you don't understand the way language works and how everything is put together, and how important this is in discourse, then you can wave your analysis bye-bye. Luckily for you, we're about to get into a bit more detail, so get ready to become a world-class word-classer...

Nouns and Adjectives

Nouns are often called naming words, but at AS, it's all a bit more complicated than that. Nouns do give the names of places, people and things — but they can also refer to groups, states, emotions, and more.

Nouns can be **Divided** into **Categories**

There are different **types** of nouns. They can refer to unique **people** or **places** (**proper nouns**), or identify more general **objects**, **states** or **groups** (**common nouns**). See below for some examples.

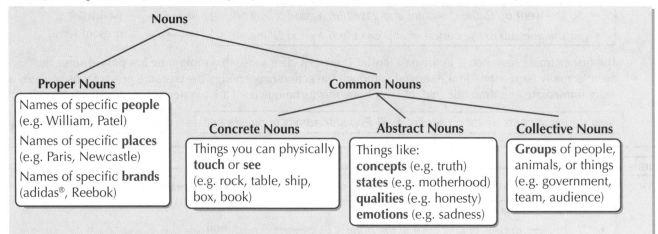

Nouns can be either **Singular** or **Plural**

1) To form the **plural** of a noun you usually add an -s or -es so that you get, for example, *birds,* or *bus**es***.

2) Where a noun ends in a consonant and then -y, the -y is replaced with -ies e.g. *lady* ⟶ *lad**ies***.

3) Word endings that include an *f* like *knife* and *dwarf* often replace the *f* with -ves ⟶ *kni**ves*** and *dwar**ves***.

4) Some other nouns form **irregular plurals**, different from the **standard** pattern, e.g.
   woman ⟶ *women*   *foot* ⟶ *feet*   *mouse* ⟶ *mice*

5) There are some nouns that **don't change their form** at all, whether they are singular or plurals, e.g. *deer* and *sheep* stay the same even when you are referring to more than one.

Nouns can be classified as **Count Nouns** or **Mass Nouns**

1) **Count nouns** (a bit obviously) can be **counted** — like *brick*. You can have *one brick, two bricks, three bricks,* and so on. Nouns that form irregular plurals can be count nouns too — *one mouse, two mice,* etc.

2) **Mass nouns** can't be counted. Nouns like these **don't** have a **plural**, e.g. you talk about *information* rather than *information**s***.

3) Some nouns can function as **both** count and mass nouns, depending on the **context**. For example, in the phrase *war is evil*, *war* is a **mass noun** — it refers to war in general. However, *war* becomes a **count noun** when you use a determiner — e.g. *the war is evil*. This time *war* refers to a **specific** war rather than war in general.

Nouns can be **Modified** to give **More Information**

Nouns **don't usually stand alone**. They're often accompanied by words that **modify** them or that tell you **more** about them. There are two types of modifier — **pre-modifiers** and **post-modifiers**.

- **Pre-modifiers** — these come **before** the noun, e.g. a sign that reads <u>*Dangerous Animal*</u>. The adjective *dangerous* pre-modifies *animal* and tells you something about it. You can also have **more than one** pre-modifier, e.g. *very dangerous animal* — *very* and *dangerous* are both pre-modifiers.

- **Post-modifiers** — these come after the noun, e.g. *Examination <u>in progress</u>*. The noun *examination* is post-modified by *in progress* — it tells the reader something about the examination.

In **noun phrases**, the noun is called the **head word** — the most important word of the phrase. The other words **modify** it.

determiner	pre-modifier	head word	post-modifier
the	largest	whale	in the world

Nouns and Adjectives

Adjectives Describe Nouns

Adjectives are classified according to their **position** — **before** or **after** the noun.

1) **Attributive** adjectives are **pre-modifying**, e.g. *the **sudden** noise*, or *the **red** balloon*.

2) **Predicative** adjectives are **post-modifying**. They're usually **linked** to the noun they are modifying by a form of the verb *be*:

> **Examples of predicative adjectives**
> - *Revision is **brilliant*** — the adjective is **linked** to the noun by a form of the verb *be*.
> - *The food looked **amazing*** — although forms of *be* are the most common links, **other verbs** can link the adjective to the noun (e.g. *looked, seemed, felt*).

Adjectives also make Comparisons

Adjectives are **gradable** — they can show **how much** of a certain property a noun displays.

1) **Comparative adjectives** are generally formed by adding an *-er* **inflection**. For example, the simple adjective *long* becomes the comparative adjective *longer*.

2) **Superlative adjectives** are generally formed by adding *-est*. For example, *long* becomes the superlative *longest*.

Look back at p.5 to see the effects of gradable adjectives in the holiday advertisement texts. Gradable adjectives make you interpret the sentences and the type of accommodation they advertise differently:

fine accommodation
simple adjective

finer accommodation
comparative adjective

finest accommodation
superlative adjective

3) Some adjectives are **irregular** in the way they form comparatives and superlatives:

Adjective	Comparative	Superlative
good	better	best
bad	worse	worst
much	more	most

4) Some adjectives need *more* and *most* to form comparisons. For example, you can't say *significanter* or *significantest*. You use ***more** significant* or ***most** significant* to make the comparison.

Practice Questions

Q1 In the following list of common nouns, identify three concrete, three abstract and three collective nouns:
love, table, purity, family, government, disgust, team, wall, sock

Q2 Which of the following are count nouns and which are mass nouns?
house, isolation, monkey, furniture, rat, gratitude, hall, courage, jug

Q3 Identify the determiner, pre-modifier, head word and post-modifier in the following noun phrase:
One fine morning in July

Q4 Identify the attributive adjective and the predicative adjective in the following phrases:
The storm was terrible   *The terrible storm*

Be Here Noun — and other great language albums...

'Like 'Noun That's What I Call Music... 88'. Or 'Urban Hymns', by The Verb. Or... never mind. Remember that nouns don't just name specific objects like pencils or sheds — they can refer to states or emotions as well. Get that idea firmly wedged into your head, and then you can go back to making up amusing grammar-based band names. If you want to, obviously.

Verbs and Adverbs

Without verbs, everything in language would stand still. That's why they're sometimes called 'doing' words.

Verbs tell you exactly **What Happens**

The base form of a verb is called the **infinitive** — it normally follows 'to', e.g. to *be*, to *laugh*, or to *think*. You can describe verbs in two ways:

1) **Main Verbs** (lexical verbs) identify the action of the sentence — e.g. *she sings like a hyena*, *he gave me his shoe*. The **verbs** *sing* and *gave* tell you the **action** involved.

2) **Auxiliary Verbs** go **before** the main verb in a sentence. They give **extra information** about the main verb and can affect the **meaning** of the sentence. There are **two** types of auxiliary verb:

Primary auxiliaries	Modal auxiliaries
There are three primary auxiliaries — *do*, *have*, and *be*. • I **do** like you • I **am** leaving tomorrow Primary auxiliaries can also be **main verbs**: • I **have** a surprise for you	Modal auxiliaries can **only** occur with reference to a main verb. There are 9 modal auxiliary verbs: *can could will would must* *may might shall should* • I **can** play the drums • I **must** do something

Verb endings **Change** depending on **Who** is **Doing** the **Action**

The **endings** of verbs can alter depending on **who** is doing the action — the first, the second or the third **person**.

Person	Singular Pronoun	Verb	Plural Pronoun	Verb
First	I	play	We	play
Second	You	play	You	play
Third	She/He/It	play**s**	They	play

Only the verb in the third person singular changes its ending — you add an -s to get plays. This rule applies to most of the verbs in English.

Changes to the ends of words that affect the grammar of the sentence are called **inflections**.

Verbs can tell you **When** something happens

Verbs change depending on whether something is happening in the **past**, **present**, or **future**.

1) **Present tense** tells you about 'now' and uses the **base form** of the verb, e.g. *I write* or *they dance* — unless it's the third person singular (see above), when you need to add the *-s* **inflection**, e.g. *she/he/it talks*.

2) **Past tense** tells you about the past (obviously), e.g. *I danced yesterday*, or *He missed the bus*. For most verbs, you form the past tense by **adding -ed** on the end — another **inflection**.

3) **Future tense** — Some people say that there's no future tense in English. This is because there **isn't** anything specific (like *-s*, or *-ed*) that you can **add** to a verb to show that the action will happen in the future. The future is expressed in **other ways** — often by using **modal auxiliary** verbs like **will** or **shall**.
   e.g.   I **shall** see you tomorrow.   I **will** pick you up at eight.

4) You can also use the **present tense** to talk about **future events** — e.g. *Rachel is **playing** hockey on Saturday.*

Verbs **Don't** always change in the **Same Way**

1) Most verbs are **regular** — they follow the same patterns outlined above.

2) Some verbs are **irregular** — they don't change like you'd expect, e.g. *I drink* becomes *I **drank***, not *I **drinked***. Other verbs with irregular past tenses include ***run***, ***sing***, ***write***, and ***speak***.

3) The verb *be* is very irregular — the forms it can take are the infinitive *to be*, plus *am*, *are*, *is*, *was*, and *were*. It changes more than any other verb according to **person** (first, second or third), **number** and **tense**.

Verbs and Adverbs

Verbs can create an *Active* or *Passive* voice

Sentences that involve an **action** can focus on either the **subject** or the **object** (see p. 12 for more on this).

Active Voice

The **active voice** is when the **subject** is the focus and **performs** the action described by the verb, e.g:

- *Ahmed **kicked** the ball.*

The subject, *Ahmed*, acts **directly** upon the object — *the ball*. The object **receives** the action of the verb.

Passive Voice

The **passive voice** is less direct. It focuses on the **object**. The **order changes** so that the object comes first, followed by the subject, e.g:

- *The ball **was kicked** by Ahmed.*

The passive voice makes sentences seem more **formal**.

Verbs can change depending on the *Aspect*

Aspect shows whether the action described by the verb has **finished**, or is still **being performed**.

PROGRESSIVE ASPECT

1) The **progressive** (or **continuous**) aspect refers to actions that don't have a definite end.

2) It's made up of one of the auxiliary forms of *be* and the **present participle** of a verb, which is the **base form** + *-ing*.

3) For example, in the sentence *They **are doing** well*, *are* is an auxiliary form of *be* and *doing* is the present participle of *do*.

PERFECT ASPECT

1) The **perfect aspect** tells you about actions that have a definite end.

2) It's made up of one of the present forms of *have* (has/have) and the past tense form of the verb, e.g. *They **have bought** a car.*

3) The **past perfect** aspect is formed in the same way but with the past tense of *have* (had), e.g. *I **had missed** it.*

Adverbs are used to *Modify* verbs

Adverbs are mostly used to modify verbs, but they can modify nouns and adjectives too. Most people recognise adverbs as '**-ly** words' but many have different endings. Here are a **few ways** that adverbs **modify meaning**:

- Adverbs of **manner** — how something is done — e.g. *He talks **incessantly**.*
- Adverbs of **place** — where something is happening — e.g. *The book is **here**.*
- Adverbs of **time** — when something is happening — e.g. *The exam is **tomorrow**.*
- Adverbs of **duration** — how long something happens for — e.g. *The bridge is closed **temporarily**.*
- Adverbs of **frequency** — how often something takes place — e.g. *Mandy visits **sometimes**.*
- Adverbs of **degree** — the extent to which something is done — e.g. *We **completely** understand.*
- Adverbs of **direction** — the direction something happens in — e.g. *Jemima walked **towards** the door.*

Some adverbs **express feelings** or opinions — ***Hopefully**, we'll find out where the garage is.*

Adverbs can also **link** sentences together — *The man was a great athlete. **However**, he didn't have a clue about adverbs.*

Practice Questions

Q1 Identify the verbs in the following sentence and state what tense they are written in.
Aiden went to see his friend Sally, but she was not in.

Q2 Identify one primary auxiliary verb, one modal auxiliary verb and one progressive verb in the following sentence.
Mohammed is going into town after college and therefore will be home late.

Q3 Rewrite this sentence in the active voice.
The glass was dropped by the waitress.

Q4 Identify two adverbs in the following sentences and explain their function.
Frankly, I disagree. Furthermore, I think your manner is despicable.

A'spect your head's still spinning after that lot — time for a lie down...

Verbs are pretty tricky customers, so it's vital that you get all this information inside that head of yours. The best way to practise all this stuff is to apply it to real life — you'll notice verbs and adverbs popping up all over the place fairly frequently. Like in that sentence — four main verbs, one modal auxiliary (in you'll), and two adverbs. I spoil you, I know.

Pronouns and Determiners

Pronouns and determiners are both related to nouns, but you never see them in the same place at the same time. They're like Bruce Wayne and Batman — and only a teensy bit less exciting.

Pronouns **Take** the **Place** of **Nouns**

Pronouns are a **sub-class** of **nouns**. They can identify subjects and objects, just like nouns do.

1) **Personal** pronouns can replace people or things who are the **subject** of a sentence.
They're classified in terms of **person** and are either **singular** or **plural**:

	Singular	Plural
First Person	I	we
Second Person	you	you
Third Person	he, she, it	they

e.g.   *Sarah thanked Sanjay*
↓
She *thanked Sanjay*
(3rd person singular subject pronoun)

2) Pronouns can also be used to replace the person or thing who is the **object** of the sentence:

	Singular	Plural
First Person	me	us
Second Person	you	you
Third Person	him, her, it	them

e.g.   *Graham thanked Adam*
↓
Graham thanked **him**
(3rd person singular object pronoun)

Pronouns are used in **Other Ways** too

1) **Interrogative** pronouns are used to **ask questions**. They are *which, what, who,* and *whose*. As with other pronouns, they help you **simplify** your sentences by **replacing nouns**, e.g:

- *Give me the name of **the person** you're looking for.* ⟶ **Who** *are you looking for?*
- *Tell me **the thing** you are going to do.* ⟶ **What** *are you going to do?*

2) These aren't the only words you use at the start of questions. *Why, where, how* and *when* are also interrogatives, but they are **adverbs**. Interrogative pronouns and adverbs are usually **classed together** as *wh-words*.

3) **Demonstrative** pronouns like *this, that, these* and *those* can **replace** people and things in a sentence where there's some **shared understanding** of what's being referred to, for example:

- If you're in the kitchen, you might ask *is this my coffee?* — only people who are also in the kitchen will be able to tell you.

- You use different demonstratives depending on the **distance** of the object from the speaker — *this* and *these* are objects **near** the speaker. You use *that* or *those* for objects **further away**.

Determiners show what the noun is **Referring To**

There are several determiners, which all **go before** the noun and show what it's referring to.

1) The **definite article** *the* and the **indefinite article** *a* refer to nouns. The definite article indicates something **specific**. The indefinite article indicates something more **general**, for example:

> *Is that **the** frog?* (we are looking for, specifically)   **or**   *Is that **a** frog?* (or is it a toad?)

2) **Numerals** such as *one, two* and *three* (cardinal numbers) and *first, second* etc. (ordinal numbers) are determiners.

3) **Possessive determiners** like *my, your, his, her, its, our,* and *their* are possessive pronouns used as determiners. They're used before a noun to show **possession** e.g. **my** *car,* **his** *friend,* **their** *problem*.

4) **Quantifiers** are determiners that show **quantity**, like *few, many* and *enough*.

5) **Demonstrative adjectives**, e.g. *this, that, these,* and *those* are also determiners. They **look the same** as demonstrative pronouns but there is a **significant difference** between them. They refer to specific objects or people that the participants are close to, rather than replacing them like pronouns do:

> *I like **those***   **or**   *I like **those** shoes*
> *(**those** replaces the noun — pronoun).*   *(**those** precedes the noun — adjective / determiner).*

Prepositions and Conjunctions

Prepositions show Relationships between things

Prepositions show the **relationship** between things in terms of **space**, **time** or **direction**. The preposition usually goes before the determiner and noun.

- *The books are **underneath** the bed* (spatial)
- *She left **before** the end* (time)
- *He moved **towards** the door* (directional)

Sometimes there's no determiner e.g. ➡
- *See you **at** breaktime.*
- *We'll talk more about it **on** Friday.*

Conjunctions are Linking Words

There are **two types** of conjunction — **coordinating** conjunctions and **subordinating** conjunctions.

1) **Coordinating conjunctions** are words like *and*, *but* and *or*. They **connect** single words or longer units of language (phrases and clauses) that have **equal status**:

*Robert **and** Bethany*	*A white shirt **or** a pink shirt*	*He kissed her on the cheek **and** she ran away*
The **coordinating conjunction** *and* connects the two names — neither is given more importance.	The **coordinating conjunction** *or* links **two phrases**.	The coordinating conjunction *and* links two **equal statements**.

2) **Subordinating conjunctions** are words like *since*, *although*, *because*, *unless*, *whether* and *whereas*. They link a main clause to one that's **less important** to the subject of the sentence:

More about clauses on p. 12-13.

*Some people find Maths really difficult, **whereas** others find it easy.*

The main clause is *Some people find Maths really difficult*. This is the subject of the sentence. The **subordinating conjunction** *whereas* introduces a less important clause *others find it easy*.

Other subordinating conjunctions give **different meanings**.
Some, like *after*, *before* and *until* are to do with **time**. Others, like *where* and *wherever* are about **place**.

1) Conjunctions are an important **cohesive device** — they help a discourse to flow smoothly.
2) A discourse **without** conjunctions seems very **disjointed** — e.g. *Last night I went out. I bumped into my friend Hayley. We talked for a while. She had to leave early. She was babysitting for her auntie.*
3) If you add **conjunctions**, the discourse is much more **fluent** — e.g. *Last night I went out **and** I bumped into my friend Hayley. We talked for a while **but** she had to leave early **because** she was babysitting for her auntie.*

Practice Questions

Q1 Identify three personal pronouns in the following sentence.
I doubt whether you will like it.

Q2 Identify an interrogative pronoun and a demonstrative pronoun in the following sentence.
Where are you going with that?

Q3 Identify the determiners in the following sentence:
There were twenty fish in my pond this year.

Q4 Find a coordinating conjunction and a subordinating conjunction in the following sentence.
The teacher and her pupils fled the building because it was on fire.

Just when you thought classes were over, it's time for two more terms...

But at least they're short. Like gnomes. Nouns, verbs, adjectives and adverbs are known as open-class or lexical words. Pronouns, determiners, conjunctions and prepositions are known as closed-class or grammatical words. The lexical words are the content of a sentence, and the grammatical words perform functions that link them all together. Ah, unrivalled joy...

Phrases and Clauses

When you're analysing word classes, you need to focus on the function of individual words. The next level of analysis after this is to look at larger units of language like phrases and clauses. Onwards and upwards, and all that...

Phrases are **Units** of **Language** that have a **Head Word**

Phrases are units of language built around a **head word** that identifies the type of phrase, e.g. in the noun phrase *the empty house*, the noun *house* is the head word. Basic sentences are created from a combination of phrases.

1) The simplest noun phrase (NP) possible is just a **noun itself**.
   It can be accompanied by a **pre-modifier**, a **post-modifier**, or both.

Pre-modifiers come before the noun. They're often a determiner, followed by an adjective.

pre-modifiers		head word	post-modifiers	
determiner	adjective	noun	preposition	noun
the	*new*	*mayor*	*of*	*Bradford*

Post-modifiers come after the noun.

2) A very simple verb phrase (VP) has **one verb**, but you can also make up a verb phrase from the head word (a main verb) and one or more **auxiliary** verbs.

auxiliary	auxiliary	head word
should	*have*	*passed*

3) For example — the **noun phrases** and **verb phrases** are underlined in the following sentences:
   The wealthy woman has been to London many times. Now she is planning a trip to Paris.

A **Clause** is a **Unit** of a **Sentence**

1) Sentences are made up of **clauses** — the **simplest meaningful units** of the sentence.

2) A **sentence** can be made up of **one clause** — e.g. *Katherine likes going walking*.

3) Or it can be made up of **more than one** clause. When there's more than one clause in a sentence, the clauses are separated by **conjunctions** — e.g. *Katherine likes going walking **but** she doesn't like running*.

4) **Clauses** can be made up of a **subject**, **verb**, **object**, **complement** and **adverbial**.

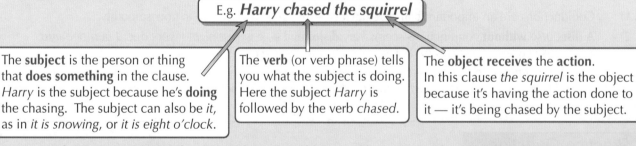

E.g. ***Harry chased the squirrel***

The **subject** is the person or thing that **does something** in the clause. *Harry* is the subject because he's **doing** the chasing. The subject can also be *it*, as in *it is snowing*, or *it is eight o'clock*.

The **verb** (or verb phrase) tells you what the subject is doing. Here the subject *Harry* is followed by the verb *chased*.

The **object** receives the **action**. In this clause *the squirrel* is the object because it's having the action done to it — it's being chased by the subject.

A **complement** gives more **information about** the **subject** or **object**. It **completes** the **meaning** of the sentence it appears in, for example:

- In *Harry is a great guitarist*, the noun phrase (NP) *Harry* is the subject. The second NP in the sentence, *a great guitarist* is a **subject complement**. It **completes** the meaning of the sentence by giving information about the subject.

- In *Harry found the film appalling*, *Harry* is still the subject. But the adjective *appalling* refers to *the film*, which is the object, so *appalling* is the **object complement**.

An **adverbial** is a word or group of words that **refers back to the verb**. The simplest adverbial is just an adverb e.g. *Harry kicked the ball **quickly***. In *Harry is playing on Sunday*, the adverbial is *on Sunday* as it relates to the specific time that Harry will play. Adverbials usually describe **time**, **place** or **manner**.

5) The verb, complements and adverbials of a clause or sentence are sometimes also called the **predicate**.
   The term 'predicate' refers to any part of the clause that is **not the subject**, but that **modifies** it in some way.
   The verb is sometimes referred to as the **predicator**.

Phrases and Clauses

There are **Seven** Common Types of **Clause**

These are created by **different combinations** of subject (**S**), verb (**V**), object (**O**), complement (**C**) and adverbial (**A**):

S + V	Harry + played
S + V + O	Harry + played + a game
S + V + C	Harry + was + great
S + V + A	Harry + played + on Tuesday
S + V + O + O	Harry + gave + him + a drink
S + V + O + C	Harry + thought + his performance + disappointing
S + V + O + A	Harry + passed + the ball + quickly

Harry + fluorescent trunks + chest wig = one hot look.

Clauses are defined by **Status**

The **status** of a clause depends on its **constituents** and whether it can **stand alone** as a meaningful unit of language.

1) **Main clauses (independent clauses)** can stand alone and still make sense:

> Harry played.

2) **Coordinate clauses** occur in sentences where there are **two or more** independent clauses.
   - They're joined together by a **coordinating conjunction** like *and* or *but*. For example:

   > The band played for two hours **but** I had to leave early.

   - The clauses could **stand alone** and still **make sense** — *The band played for two hours. I had to leave early.*

3) **Subordinate clauses** can't stand alone. They have to be with a **main clause**.
   - A subordinate clause gives **extra information** about the main clause.
   - In most cases, a subordinate clause is led by a **subordinating conjunction** (like *since, although, because, unless, if, whether, while, whereas etc.*). This links it to the main clause. For example:

   main clause ⟹ *Will you pop in to see me **while** you're here tomorrow?* ⟸ subordinate clause
   (the clause can't stand alone in a meaningful way)

   subordinating conjunction

4) **Combining clauses** — you can combine coordinate and subordinate clauses in the same sentence:

   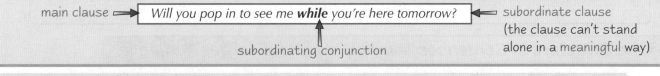

   > *He went to London **and** she went to Manchester **because** of a terrible row.*

   coordinate clause — coordinating conjunction — coordinate clause — subordinating conjunction — subordinate clause

Practice Questions

Q1 Identify the head word, pre-modifiers and post-modifiers (where applicable) in the following noun phrases:
the gold bracelet   *a cold, frosty morning in spring*   *fish and chips from the shop*

Q2 Identify verb phrases in the following clauses:
Joshua should tell her   *You should have seen it*   *I will be leaving early tomorrow*

Q3 Which is the main clause and which is the subordinate clause in the following sentence?
It was still dark when the travellers rose from their slumbers.

Don't let all this stuff get on top of you... it'd be dead clause-trophobic...

To get the hang of how these phrases and clauses work, practise identifying them — have a look at some articles or listen to the news and see if you can work out how the sentences all fit together. Refer back to these pages if you need to, and just keep going until it's a piece of cake. Mmm cake... Almost as much of a treat as learning about clauses, but not quite.

Sentences

So far you've seen how word classes, phrases and clauses fit together. Now for the big surprise. It turns out that they're all building blocks in sentences — the largest grammatical units. Well, who'd have thought it...

Sentences can be anything from very **Simple** to really **Complex**

There are **five** types of sentence — **minor**, **simple**, **compound**, **complex** and **compound-complex**.

1) **Minor sentences** are complete and meaningful statements that **don't have** a subject and verb combination. Lots of everyday sayings are minor sentences, e.g. *Be quiet. Goodbye. Sounds good.*

2) A **simple sentence** must have a **subject** and a **verb**. It should express a **complete thought**, e.g. *The snow falls.* *Snow* is the **subject**, *falls* is the **verb**.

3) A **compound sentence** is an independent clause linked to another independent clause by a **coordinating conjunction**. Either one could be a main clause in a different sentence.

independent clause ➡ *I went to Manchester **and** I went to Liverpool.* ⬅ independent clause

⬆ coordinating conjunction

Upset the grammar sheriff — get a really long sentence.

4) A **complex sentence** consists of a main clause and a subordinate clause (or subordinating clauses). A **subordinating conjunction** connects the clauses together:

main clause ➡ *The workers left the building **when** they heard.* ⬅ subordinate clause

⬆ subordinating conjunction

5) A **compound-complex sentence** is made up of at least two **coordinate clauses** connected by a **coordinating conjunction**, and **at least one** subordinate clause.

*Some of the children went home early **but** the others remained **because** they had no transport.*

first coordinate clause   second coordinate clause   subordinate clause
coordinating conjunction   subordinating conjunction

The **Structure** of **Sentences** tells you about the **Target Audience**

1) The length and complexity of sentences can be varied according to the **content** and **audience** of a text.
2) A good example of contrasting sentence structures is the difference between **broadsheet** and **tabloid** newspapers.

BROADSHEET NEWSPAPER

The scientific community is under the microscope as it nears hybrid embryo creation.
(Complex sentence: main clause + subordinate clause)

This is a serious ethical issue since it questions the very nature of what it is to be human.
(Complex sentence: main clause + subordinate clause)

The intention to find new ways of treating diseases that have so far proved untreatable is clearly laudable, but the magnitude of the moral issue can't be ignored, as the procedure will involve destroying live embryos after fourteen days.
(Compound-complex sentence: main clause + main clause + subordinate clause)

TABLOID NEWSPAPER

Mad scientists are on the verge of creating monsters.
(Simple sentence)

They will take the sperm and eggs of humans and animals and mix them up.
(Compound sentence: coordinate clause + coordinate clause)

Living embryos will be trashed after fourteen days.
(Simple sentence)

3) The writers create a different **mood** and **tone** depending on the types of sentences they use. They're intended to appeal to different **audiences**.
4) The first example is more complex — it has a **measured** and **serious tone**. The second, relatively simple set of sentences is more **emotive** and **subjective**.

Sentences

You can **Classify Sentences** by their **Function**

Sentences have **four** functions.

1) DECLARATIVES

- **Declarative** sentences are statements that **give information**, e.g.

> *This summer was the hottest on record.*
> *I don't like cheese.*

2) IMPERATIVES

- **Imperative** sentences **give orders**, **instructions**, **advice** and **directions**.
- They **start** with a **main verb** and **don't** have a **subject**, e.g.

> **Go** *left and it's first on your right.*
> **Answer** *one question from each section.*

3) INTERROGATIVES

Interrogative sentences ask **questions**.

- Some questions are formed by **inverting** (swapping round) the **verb** and the **subject** of a sentence.

E.g. **You are coming** *out tonight.* → **Are you coming** *out tonight?*

Subject **Verb** **Main verb**   **Verb** **Subject** **Main verb**

- Interrogatives can start with *wh-* **words**, e.g.

> **Wh**ere *are you going?*
> **Wh**en *will you be back?*

- They can also be added to the **end of a statement**. These are called **tag questions**, e.g.

> *It's cold,* **isn't it**?
> *She said she was on her way,* **didn't she**?

- In **spoken discourse** you can turn **declarative statements** into questions using **stress** and **intonation**. This is called a **rising inflection**, e.g.

> *He will get better?*

4) EXCLAMATIVES

- **Exclamative** sentences have an **expressive function** — they convey the force of a statement, and end with an **exclamation mark**, e.g.

> *I will not do this any more!*
> *That was fantastic!*

Practice Questions

Q1 Identify whether the following sentences are minor or simple:
Good afternoon   the doctor is here   the band was late   your turn

Q2 Identify the coordinate clauses and the coordinating conjunction in this compound sentence:
Ravina is going to Delhi but I will stay in Calcutta.

Q3 Identify the main clause, the subordinate clause and the subordinating conjunction in this complex sentence:
I will stay in bed today because I'm not feeling very well.

Q4 In this compound-complex sentence, identify two coordinate clauses and one subordinate clause:
The band played brilliantly and the crowd screamed for more until the lights went out.

Minor sentences — great if you're down 'pit, rubbish if you're in an exam...

Brilliant. That was sentences. Learn this stuff and you'll be OK. It's very important because sentence structure can help identify a target audience. It might seem tedious, but you need to do it, because knowing all this syntax malarkey is useful. Ah, grammar — the most fun you can have in an empty room with no windows, lights, friends or board games.

Morphology

AQA A and B can ignore this. It's a shame though really, cos these pages look like a right jolly old romp. Morphology is about the internal structure of words — basically, how they're formed and how this can affect their meaning.

Morphemes are the Basic Units that make up words

1) **Morphology** is the study of **word formation**. It looks at how the **form** of a word **changes** because of **grammar**, and how the **meaning** of a word can **change** by adding an **affix** — a **unit** of a word like *un-* or *-ness*.

2) The separate units that make up words are called **morphemes**.

- Simple words are **morphemes** in their own right, such as *man*, *dog*, *ignore* and *journey*. They **can't** be **broken down** any further (e.g. *ig+nore*). They're called **free morphemes**, or **base**, **root** or **stem** forms.

- **Bound morphemes** are morphemes that are **not** words on their **own**. They're things like *-ful*, *-s*, *-ness* and *-est*, which can be added to **free** morphemes to create words like *thankful*, *cups*, *darkness* and *largest*.

EXAMPLES

The word 'thankful' is made up of the base form 'thank' and the bound morpheme '-ful'.

base form	bound morpheme
thank	*-ful*

Some bound morphemes occur after the base form, some occur before it.

bound morpheme	base form	bound morpheme
un-	*help*	*-ful*

Prefixes can create New Words in the same Word Class

Prefixes are **morphemes** added to the start of a word. They change the **meaning** of nouns, verbs, adjectives and adverbs.

prefix	noun	new word
dis- ⟶	parity ⟶	*disparity*

prefix	verb	new word
inter- ⟶	act ⟶	*interact*

prefix	adjective	new word
ir- ⟶	relevant ⟶	*irrelevant*

prefix	adverb	new word
super- ⟶	naturally ⟶	*supernaturally*

Suffixes can change a word's Class and Meaning

Suffixes are **morphemes** added to the **end** of a word.

The tables below show how you form different words and word classes by adding **different suffixes** to the **base form**.

1) Base form is a **noun**:

noun	adjective	verb	adverb
type	*typical*	*typify*	*typically*

2) Base form is an **adjective**:

adjective	noun	verb	adverb
legal	*legality*	*legalise*	*legally*

3) Base form is a **verb**:

verb	noun	adjective	adverb
explode	*explosion*	*explosive*	*explosively*

Suffixes and prefixes are both types of affixes.

Mixing up words is nowhere near as dangerous as whatever this lady is doing.

Morphology

Adding Morphemes to existing words is called Affixation

Affixes are **bound morphemes** that are added to words. There are **two** kinds of affixation — **inflectional** and **derivational**.

Inflectional affixation

1) **Inflectional affixation** changes the **grammar** of the word — e.g. its **number** or **tense**.

2) Inflectional affixes are always **suffixes** (they go after the base).
   For example, *pushed*. The bound morpheme *-ed* attaches to the verb *push* to change the action from the **present tense** to the **past tense**.

3) Here are some common kinds of inflectional affixation:

Plural -s (also -ies, -oes)	*dogs, ladies, tomatoes*	**Past participle** -ed	*He has recovered*
Possessive -'s	*Bernie's car*	**Present participle** -ing	*He is recovering*
Third person singular -s	*She says*	**Comparative** -er	*Quicker*
Past tense -ed	*He recovered*	**Superlative** -est	*Quickest*

Derivational affixation

1) Derivational affixation has a **semantic function** — it changes the **meaning** of a word.

2) The **noun** *player* is formed by adding the **suffix** *-er* to the **verb** *play*. The word changes from being an **action** to the **performer** of the action.

3) **Prefixes precede** (go before) the **base form**, **suffixes** come at the end — both **change** the meaning of a word:

Prefix	Meaning	Example	Suffix	Meaning	Example
auto-	self	*auto*biography	-archy	leadership	hier*archy*
inter-	between	*inter*active	-less	absence of	shame*less*
un-	not, opposite	*un*necessary	-phobia	fear	claustro*phobia*

Morphology and Coining Words

Coining is the general term for creating words. Many new words are formed through **derivational affixation**.
There are **four main ways** that new words are coined:

1) **Clipping** — sometimes prefixes or suffixes are **dropped**. For example, *the gymnasium* is now usually referred to as *the gym*, and you're more likely to say *phone* than *telephone*.

2) **Compounds** — new words are created by **combining** two free morphemes, e.g. *mankind*, *blackbird* and *sleepwalk*.

3) **Back-formation** — this involves a free morpheme that **looks like** it has a suffix, like *editor*, being adapted to create a word like *edit*. **Historically** the word *editor* is a **free morpheme**, but the verb *edit* has been created **from** it. This is also true of *writer* (historically a free morpheme) producing the verb *write*.

4) **Blends** — new words are also created by **fusing** two words into one. These words are referred to as **blends**.
   For example, *alcoholic* has been fused with *chocolate* to form *chocoholic*, and with *shopping* to form *shopaholic*.

Practice Questions

Q1 Divide the following words into individual morphemes, identifying the base form and the bound morpheme:
   singer   *information*   *atomic*   *friendly*   *incomprehensible*   *brotherhood*

Q2 Identify prefixes and suffixes in the following words:
   inconsolable   *undemonstrative*   *inconceivable*   *antidisestablishmentarianism*

Q3 Which of the following words contain inflectional morphemes and which contain derivational ones?
   singing   *delightful*   *unnecessary*   *smartest*

Blending words seems a bit harsh — and a total waste of equipment...

Couldn't you just have a smoothie instead? Anyway — it's too late to worry about that now, because this is the end of section one. By now you should be pretty clued up on the delights of word classes, phrases, clauses and sentences, and how they're all gloriously linked under a big grammatical umbrella. Although it's not very waterproof and it won't keep you dry. Sorry.

Lexis

These pages are for everyone. What a big happy family. Lexis is just a fancy word for words. If you're thinking that words is a perfectly good word for words, then you'll be eating your words after you read these words. No word of a lie.

Lexis means Words

1) **Lexis** is the linguistic term for **vocabulary** — the words of a language.

2) When you're **analysing language**, you'll start by looking at the lexis.

3) It's divided into **word classes** — also called the **parts of speech** (see page 4), e.g. nouns, verbs, adjectives.

4) Lexis can also be analysed in chunks or phrases, known as **lexical phrases**. These are well-known groups of words like *on the other hand* and *once upon a time*. There are hundreds of these phrases and they're used all the time.

English has been Influenced by Other Languages

1) A lot of the most frequently used words in the English vocabulary come from **Old English**. They're mostly **everyday** words like *that, house, on, be, bread*.

2) English developed from Old English with lots of borrowings from **French** and **Latin**.

3) This is one of the reasons why English has lots of **synonyms** (different words for the same thing, see p.21) — some are from one language, some from another.

4) Words with **Latin** origins tend to feel more **formal** than Old English ones — e.g. *chew* comes from Old English, *masticate* comes from Latin.

English is always Changing

1) English is still influenced by other languages. Words that are **borrowed** from other languages are called **loan words** — e.g. *shampoo* from Hindi, *bluff* from Dutch, *schmooze* from Yiddish. They become part of English through contact with other cultures.

2) Words also enter the language through advances in **science** and **technology**, which creates the need for **new words** (**neologisms**) — e.g. *email, genome*.

3) Once a word has entered the language, it can become part of **everyday English** in different ways:

Adding an affix

1) **Suffixes** are put **after** the root or stem of a word (see p.16). These can alter the **meaning** of the word they're attached to and change its **word class**.

2) **Common** English suffixes are *–tion, -ness, -ish* and *–able*.

3) When nouns from other languages become part of **everyday English**, the plural is made by adding an *-s*. For example, the German word *Kindergärten* (meaning *more than one Kindergarten*) becomes *kindergartens* in English.

4) **Prefixes** are put **before** the root or stem of a word. They alter the meaning of the word, often **reversing** the original meaning.

5) Common English **prefixes** include *multi-, dis-, trans-* and *sub-*.

Conversion

1) This is where the **word classes** of existing words are **altered**.

2) For example — *water* can be a **noun** (*the water*), but it can also be used as a **verb** (*to water*).

3) *Empty* is an **adjective**, but it can also be converted to a **verb** (*to empty*).

Creating compound words

1) **Compound words** are created by **joining** two or more words together.

2) For example, *rainbow* joins *rain* and *bow*.

3) The separate words are combined to create a **new meaning**, which is **different** to the meanings of the original words — e.g. *laptop* specifically refers to a computer you could rest on your knees.

Lexis

The **Lexis** people use depends on the **Situation**

Lexis has different **levels** of **formality**.

1) **Informal lexis** is relaxed, familiar and conversational.

2) It's **colloquial** and often **non-standard**, so it will contain **dialect** words and **slang** (see p.36-37 and p.42-43) — e.g. you might describe someone as being *tapped* or a *loony*.

3) It tends to be **smaller** than **formal lexis** and contain more **monosyllabic** words (see p.24) like *nice* and *grub*.

4) It contains lots of **abbreviations** like *can't*, *you'll* and *would've*.

5) Informal lexis for **ordinary** things often has **Old English** roots — e.g. *house*, *home*.

---

1) **Formal lexis** is more serious and impersonal.

2) It tends to be made up of **Standard English** words, so it's unlikely to contain **dialect** words or **slang**, e.g. someone might be described as *mentally ill* or *not in possession of their faculties*.

3) It's bigger and more complex than informal lexis, so there are more **polysyllabic** words (see p.24) like *enjoyable* and *comestibles*.

4) Words are less likely to be **abbreviated** — e.g. *do not* will be used rather than *don't*.

5) Formal lexis often has **Latinate** roots (it comes from Latin) — e.g. *residence*, *habitation*.

The **Lexis** of **Written** and **Spoken** English is very different

1) As a general rule, **written** language is **more formal** than **spoken** language.

2) The most **informal** language is found in **speech** between friends and family. The most **formal** language is found in **writing** between people who don't know each other — e.g. essays, business letters and broadsheet newspapers.

3) One of the main reasons for this is because **speech** tends to be **spontaneous**, so the lexis is **smaller** and there's lots of **self-correction** — speakers notice their own errors and correct them in mid-sentence.

4) Speech also tends to contain lots of **abbreviations**, like *shan't* and *gonna*. This is even the case with **planned speech**, which can sound strange and stilted if the speaker doesn't abbreviate some words.

5) However, there are situations where **speech** is more **formal** than **writing**. This is especially the case when it's **planned** — e.g. a politician's speech, or in a formal situation like a job interview.

6) Likewise, there are situations where **written language** is informal, e.g. an email between friends.

Practice Questions

Q1 What is lexis?

Q2 Outline how English has been influenced by other languages.

Q3 What is conversion?

Q4 Outline two differences between informal and formal language.

Essay Question

Q1 Outline how English has developed through the influence of different languages, and how it continues to change.

Lexis a nice name — short for Alex you know...

I've got that thing now where I've read the word 'word' so many times that it's started to look ridiculous. Word word word word word. It looks a bit gross somehow, like 'worm'. If this happens to you in the exam you may be forced to replace it with a substitute until the affliction wears off — something neutral like 'gentleman' or 'rice' would probably be best...

Semantics

Everyone can enjoy these pages. Although there are no guarantees that everyone will. Semantics means meaning, so if you've ever understood the meaning of a word then you shouldn't find the idea too difficult to grasp.

Semantics is the Study of Meaning

Semantics looks at how the **meanings** of words are **constructed** and **interpreted**.

Denotation

1) Denotation is the **straightforward meaning** or **definition** of a word, which you'd find if you looked the word up in a **dictionary**.

2) For example, *red* is *'a primary colour that lies next to orange on the visible spectrum'*.
Cloud is *'a mass of water or ice particles in the sky'*.

3) It's especially **important** for the denotation of words to be **clear** when people are giving **instructions** and **information**, e.g. in safety notices and scientific documents. Writers have to be careful to **avoid ambiguity** (see below), otherwise people might not understand the meaning properly.

Connotation

1) Connotation refers to the **associations** a word has, or the **emotions** raised by a word.

2) For example, *red* can be associated with love and passion, or with blood and danger.
Cloud can be associated with fluffiness, blue skies and rainbows, or dreariness and sadness.

3) The **connotations** of words can be **ambiguous**, so **interpretations** can **vary** from person to person.

Implication

1) This is when the meaning is **suggested**, rather than being stated directly.

2) For example, if a child arrives home late from a party, their parents might say *'You're late!'*.
Literally, all they're saying is that the child was expected home earlier. But the **implication** behind the words is *'You're in trouble — explain why you're late'.*

Ambiguity

1) This is where a word, phrase or argument can be **understood** or **interpreted** in **more than one way**.

2) For example, *men can't bear children* could mean *men can't give birth to children*, or *men hate children*.

3) Sometimes this is **unintentional**, and a case of the writer not checking carefully.
Sometimes it's done **deliberately** to raise questions in the readers' minds.

Structural Semantics is about the Relationships between Words

Structural semantics looks at the different ways that **words relate** to **each other** through **meaning**.

1) Semantic Fields

1) **Semantic fields** (also called **lexical fields**) are **groups** of words that are **connected** in **meaning**.

2) E.g. the words *classroom, teacher, assembly, lesson* and *homework* are all in the **semantic field** of '**school**'. Although the **meaning** of each word is different, they're all part of the same **framework**.

3) The words (lexis) that make up the semantic field are known as **field-specific lexis**.

Here are some more examples of **semantic fields** and **field-specific lexis**...

Semantic field of **war**

artillery   bomb   naval
air force   gas   insurgence
combat   weapon

Semantic field of the **body**

hair   circulation
respire   skin   muscle
legs   cell   heart

Semantics

2) Synonyms

1) **Synonyms** are words that have **similar meanings**, e.g. *grub* and *comestibles* are synonyms for *food*.

2) Synonyms can have different **connotations**, so their meaning isn't identical, e.g. *grub* is informal and suggests that the food is quite plain, *comestibles* is more formal and old fashioned. Talking about someone's *children* has different connotations to talking about their *brats*.

3) Using a particular synonym over another can be a **regional variation** (see p.36), e.g. saying *bairn* instead of *child*, or *mardy* instead of *grumpy*.

4) You use different synonyms depending on the **situation**, e.g. in a formal letter you might write about *working*, but in informal speech you might talk about *beavering away*.

It seemed that Max thought 'girlfriend' was a synonym for 'foot rest'.

3) Antonyms

1) **Antonyms** are words with **opposite meanings**.

2) For example — *hot / cold, male / female, day / night, sweet / sour*.

3) Antonym **pairs** are often used together as **comparisons** — e.g. *I'm always tired during the **day** but I wake up at **night**,* or *you're blowing **hot** and **cold** with me.*

4) They tend to be quite **rigid**, so they don't necessarily work with **other synonyms** — e.g. you wouldn't say *hot / cool, male / feminine, day / evening*.

4) Hypernyms and Hyponyms

This can be a bit confusing at first, but bear with it because it becomes clearer once you've seen some examples:

1) Basically, a **hyp<u>e</u>rnym** is a **general** word. A **hyp<u>o</u>nym** is **specific** word with a meaning that's **linked** to the hypernym.

2) E.g. ***school*** is a **hypernym**. Words describing more **specific types** of school, such as ***primary***, ***secondary***, ***grammar***, ***comprehensive*** are **hyponyms**.

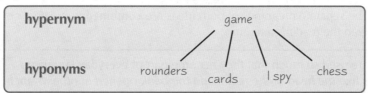

3) Words can be **hypernyms** in one context and **hyponyms** in another. E.g. ***fruit*** is a **hyponym** of ***food***, because it's a **specific type** of food. But it's also a **hypernym** for ***melon***, because ***melon*** is a **specific type** of fruit.

Practice Questions

Q1 Which semantic fields could these words belong to — bed, wine, wicket?

Q2 Explain the difference between a synonym and an antonym.

Q3 Explain the difference between a hypernym and a hyponym.

Essay Question

Q1 Place the word **adult** into each of the categories on these pages, and explain how it fits there. E.g. its connotations, how it's ambiguous, which semantic fields it fits into, and some synonyms for it.

Relationships between words can be very meaningful...

Lots of technical words to get to grips with here, but it'll look really good if you can use some of them. All this hypernym / hyponym stuff can be a bit of a nightmare, but a handy way of remembering which is which is that hypernym is a longer word, for a bigger, more general thing. I'd like to say that antonyms had something to do with ants, but that would be a lie.

Semantics

This is for everyone. You can get your meaning across literally (he's ugly), or inject a bit more interest with figurative language (he's fallen out of the ugly tree and hit every branch on the way down). This lets writers be a bit more creative.

Figurative Language isn't Literal

Figurative language (or **figures of speech**) **isn't** meant to be taken **literally**.
It's used to add colour to the language, and is classified into **different types**.

Figurative language	Explanation
Similes	1) Similes are comparisons that use the words 'like' or 'as'. 2) For example — *his hair was as white as snow, she can swim like a fish*. 3) The comparison is always stated **explicitly**, e.g. in the example above, she isn't **actually** a fish, she's just said to be **like** one.
Metaphors	1) Metaphors are comparisons that **don't** use 'like' or 'as'. 2) They describe a person, object or situation as if it actually were something else. 3) For example — *there was a blanket of snow on the ground*. The snow isn't actually a blanket, it's just **like** one. Because the comparison is **implicit** it's more **powerful** than a simile. 4) An **extended metaphor** is when the same metaphor is continued throughout a text to create a chain of images — e.g. if the *rain* is referred to as *tears*, then it's also referred to using other words relating to crying, e.g. *weeping, miserable*.
Personification	1) Personification is a type of **metaphor**, where an object or situation is given **human qualities**. 2) For example — *the wind wailed* creates the image of the wind having a mouth and being able to wail like a human.
Metonymy	1) Metonymy is using a **part** of something to describe the **whole** thing. 2) For example — the term *the crown* can be used to mean the *monarchy*, because one of the **attributes** of monarchs is that they wear a crown.
Oxymoron	1) An oxymoron brings two **conflicting ideas** together. 2) E.g. *bittersweet, living death, gentle tyrant*. 3) The separate meanings of both ideas are **combined** to create a new one, and to grab the reader's attention.

1) Some **figurative expressions** are used so much that they become part of **everyday language**, e.g. metaphorical expressions like *the **head** of the table*, and *the bank opened another **branch***.

2) These are known as **dead metaphors**, because they're not seen as comparisons any more, but just expressions in their own right.

3) When a figurative expression is **overused** then it can lose its impact or novelty value and become a **cliché**, e.g. the **similes** *as good as gold* and *as plain as the nose on your face*, and the **metaphors** *it's a piece of cake* and *I'm all ears*.

Jargon is the Specific Language people use at Work

There's loads more about **jargon** on p.52 and p.62-63, so this is just a quick glance at how it fits in with **semantics**.

1) Jargon is **specialist vocabulary** associated with a particular **occupation** or activity.
2) It tends to be more **formal** than everyday language, because it refers to **specific**, **technical** things.
3) This means it can be **difficult** for **non-specialists** to **understand**.
4) **Existing** words can take on **new meanings** within a specific environment. For example, online advertisers might talk about *spiders* and *sticky*. These words have completely **different meanings** in the **context** of online advertising — a *spider* is a software program that automatically follows links, a *sticky* website is one that people stay on for longer than usual.

Semantics

Rhetorical Language is designed to Persuade

There are loads of **rhetorical devices** — here are some of the most common ones.

Three-part list
1) This is where three elements are used in a list to give **emphasis** and build to a **climax**.
2) E.g. *blood, sweat and tears* is a list of three **nouns**, *he came, he saw, he conquered* lists three **verbs**.

Repetition
1) **Repetition** is when a word or phrase is repeated for **emphasis**, for **emphasis**.
2) E.g. *it's not good enough, simply not good enough*.

Hyperbole
1) Hyperbole means using **exaggeration** for **effect**, e.g. *I've told you a hundred times*.
2) The **media** use hyperbole to make stories seem more important, interesting or entertaining, e.g. describing a football referee's unfair decision as the *crime of the century*.

Rhetorical questions
1) A rhetorical question doesn't require an **answer**, because it's phrased in a way that **assumes** the answer is obvious.
2) E.g. *how would you like to be in this position?*

Meaning depends on Context

1) Words can have different **meanings**, so readers have to rely on **context** to understand which meaning applies.
2) For example — the word *book*. When it's on its own, it's impossible to know whether it's the **noun** *book*, as in 'printed pages bound in a cover', or the verb *to book*, as in 'to book a hotel room'.
3) Writers sometimes take advantage of **double meanings** to suggest different ideas and make their work more layered. For example, in the sentence *Jonathan was trying*, *trying* could be a **verb**, suggesting that Jonathan was *trying* his hardest, or it could be an **adjective** suggesting that his personality was *trying* (irritating).

Practice Questions

Q1 Outline the difference between similes and metaphors.
Q2 What is the purpose of rhetorical language?
Q3 Why is hyperbole frequently used in the media?

Essay Question

Love's not Time's fool, though rosy lips and cheeks
Within his bending sickle's compass come:
Love alters not with his brief hours and weeks,
But bears it out even to the edge of doom.
If this be error and upon me proved,
I never writ, nor no man ever loved.

Sonnet CXVI, William Shakespeare, 1609

Q1 Analyse the use of figurative and rhetorical language in this extract.

These linguists seem to get up to sem very silly antics...

A good way to remember the difference between a simile and a metaphor is that a simile says something is similar to something else, because it uses 'like' or 'as'. But if you really can't decide which one it is then you can just say that the language is figurative and leave it at that. What a great topic. And to top it all, simile looks a bit like smile — awww...

Phonology

Everyone needs to look at these pages. Oh go on, please. They'll tell you all the basic stuff you need to know about phonology. Phonology is all about what the language sounds like. And I know one thing it sounds like — fun...

Phonetics and *Phonology* are *Different*

Phonetics

1) **Phonetics** is the study of how speech sounds are **made** and **received**.

2) It covers all **possible sounds** that the human vocal apparatus (vocal chords, tongue, lips, teeth, etc.) can make.

3) It focuses on **differences** in **articulation**, e.g. different accents.

Phonology

1) **Phonology** is the study of the **sound systems** of languages, in particular the **patterns** of sounds.

2) It focuses on **units** of sound, called **phonemes** (see below).

3) Unlike phonetics, in phonology you **don't** look at **differences** of **articulation**, e.g. if someone pronounces *stupid* as *shtupid*, the *s* and *sh* are still classed as the **same phoneme**, because the different pronunciation doesn't create a **different meaning**.

Phonemes are *Units* of *Sound*

1) The **smallest units** of **sound** are called **phonemes**. There are only about **44** phonemes in English, and combinations of them make up **all** the **possible** words and sounds in the language.

This is the International Phonetic Alphabet (IPA). It's different to the normal alphabet because it's used for writing all the possible phonemes (sounds) that humans can make in any language. Slanting brackets are used to distinguish between phonemes.

2) For example, the word *cat* has **three** phonemes — /k/ (like the *c* in *coat*), /ae/ (like the *a* in *bat*) and /t/ (like the *t* in *toy*). By **changing** one of these phonemes (e.g. /f/ for /k/) you can create a new word, *fat*.

3) The 26 letters of the **alphabet** can express **all** the possible sounds in English, e.g. **pairs** of letters (**digraphs**) like *sh-* and *ch-* can be used to represent **single phonemes**.

4) The study of phonemes is divided into **vowel sounds** and **consonant sounds**.

Vowel Sounds

1) There are about **twenty vowel sounds** in English, even though there are only **five** vowels in the alphabet.

2) E.g. the vowel *a* has a different sound depending on the word in which it appears. In *ape* it sounds different to when it's in *sat*, *care* and *saw*.

3) Vowel sounds are usually in the **centre** of a **syllable**, e.g. b<u>a</u>g, c<u>oa</u>t.

4) When a vowel sound is spoken, the **vocal tract** is always **open** — the **airway** is clear and your **vocal chords** rub together to 'voice' the sound. Vowel sounds are made by **altering** the **shape** of the **mouth**. The way vowel sounds are **pronounced varies** in **different** regions. This is how people can tell the difference between accents (see p.36-37).

Consonant Sounds

1) The number of **consonant sounds** in English is close to the **actual** number of **consonants** in the **alphabet**.

2) Consonants are mostly found at the **edges** of **syllables**, e.g. <u>b</u>oy<u>s</u>, <u>g</u>irl<u>s</u>. Sometimes they can appear in **sequences** of three or four consonants **together**, e.g. <u>str</u>ing or twe<u>lfth</u>.

3) Unlike vowels, they're mostly articulated by **closing** the vocal organs.

4) Some consonants are formed by **vibration** of the vocal cords, e.g. /b/ and /n/. The amount of vibration depends on the **position** of the consonant within the word. At the end of the word, the consonant is less pronounced. Other consonants don't use the vocal cords at all, such as /p/ and /s/.

Words are made up of *Syllables*

Syllables are a word's **individual units** of pronunciation. They are normally **combinations** of consonants and vowels.

1) The **centre** of a syllable is usually a **vowel sound**, e.g. b<u>u</u>n, t<u>y</u>ke.

2) Syllables can have one or more **consonants before** the **vowel**, e.g. <u>b</u>e, <u>sl</u>ow.

3) Many syllables have one or more consonants **following** the **vowel**, e.g. a<u>nt</u>.

4) They can also have consonants before **and** following the vowel, e.g. <u>pl</u>ay, <u>r</u>ea<u>d</u>.

5) **Monosyllabic** words have **one syllable**, e.g. *plate, car*. **Polysyllabic** words have **more than one** syllable, e.g. *amazing* (a-maz-ing), *cryogenic* (cry-o-gen-ic).

Phonology

Words Sound Different when they're Connected

Words are often pronounced **differently** than you'd expect when you see them **written down**.
This is because spoken language **combines** and **runs** sounds together.

Elision is when sounds are **left out**.
1) It happens especially in **rapid speech**, with words that have **clusters** of **consonants** or **syllables**.
2) For example, *library* is usually pronounced *libry*, and *everything* can become *evrythn*.

Assimilation is when sounds that are next to each other become **more alike**.
1) This happens especially in **rapid speech**, because it makes the words **easier** to say quickly.
2) For example, in the word *handbag*, *hand* becomes *ham*, to make it **easier** to **pronounce** with the syllable *bag*.

Liaison is when a **sound** is **inserted between** words or syllables to help them run **together** more smoothly.
1) For example — pronouncing /r/ at the **end of words**. When a word ending with *r* is **followed** by a word that **begins** with a **vowel**, the /r/ is **pronounced**, e.g. *mother ate* **sounds like** *mother rate*.
2) This is to avoid a gap between the words, known as **hiatus**.
3) Sometimes it's easier to link words with /r/ even if there's no r in the spelling — e.g. *media(r) interest*.

Phonological Frameworks are used to Analyse Sound Patterns

Part of **phonology** involves looking at how sounds can convey **meaning** and **association**.

1) **Rhythm** is very clear in **poetry**. Lines are often **constructed** so that the **stress** falls on **important** words, emphasising their meaning, e.g. *But to **go** to **school** in a **summer** morn, / Oh! it **drives** all joy away.* **Advertising** also uses rhythm, particularly in **slogans**, to help the audience **remember** the **product**.

2) **Rhyming** is when words have **similar endings**. It's usually associated with poetry and songs, but it's also used in planned speeches and in advertising. The rhyme words in a speech or text always **stand out**, and their meanings are often **linked**.

3) **Alliteration** is where two or more words close to each other **begin** with the **same sound**, e.g. *six sizzling sausages*.

4) **Assonance** is when the **vowel sounds** in the middle of two or more words are similar, e.g. *spoke* and *hope*. When vowel sounds **clash** with each other it's known as **dissonance**.

5) Alliteration and assonance are used in **creative writing** to **emphasise** words and show that the **meaning** is **linked** in some way. They're also used in **persuasive writing** to make phrases catchy and more memorable.

6) **Onomatopoeia** — this is when a word **sounds like** the noise it describes, e.g. *buzz, pop, bang, snap*.

7) Sometimes sounds can appear **symbolic** for other reasons, e.g. **closed vowels** in words like *chip* and *little* can suggest smallness, while **open vowels** in words like *vast* and *grand* can suggest largeness. It's not always the case, but it's worth noting **sound symbolism** like this when you're analysing a text.

Practice Questions

Q1 What is a phoneme? Give examples.
Q2 Give three features of consonants.
Q3 How can pronunciation be affected when words are connected?
Q4 What is the difference between alliteration and assonance?

Essay Question

Q1 How can the techniques of phonetics and phonology be applied in the analysis of a text or speech?

Mobiles, ringtones, texting — this phonology lark is pretty easy...

Apparently when phones were first invented, Alexander Graham Bell thought the best thing to say when you picked up was 'ahoy hoy'. But his rival Thomas Edison didn't like this so he used 'hello' instead, and that's what stuck. I reckon it's about time 'ahoy hoy' made a comeback — remember it next time you answer the phone, and make a poor dead inventor happy.

Non-Verbal Communication

AQA A, AQA B and WJEC need to know this first page. People don't just use words to communicate — lots of communication is non-verbal. Writing about this in a language exam can seem weird, but you may as well give it a whirl...

Non-Verbal Communication has Different Functions

Non-verbal communication (NVC) just refers to any way of getting your point across **without** using **words**. It's used for loads of different reasons.

- To **reinforce** what's being said, e.g. using gestures like pointing to support what you're saying.
- To **reveal feelings** that don't come across in the words that are being spoken, e.g. smiling while you say something nasty, to show that it's meant as a joke.
- To **take the place of speech**, e.g. waving instead of saying *hello*.
- As part of **social rituals**, e.g. greeting someone by shaking hands.
- To **present** yourself to others in a particular way, e.g. speaking in a high-prestige accent (see p.38), or dressing like a goth.

Prosody is the Non-Verbal Aspects of Speech

1) **Prosody** is about **how** you say things, rather than what you say.
2) These **non-verbal aspects** of **speech** help **communicate** attitudes and meaning.

'Non-verbal aspects of speech' just means all the aspects of speech that aren't words.

Pitch
- The **level** of the voice is most noticeable if it's particularly **high** or **low**.
- People might speak with a low pitch if they're relaxed, or depressed. They might speak in a high pitched voice if they're excited or frightened.

Volume
- Loudness can show **excitement** or **anger**.
- **Confident** speakers tend to speak more **loudly** than **nervous** speakers. Speaking quietly can also be a politeness strategy.

Pace
- The **speed** of speaking is another example of non-verbal communication.
- Slow, controlled speech can be calm and authoritative. Rapid speech can suggest excitement or panic.

Pauses
- Pauses can often be **awkward** in conversations, so people often try to fill them.
- They can show that speakers are **thinking** about what they say, or are **unsure** of themselves.

Intonation
- The same words can mean different things depending on how you say them, so **variation** in **tone** is important for getting the right meaning across.
- E.g. you could say something angrily or sarcastically. This is covered in more detail on p.30.

Stress
- Each word or phrase has a pattern of **stressed** and **unstressed syllables**. This is called **natural stress**.
- **Changing** the way these words are usually stressed can **change** the **meaning** — **emphatic stress**.

Rhythm
- This is similar to **stress**. Prepared speech often has a more strict rhythmic pattern of **stressed** and **unstressed** syllables than spontaneous speech.
- This is especially true if the speech has a **persuasive** purpose.

- The way that people **pronounce** words can also show how they want to **present themselves** to others.
- On formal occasions people might adopt a **higher social class accent** that's closer to **Received Pronunciation** (see page 39). Or they might use a **regional accent** to try to fit in, or to emphasise their background.

Non-Verbal Communication

This page is just for WJEC.

You can tell a lot from a person's Body Language

The way people use **non-verbal communication** sends messages about how they feel and what they mean. There are **three** main types of **body language**:

Gestures

1) **Gestures** can be used to **emphasise** meaning, or **instead** of words, e.g. you might point in the direction you've come from, or wave to mean *hello* or *goodbye*.

2) The **meanings** of gestures depends on the **context**, e.g. people might **point** to be **helpful** when they're showing someone where to go, or they might point at someone **aggressively** in an argument.

3) Meanings can also **differ** from one **culture** to another, e.g. in Bulgaria people shake their heads to mean *yes* and nod them to mean *no*.

Proximity and Posture

1) **Proximity** is the **distance** between speakers.

2) How you interpret the relationship between people can depend on the **context**, e.g. **closeness** can indicate **intimacy**, or it can be **threatening** because you're invading somebody else's space.

3) **Posture** can convey meaning, e.g. if someone has hunched shoulders, it could suggest a lack of confidence.

4) Sometimes people subconsciously adopt the **same posture** as the person they're talking to, e.g. both rest their chins on their hands. This is called **echoing**, and can show that the speakers agree with each other.

Facial Expressions

1) Lots of facial expressions are **universal**, e.g. a smile is a sign of pleasure or welcome in all cultures.

2) **Interpretation** still depends on **context** though, e.g. in some cultures it's seen as aggressive to maintain eye contact for a long time.

Steven's smile said it all.

People Communicate their Identity through their Appearance

It can feel strange to be talking about this in an English Language exam, but **meanings** are also conveyed through what people **look like**.

1) People **communicate** aspects of their **personality** and **social role** through their **appearance**. This includes things like clothing, hairstyles, physique, tattoos and jewellery.

2) For example, a uniform can show what a person's job or hobby is.

3) Appearance can show that you **identify** yourself as part of a **social group**, e.g. goths or emos.

4) It can also show the **formality** of a **social setting**, e.g. dressing in black tie for a ball.

Practice Questions

Q1 Explain the term 'non-verbal aspects of speech'.

Q2 Outline three examples of prosody and explain how they can help communicate meaning.

Q3 How can you detect when someone is nervous through their body language or prosody? Give two examples.

Essay Question

Q1 Explain the importance of non-verbal communication in getting meaning across.

Mmmmph mm ah ah mm — ooh erm shh mmmph mm....

It can seem a trifle odd to be talking about this stuff. Basically though, in fictional texts look out for things like stage directions and descriptions of characters. Italics or bolding might tell you which words are meant to be stressed. In transcripts of real conversations look at the amount and length of pauses — they can tell you about the situation and the speaker's mood.

Cohesion

These pages are just for AQA A and AQA B. Different ideas in a text need to be linked together, otherwise it won't make any sense as a whole. Cohesion is about the way that different parts of a text are connected.

Cohesion *refers to the* Structure *of a* Text

1) Cohesion **links ideas** in different parts of a text together.

2) Sometimes texts don't need to be particularly **cohesive** because they rely on **prior knowledge**. In this case the reader is expected to **fill in the gaps**, e.g. *The winter was one of the wettest on record. York was bracing itself.* These sentences don't appear to be connected — they rely on the reader to make a **link** between them. For them to make sense, the reader would have to know that heavy rain often causes flooding, which York is very prone to.

3) Generally, though, if a text isn't cohesive then it won't **make sense**. Cohesion is especially important in texts containing **complex arguments** or **development** of ideas.

4) Spoken language is also **cohesive**. See p.70 for how ideas are linked in prepared and spontaneous speech.

Grammatical Cohesion *is about* Linking Sentences

There are **five** main types of **grammatical cohesion**.

Reference

1) This involves **third person pronouns** (*he, she, it, they*) and **demonstrative pronouns** (*this, that*).

2) An **anaphoric reference** refers **back** to something that has already been mentioned. E.g.

   - *My grandmother went to university. **She** wanted to be a teacher.*
     The word *she* is the cohesive link between these sentences, because it refers back to the *grandmother*.

   - *He just couldn't stand ducks. **That** was the big problem.*
     Here, the cohesive word *that* refers back not to just one word, but the whole previous sentence.

3) References **forward** to something in the **future** are called **cataphoric references**. E.g.

   - *The goat gave **the following** reasons for its decision.*
     The sentence refers to something that has not actually been said yet, and will follow in the next sentences.

4) Reference to something **outside** the text is called an **exophoric reference**. The demonstrative pronouns refer to something in the **immediate**, **present context** of the utterance e.g. *that* tree over *there* (see p.10).

Identification

1) This is when **determiners** like *the, this* and *that* are used to show that a **noun** has already been mentioned. E.g.

   - *A large lorry blocked the road.*
     ***The** lorry had broken down.*

2) The **indefinite article** *a* is used the first time the lorry is mentioned. After that the **definite article** *the* is used to show that the clause is referring to the same noun.

Ellipsis

1) This is where words are **left out** of a sentence.

2) It's still cohesive if the **earlier** part of the text enables the reader to **supply** the **missing information**. E.g.

   - *His jeans were stained, his jacket was ripped and blood dripped down his face. What a state.*

3) The information given in the first sentence allows the reader to understand the second **incomplete** sentence: *What a state (he was in).*

Conjunctions

1) Conjunctions are words that **connect** different words, phrases and clauses, e.g. *and, because, then, although*.

2) They can be used to **link together** parts of a text and show the **relationship** between them. E.g.

   - *They'd been promised roast chicken **and** they were looking forward to it, **but** they were sadly disappointed.*

3) The conjunction *and* connects the second clause with the first clause — it shows that what they were *looking forward to* was *roast chicken*. The conjunction *but* qualifies what was said in the previous clause.

Adverbs

These connect clauses by referencing **space** and **time**. E.g.

   - *We're leaving London **tomorrow** morning, **before** the traffic gets bad.*

Cohesion

Lexical Cohesion is about Linking Words

Lexical cohesion links words through **meaning** and **association**, rather than through **grammatical structure**:

Repetition

1) Using the **same word** more than once can link separate sentences. E.g.
   *All we could see was **rain**. Anything would have been better than **rain**.*

2) Ideas can also be linked by using **synonyms** (see p.21) rather than exactly the same word. E.g.
   *He **wandered** slowly towards the building, then **ambled** down the corridor before **loitering** outside the door.*

3) This connects different events in the text, but ensures that there's still **variety**.

Collocation

1) Words that commonly appear together in lexical units are called **collocations**.

2) All **native speakers** of English understand its collocations easily, but non-native speakers might find them a bit bizarre. They are related by **association** rather than through any grammatically based rule.

3) Some words produce predictable collocations — you know what word will follow to complete a phrase because the collocation is so **familiar**, e.g. *neat and tidy*.

4) Collocations like this can't be **rearranged** — you'd always say *neat and tidy* rather than *tidy and neat*.

5) Collocations become well known phrases that are seen as **normal** and **acceptable**, e.g. it's perfectly normal to say *fast asleep*, but not *fast awake*, and *wide awake*, but not *wide asleep*.

6) Some words collocate more **broadly** but can still cause confusion for foreign speakers, e.g. the **verbs** that accompany certain phrases — you *make a mistake* rather than *perform* or *do* one.

7) Collocations aren't usually linked together by **meaning** — only by **familiar association**. You can be *green with envy*, but there's nothing green about envy.

8) Collocations are cohesive because they're **recognisable patterns** to the reader. If a word is paired with one that it doesn't collocate with then the **cohesion** and **fluency** of the statement is lost. E.g. you'd have to **stop and think** about the phrase *diamond clear* if you came across it in a text, because the collocation *crystal clear* is much more familiar.

Layout and Presentation can make a text Cohesive

This is a nice easy one to finish with...

1) **Graphological cohesion** is about making a text **look** cohesive.

2) It's particularly important in writing that's designed to be **persuasive**, e.g. adverts. The aim is to draw the reader's eye to the most important points, and make sure that the text looks **consistent** as a **whole**.

3) This is usually achieved by using the same **typeface** for running text, captions and headings, and by using a cohesive **colour scheme**.

Practice Questions

Q1   List five types of grammatical cohesion.

Q2   Explain how repetition has a cohesive effect on a text.

Q3   Explain what collocation is.

Essay Question

Q1   Find a newspaper and look at the front page. How has cohesion contributed to the meaning of the text?

I'm feeling strangely attracted to this page — must be the links effect...

This cohesion stuff is quite simple really, and these pages are a nice reminder of what to do in your essays too — if they don't have cohesion then they won't make any macaroni sense as a whole cheese. And nobody wants shoes like that he laughed. That might well be the case but there's no need to go on about it now. Good. Glad we've sorted those badgers out.

Pragmatics

This is for everyone apart from OCR. *It'd be a lot easier if everyone just said what they meant. Although not much fun if it turned out everyone meant to say that you smell and they hate your shoes. That's kind of what pragmatics is about.*

Pragmatics is about how Language is used in Social Situations

Pragmatics is the study of the part that language plays in **social situations**.

1) The meaning of what people say **isn't** always as **clear-cut** as it might seem.

2) There are lots of **unwritten social rules** that **prevent** people saying certain things, e.g. you probably wouldn't ask the Queen to *'put the kettle on, love'*.

3) There are also social conventions that make people say things in particular situations, e.g. saying *thank you* when somebody gives you something.

4) Pragmatics looks at **how** people get their **meaning** across within different **social contexts**. People often have to **imply** meanings rather than state them **directly**, so pragmatics concentrates on the meaning **behind** what's actually being said — the **subtext**.

> **EXAMPLE:**
>
> - In a meeting, an employee might say *it's a bit chilly in here*. What they actually mean is *can we close the window?* Saying it **indirectly** seems **less controlling** — it gives other people the opportunity to agree that it is chilly, and sets up a situation where **someone else** will offer to close the window.
>
> - Someone might say *I seem to spend all my time washing up* to their housemates. This is an **indirect request** for help, as what it actually means is *can someone else help?*

Prosody can Change the Meaning

Getting your meaning across isn't just about **what** you say, it's also about the **way** you say it.

Computers make the best friends — they're never sarcastic and they don't shout.

1) Prosody is part of non-verbal communication (see p.26). It includes **pitch**, **volume**, **pace**, **pauses**, **intonation** and **stress**.

2) The way that something is said can completely change its meaning, so looking at **prosodic features** is really important in **pragmatics**.

3) For example, there are loads of ways of saying this sentence that would **change** its **meaning**:

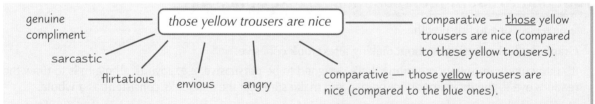

genuine compliment — *those yellow trousers are nice* — comparative — <u>those</u> yellow trousers are nice (compared to these yellow trousers).

sarcastic

flirtatious envious angry

comparative — those <u>yellow</u> trousers are nice (compared to the blue ones).

4) It can be really **difficult** to convey **prosodic features** in **writing**. Writers sometimes use **bolding**, <u>underlining</u> or *italics* to show where the emphasis should be. In fiction, they often have to **explain** how a character says something, e.g. *He answered quickly and angrily.*

The Words people Choose depend on the Audience and Context

This stuff is useful to know in your exam, because you can pick up on the **relationship** between speakers and the **context** they're in from how they speak to each other. For example:

1) If a speaker tells someone to *shut the door*, you might assume they were speaking to a **friend**, a **family member**, or someone they have **authority** over. You might also assume that they were in quite an **informal setting**.

2) If they said *I'm sorry but would you mind closing the door — there's a terrible draught* then you might assume that they were talking to a **stranger** or a **superior**. Friends or relatives would probably only speak to each other like this in a **formal setting**.

3) Any analysis like this is open to your **interpretation**, so it's good to discuss it even when speakers don't address each other as you might **expect** them to, e.g. family members might speak formally because they don't get on and feel uncomfortable around each other.

Pragmatics

Politeness Strategies ensure speakers Don't Cause Offence

No one knew how to tell Liz that the all-in-one body stocking wasn't a good look.

1) There are lots of **different ways** to communicate an idea. The way you do it depends on the **situation** — where you are and who you're with.

2) You might need to be **tactful** and **diplomatic**, or very **forceful**.

3) People use different **politeness strategies** depending on how they want to come across, even if the **underlying meaning** is still the **same**.

4) Here are some of the possible strategies for saying **no** in response to the question **would you like to go and see a film tonight?**:

Politeness Strategy	Example
Definite with negative word (e.g. *no, not, never*)	*No / no way / not a chance*. This sort of direct response would normally just be used with friends or family, because it's generally thought to be a bit rude.
Definite without negative word	*Are you serious? / I'd rather die*. These could be used for humorous effect, or if you really didn't care about being offensive.
Excuse	*I'd love to but I'm busy / Tonight isn't a very good night*. Excuses are used to justify why the answer is no.
Evasive	*Can we talk about this later / Now's just not a good time*. Evasive responses are used to avoid having to say no.
Apologetic	*Sorry... / I'm afraid...* People often apologise when they're saying no to soften their negative response.
Inarticulate	*Erm / Ah / Hmm* This usually shows that the person feels awkward and is trying to think of an excuse or a way to say no politely. If they stall for long enough, the meaning will become clear anyway.

5) People often use **more than one** politeness strategy in their response, e.g. if they were saying no, they might say *erm sorry no I can't tonight, I'm really busy*.

6) Politeness strategies also act as **conventions** for what to say in certain situations, e.g. it's normal in the UK to hear shop assistants and customers saying *thank you* to **each other** when a transaction is carried out at a till. Some politeness strategies like this are used **more** in the **UK** than in other countries.

7) Sometimes following the rules of politeness can lead to strategies being used in **strange ways**, e.g. people often say *sorry* when someone else bumps into them in the street.

Practice Questions

Q1 How do social conventions affect the way we speak?

Q2 Describe how prosody can affect meaning.

Q3 Name and describe the six politeness strategies you could use to turn down an invitation.

Essay Question

Q1 Explain how and why people alter the language they use depending on the social situation they're in.

Pragmatics — make sure you Czech your meaning...

This stuff can sound quite obvious, but until you start learning about all these social rules you often don't notice how weird they are. There's no actual law against going up to a stranger, giving them a hug and telling them how much you've missed them, but most people don't do it. It's a shame really — you never know, you might end up making a lovely new friend.

Graphology

AQA A, AQA B and Edexcel here. Graphology is about what pages look like, and how things like the layout can help get the meaning of the text across. It's also a chance to talk about pretty doodles and colours and borders.

Layout and Presentation can Emphasise Meaning

1) Text and images can be placed **next to** each other in **effective** ways. This is called **juxtaposition**. For example, **newspapers** might place **similar** stories next to each other on the page. They might also put **adverts** next to stories that they **correspond** with, e.g. an advert for an airline next to an article about holiday destinations.

2) If the **text** is **broken up** with **borders** or **boxes** then it's designed to draw the reader's **attention** to a particular section. It also makes the text seem more **appealing**. **Colour** and **graphics** can have the same effect.

3) It's good to mention whether the layout fits in with the **form**, e.g. you'd expect a newspaper article to have a bold heading and text set out in columns. Sometimes texts adopt the conventions of **different forms** for **effect**, e.g. a newspaper article might be set out like a letter or a diary.

Typeface is often called Font

This is a bit of a confusing one — until everyone started using computers, **typeface** and **font** were seen as completely **different** things.

1) **Typeface** was things like Arial and Times New Roman, and **font** just referred to the size of the text and whether it was **bold** or *italic*.

2) But now the terms tend to be used **interchangeably**, and most people would call t̶h̶e̶s̶e̶ **different fonts** ̶n̶o̶t̶ ̶d̶i̶f̶f̶e̶r̶e̶n̶t̶ typefaces.

3) When you're talking about the style of the lettering in the exam, it's probably best to stick to saying **typeface**.

Magda had never seen such a gorgeous typeface.

There are some general things to look out for:

Ascenders and Descenders
- These are the '**stems**' of letters.
- The bits that extend **upwards** are the **ascenders**, on letters like 'd', 'h' and 'l'.
- The bits that extend **downwards** are **descenders**, on letters like 'j', 'q' and 'y'.
- **Long** ascenders and descenders could be used to indicate **sophistication** or **elegance**.

Leading
- This is the amount of **vertical space** between **lines** of type.
- It can affect whether the text is dense and difficult to read, or very spaced out.

Serif
- These are small **strokes** on the **ends** of letters.
- Typefaces that don't include them are called *sans serif* (**without serifs**).
- Typefaces with serifs tend to seem **traditional**, while *sans serif* typefaces are considered more **modern**.

A — serif

A — sans serif

Typeface is used to create Different Effects

In any text the **typeface** has been chosen for a particular **reason**, so you need to consider the **effect** it has.

1) The choice of **typeface** tells you about the **tone** of the text. Typefaces can seem traditional, informal, youthful, elegant, etc. They can be can be made to look like handwriting, for example.

2) Bold, italics and underlining can place **emphasis** on certain parts of the text to show that it's **important**.

3) The use of **upper** and **lower case** letters can also be significant. Words can be **capitalised** to draw attention to them. Sometimes the typeface is all **lower case**, which can appear **stylish**, **modern** or **experimental**.

Graphology

Graphemes are Units in a Writing System

1) **Graphemes** are the **smallest units** that can create **contrasts** in **meaning**, e.g. letters of the alphabet like <f> and <e>, and symbols like <,> and <&>.

2) For linguistic analysis they're usually written in **angle brackets** — e.g. <m>, <?>.

3) They can appear in loads of **different** forms, depending on things like **typeface** and **handwriting style**, e.g. <a> can be written as A *A* **a** *a* etc.

4) A different form of a grapheme is called a **glyph**. When **different glyphs** can be used for the **same grapheme**, e.g. A *A* **a** *a* for the grapheme <a>, then they're called **allographs**.

5) Most **graphemes** don't mean anything on their own — their role is to **combine** and **contrast**.

6) However, some **graphemes** can be **interpreted** in **more than one way**, so the **context** they're used in is important:

For example, <x> has many uses — it can mean:

> **EXAMPLE:**
>
> - A **kiss** at the end of a letter.
> - An **incorrect answer**.
> - For **adults only** — X-rated.
> - '**Illiterate**' when it's used on a form in place of someone's name.
> - '**Location**' — X marks the spot.
> - An indication of **choice**, e.g. when a **ballot paper** is marked with an x.

Graphics can Convey Meaning

1) Graphics can be cartoons, illustrations, tables, photographs and diagrams.

2) Graphics can **break up** the layout of **dense text**, making it more accessible and less formal.

3) They're usually **visual representations** of the text, which help to **illustrate** and **develop** its meaning.

4) They might have the simple **function** of making the meaning **clearer**. This is especially true of **instructional texts** which often use diagrams, and **children's texts**, which might be illustrated to help children learn to read.

5) They could also be used to set the **tone** of a piece, e.g. a cartoon might be used to add humour.

6) Sometimes a graphic will be a deliberate **contrast** to the text, e.g. in a parody or satirical piece of writing.

Don't dwell on graphics for too long — make sure you talk about language by linking your analysis to the text.

Practice Questions

Q1 Give four effects that using different typefaces can create.

Q2 What is a grapheme?

Q3 What function can graphics have in a text?

Essay Question

Q1 Look at two different newspapers, one tabloid and one broadsheet.
Analyse the effect of graphological features like typeface and graphics, and the relationship they have with the text.

This is a nightmare — I can barely remember how to draw a bar chart...

It's one of those cruel ironies — you can harp on all you like about how colours and borders can help emphasise meaning, and how a picture paints a thousand words, but the minute you choose to answer your exam in cartoon form, or perhaps create a little flip book in the corners to help get your point across, suddenly everyone changes their tune...

Register and Mode

Everyone back on board here: AQA A, AQA B, OCR, Edexcel and WJEC. These pages are about the 'type' of language you use in certain situations.

Register is the Type of Language used in different Situations

Registers are the different **varieties** of language used in different **situations**. Deciding which register is **appropriate** to use depends on several factors.

Audience
- This is to do with the **relationship** between the speaker or writer and the audience.
- E.g. if the speaker or writer knows the audience personally, the **register** they use will usually be quite **informal**. It might include informal lexis, like slang and abbreviations (see p.18-19 for more on lexis).
- This may be more apparent in informal speech than in informal writing.

Purpose
- E.g. a **report** will use a **formal register**, as its **purpose** is to convey information accurately.
- When the purpose is more **persuasive**, e.g. an advert, the register will often be more **informal** as the text needs to get the audience's attention in order to persuade them.

Field
- This is the subject being talked about.
- E.g. if the topic is **football**, the **lexis** will include words linked to football, like *match, penalty*, etc.
- Some fields have a larger specialist lexicon (stock of words), like **biochemistry**. Most workplaces have their own lexicon connected solely with that field, from car repair shops to hospitals (see p.60-63 for more on occupational language).

Form
- E.g. business letters will be written in a **formal register** because of the **professional context**. Text messages, on the other hand, tend to use a more **informal register**, as the context is generally social.

Whether the register is **appropriate** depends on the **context** it's used in — using an **informal register** in a **formal situation** is **inappropriate** because it could seem **disrespectful** or **rude**. Using **formal language** in an **informal situation** could sound **unfriendly** and **stuffy**.

Registers Vary in terms of Lexis, Grammar and Phonology

Different **registers** use different **lexis** and **grammar**, and the way they're **pronounced** can **vary** too. For example:

Lexis
- A conversation between two **specialists** would contain **technical vocabulary** that they would both understand. (see p.60-63 for more on occupational language).
- For example, the lexis in the registers used by **mechanical** and **medical** specialists would be very different.

Grammar
- **Register** can affect syntax — the **structure** of clauses and **complexity** of sentences.
- Some registers even have grammatical constructions that are **specific** to them, like the legal register (known as **legalese**), which uses lots of clauses and mainly passive sentences.

Phonology
- This is to do with how the words in a particular **register** are **pronounced**.
- The **informal register** people use when speaking to friends involves things like dropping the <h> from words like *have* and missing a <g> off words like *thinking*.
- Generally speaking, the more **formal** a situation is the more likely people are to **modify** their **accent** so it's closer to **Received Pronunciation** (see p.39).

Register and Mode

Modes can be Written or Spoken

Written modes

1) Written modes include letters, essays, novels, recipes and reports. Written modes tend to be the **most formal**.

2) In written modes the words have to make the **meaning** clear, because there's no opportunity for **non-verbal communication** between the writer and the reader.

3) Sometimes writers try to convey **prosodic features** like tone, intonation and pitch to make the meaning clearer, using **features** like *italicising*, underlining, CAPITALISATION, and **punctuation** like exclamation marks.

Spoken modes

1) Spoken modes are things like interviews, broadcasts and presentations. Spontaneous speech (like a conversation between friends) is normally the **least formal** mode.

2) In **spoken modes** speakers can rely on **non-verbal communication** like gestures and **prosodic features** (see p.26-27 and p.30) to get their point across.

3) The grammar of informal speech is often **disjointed** — it contains lots of **interruption** and **incomplete sentences**. It also contains **non-fluency features** (things that interrupt the flow of speech) like **self-correction, pauses, repetition, fillers** (*you know, sort of, I mean*) and **false starts**.

4) Speech also tends to contain **phatic expressions** (small talk expressions that have a **social function**, so their meaning isn't particularly important, like *hello* and *how's things*).

AQA A only

Modes can be **classified** in different ways — texts can be grouped according to the following approaches.

1) **Continuum classification** — position on a **scale** that places written Standard English at one end and spoken informal speech at the other. In the middle are things like telephone conversations and email (see below).

2) **Typology** — grouping together types of language that have **characteristics** or **traits** in common, e.g. sports commentaries, music reviews, formal interviews, novels, poems, etc.

3) **The dimensions approach** — looking at different aspects of modes, e.g. lexis, grammar and structure to analyse the level of formality in a certain text.

Multi-Modal Texts contain Features of both Speech and Writing

Lots of texts are a **mixture** of **spoken** and **written** modes, especially electronic texts like **emails** and **text messages**.

1) These are **written modes** that can contain elements of **spoken language**, e.g. **phatic communication** like *hello* and *bye*.

2) Very **informal** emails or messages between friends contain **phonetic spellings**, like *b4* for *before*, and *u* for *you*.

3) **Formal** business emails still tend to be **less formal** than **letters** — they tend not to use **conventions** like writing the sender's address at the top. **Paragraphs** and **sentences** tend to be **shorter**.

Practice Questions

Q1 Outline three factors that influence which register is used.

Q2 How can registers vary in terms of phonology?

Q3 Name three differences between spoken and written modes.

Essay Question

Q1 Discuss how and why writers employ different registers in different situations, giving examples.

It shouldn't be the mode difficult thing to underdand...

Modes, continuums, typology... I don't know when it all became so complicated. Makes you long for a time when all you had to worry about was sitting on the mat and watching Words and Pictures. Then a bag of crisps for morning break, a bit of a play in the sand, and home before 3.30. Yes, life really was much better back in year 11...

Accent and Dialect

Ignore these two pages if you're doing AQA A. English isn't just spoken or written in one way — there are loads of different varieties. This bit is all about dialect and accent — basically, what you say and how you say it...

Accents are Variations in Pronunciation

1) **English** words can be **pronounced** in different ways.
The different **patterns** of pronunciation are called **accents**.

2) Accents can be affected by the speaker's **regional** or **social** background.

3) An accent can be a feature of a dialect. But it's **different** to **dialect** because it just refers to **how** you say words, not the words themselves.

> You need to consider accents when you look at the phonology of spoken language (see p.24-25).

> 1) Pronunciation and intonation can vary over **large geographic areas** like countries, e.g. the difference between American, Australian and UK English.
>
> 2) In **England**, most people can tell the difference between **northern accents** and **southern accents**. The main differences are between **vowel sounds**, e.g.
>   Someone with a **northern accent** would say *path* with a short vowel sound, to sound like *cat*.
>   Someone with a **southern accent** would say *parth*, with a long vowel sound.
>
> 3) Sometimes people that live near each other can tune in to **smaller** differences in each other's accents, to the point where you can often tell if someone's from your town or one a few miles away.

Dialects are Variations in Language

1) A **dialect** is a **variation** in a language, with its own distinctive features of **vocabulary**, **grammar** and **pronunciation**. It's different to **accent** because it refers to the **specific words** you use, not just **how** you **say** them.

2) The term **dialect** is usually used to describe language that's particular to a specific **geographical region**.

3) It's also sometimes used as a **general** term for variations in language that are the result of **social background** (**sociolect** — see p.40) or **personal differences** (**idiolect** — see p.41).

> **Vocabulary**
>
> Different dialects have different words for things, e.g.
>
> - Someone from Yorkshire might say *anyroad* for *anyway*.
> - People in Lancashire might call a *bread roll* a *barm*.
> - In the West Country *acker* means *friend*.
> - In East Anglia to *mardle* is to *gossip*.

> **Grammar**
>
> The way that people form sentences can depend on their dialect. Regional dialects often contain **non-standard** grammar (see p.38), e.g.
>
> - *them* as a demonstrative adjective — *look at **them** books*
> - Double negatives — *we **don't** want **none***
> - Missing plurals — *it costs four **pound***
> - Missing the *-ly* suffix off the end of adverbs — *I walked **slow***
>
> Some grammatical variations are **specific** to a **particular** dialect, e.g. people from **Yorkshire** might miss out the definite article *the*, so they might say *I cleaned car* rather than *I cleaned **the** car*. The **Scouse** dialect has *youse* as the plural of *you* — e.g. *what are youse doing*?

> **Pronunciation**
>
> 1) Most regional dialects have an **accent** to go with them. So you'd probably expect a **Geordie** (someone from Newcastle) to say the word *town* like *toon*, or someone from **Cornwall** to pronounce the *r* in *water*.
>
> 2) But don't forget — accents are just **one feature** of a dialect. You can use words and constructions from one dialect but speak in the accent of another.

Accent and Dialect

People Have **Different Attitudes** towards **Accents** and **Dialects**

People sometimes make assumptions about others based on the variety of English they use, e.g. people from the **north** of England often think that people with **southern accents** sound '**posh**'.

1) **Workman (2008)** studied people's **perceptions** of different **accents**. Participants listened to recordings of different accents while they looked at photos of people.

2) It was found that participants rated the **intelligence** of the people in the photos differently, depending on which accent they thought they had.

3) **Yorkshire** accents were rated as sounding the **most intelligent**. When a recording of a **Birmingham** accent was played, the people in the photo were rated as being much **less intelligent**. Obviously this **isn't** actually **true**, but it shows how strong the **stereotypes** about different accents can be.

Someone's **accent** or **dialect** is often a good indication of **where they're from**. But it can also provide clues about their **social background** and **education**.

1) **Standard English** (p.38) is a **social dialect**. It's usually associated with **educated**, **middle** and **upper class** people. It's the way that you're taught to use English at school, and the language of **formal speech** and **writing**.

2) Some people **assume** that people who use **regional dialects** are **less well educated**, or **lower class**.

3) On the other hand, **regional varieties** of English are often associated with being **down-to-earth** and **modest**, e.g. there are now lots of TV presenters with regional accents, because their accents are seen as being more **accessible** to audiences (see p.39).

You need to look at **Written Language** as well

Dialect and accent don't just apply to **spoken language**.

1) **Transcripts** of speech can show features of **regional dialects**. Look out for dialect words and grammatical constructions, e.g. *we **seen** her yesterday with her **bairns***.

2) **Literary texts** can contain representations of **accents** as well as **dialects**. The author has included these features for a reason — the way characters speak **reflects** something about them. For example, in *Oliver Twist* by **Charles Dickens**, the Artful Dodger says to Oliver "*I've got to be in London to-night; and I know a '**spectable** old **genelman** as lives there, **wot'll** give you lodgings for **nothink***". These features imply things about the character, e.g. that he's from London and he's lower class.

3) Some literary texts are written **entirely** in a **regional dialect**, rather than **Standard English**. This is called **dialect literature**. Authors do this for different reasons, e.g. to make the story seem more **authentic** and **realistic**, or to make a statement about attitudes towards regional varieties of English.

Practice Questions

Q1 What is the difference between accent and dialect?

Q2 Give two examples of how regional dialects can vary from Standard English.

Q3 Outline some of the different attitudes that people sometimes have towards regional accents and dialects.

Essay Question

"I mean as 'appen Ah can find anuther pleece as'll du for rearin' th' pheasants. If yo' want ter be 'ere, yo'll non want me messin' abaht a' t' time."

She looked at him, getting his meaning through the fog of the dialect.

"Why don't you speak ordinary English?" she said coldly.

"Me! — Ah thowt it *wor*' ordinary."

From *Lady Chatterley's Lover*,
by DH Lawrence

Q1 Identify some features of regional dialect, and explain what the author is suggesting about attitudes towards them.

Ain't naw use twinin bout revision — quit yer mitherin and gerronwi'it...

It's best to think of English like a family-sized variety pack of crisps, full of different flavours. Scouse and Onion, Salt and Lancashire, Prawn Cockneytail (that's a good one) — they're all here for you to crunch loudly in your dad's ear while he's trying to watch the news. Yes, with its tasty potato-based dialects and crinkle-cut accents, English really is the king of snacks...

Standard English and RP

These two pages are just for AQA B, OCR and Edexcel. There are so many different varieties of English that it's a wonder people can understand each other. But they can, and it's down to a little thing called standardisation...

Standard English is a Social Dialect

Standard English is a dialect of English. It has distinctive features of **vocabulary**, **grammar** and **spelling**.

1) A **standard** form of a language is one that is considered to be **acceptable** or correct by **educated** speakers.

2) In **medieval England** people in different parts of the country spoke very different **dialects**. They were so varied that people from different regions would have had **difficulty understanding** each other.

3) The **Standard English** used today started off as the **regional dialect** of the East Midlands. Its influence spread around the country, and it became the dialect that was used in print.

4) As more books were printed, **variations** in **spelling** and **grammar** were ironed out — the language started to conform towards a **standard**.

5) People began to **codify** the language (decide how to write it) in **dictionaries** and books of **grammar rules**. For example, Johnson's dictionary, printed in 1755, aimed to standardise spellings and word meanings.

6) The standard form of the language became associated with **education**, **class** and **power**.

> It's difficult to give examples of **Standard English** as a dialect, because it's what other dialects are usually compared with. As a general example though, this book is written in Standard English, as it contains mostly **standardised vocabulary**, **spellings** and **syntax**.

Standard English is used in Lots of Situations

Standard English is the most widely understood version of English, so it's used in lots of different fields:

1) **Education** — Standard English is the variety of English taught in schools, and it's what people are taught when they learn English as a foreign language.

2) **Media** — it's used in newspapers and by newsreaders on the TV.

3) **Formal documents** — it's the language used in essays, business letters and reports.

4) **Formal speech** — you'd expect people to speak using Standard English in formal situations like business negotiations and public announcements.

People have Different Attitudes towards Standard English

1) As one variety of the language became standardised, other varieties became seen as **less prestigious**.

2) **Regional dialects** were associated with the **uneducated** and the **lower classes**, so it was seen as important to be able to use English '**properly**' if you wanted to be successful.

> **Standard English** is often seen as the '**correct**' or '**pure**' form of the language. Other varieties are sometimes thought to be '**corruptions**' of it. There's a view that if you use another dialect, you're not using English '**properly**'.

> However, most **linguists** argue that all varieties of English should be **valued equally**. There's **no reason** why Standard English should be seen as better than any other dialect. They claim that people shouldn't be thought of as **uneducated** or **lower class** if they **don't** use Standard English.

Standard English and RP

Received Pronunciation (RP) is a Social Accent

1) **Received Pronunciation** is an **accent**, traditionally associated with **educated** people and the **upper classes**.

2) This means it's **different** from other accents, which normally indicate which **region** the speaker's from.

3) Traditionally **RP** and **Standard English** are linked — the most **prestigious** way of speaking would be Standard English using RP. While lots of people speak Standard English (or something close) with regional accents, you don't generally hear people saying dialect words and phrases in RP.

4) The most recognisable examples of RP are how the **Queen** speaks, and the traditional speech of **BBC presenters**. Because of this, people sometimes refer to RP as the **Queen's English**, or **BBC English**.

5) Because RP has been seen as the standard, accepted way of speaking English, it's the accent many people are taught to use when they learn English as a **foreign language**.

Emma had just received some very juicy pronunciation.

> **Some features of RP**
> - **Long vowel** sounds in words like *grass* (grarss) and *castle* (carstle).
> - **Long vowel** sound in words like *come* and *under*.
> - Pronouncing **hs** and **ts** in words like *hat* and *letter*.

RP has Changed Over Time

Language is always changing, and nowadays very few people actually use RP in its 'original' form, e.g. BBC newsreaders use **Standard English**, but they speak it in a range of **regional accents**. Even the Queen's accent has changed a bit from when she was first crowned 50 years ago.

> **Estuary English**
>
> 1) Some linguists claim that **RP** is being replaced as the most 'acceptable' English accent by **Estuary English**. This is an **accent** that has roots in the speech found around the **Thames Estuary** in **London**.
>
> 2) It contains many similar features to the **Cockney** accent, e.g. dropping **hs** at the beginning of words (pronouncing *hit* like *it*), and pronouncing **th** like **f** (so *mouth* becomes *mouff*).
>
> 3) It's used by a lot of people in the **entertainment industry**, as it's seen as a **commercially acceptable** accent.
>
> 4) Because of the **influence** of the **media**, Estuary English is becoming increasingly common **outside** of London. You can't necessarily tell where someone's from if they use Estuary English — it's become a **widespread accent**.

Practice Questions

Q1 Identify which of the following statements are in Standard English and which aren't. Explain why.
'I were going home when I spotted 'im.'
'The circumference of the circle ain't 54.'
'Turn left at the end of the road. Then take a sharp right.'

Q2 What factors contributed to the rise of Standard English as the accepted dialect?

Q3 Name four instances when you might use Standard English.

Q4 What is RP?

Essay Question

Q1 The use of Standard English and RP in the media has changed over the last 50 years. Identify some of these changes and comment on why they might have taken place.

wivowt stndrd inglish we cudnt undrstnd eech uvver...

Aha, I've done something rather clever there — I've shown that we can still understand each other even without Standard English. That's OK, there's no need to applaud, it's all in a day's work. It does make you wonder why people bang on about using 'good English' so much though, and whether it's right that one variety should be seen as better than the others...

Sociolect and Idiolect

These two pages are just for AQA B, OCR and Edexcel. You don't spend all your time talking to yourself in the bathroom mirror, so it makes sense that the way you speak is affected by who you're with and what you're doing...

Sociolect *is the* Language *of* Social Groups

Sociolects (or **social dialects**) are **varieties** of language used by particular **social groups**, e.g. middle-aged lawyers speak differently from school children. The sociolects of different groups help to give them their own **identities**.

The language people use depends on different social factors:

Socio-economic status

- Studies have shown that **middle** and **upper class** people tend to use more **standard forms** (see p.38-39) than **lower class** people.
- The language of lower class people is more likely to contain features of **regional dialect** (p.36-37).

The points in this section are generalisations, so they're not true for everyone.

Education

- Studies show that **well-educated** people are more likely to use **Standard English** and **RP** (see p.38-39) than less well-educated people.
- They're usually less likely to use words and sentence structures from **regional dialects**.

Age

- Sociolects used by teenagers tend to include more **non-standard** forms and **slang** (p.42-43) than language used by adults.
- They also include more influences from, and references to, **popular culture**.

Occupation (there's more on language and occupation on p.60-63)

- Every occupation has its own specialist terms and technical vocabulary, known as **jargon**.
- You might expect a lawyer to talk about *tort* (a civil wrong) or *GBH* (grievous bodily harm), and a doctor to talk about *prescriptions* or *scrubs*.
- Sometimes these **sociolects** also have distinctive **grammatical** features, e.g. legal documents often contain **complex** sentences with lots of subordinate clauses.

Belief system and culture

- **Religious groups** use lots of **specialist vocabulary**, e.g. *Diwali* (the Hindu festival of light), *kosher* (food prepared in accordance with Jewish law), *salah* (Islamic daily prayers).
- Because UK society is **multicultural**, lots of words from other languages and cultures have become part of a **wider** sociolect.
- For example, the word *kosher* isn't just used by members of the Jewish community. It's taken on a **broader** meaning in the English language, so people often use it to mean *genuine* or *legitimate*.

The Way you Speak can Depend on the Situation

Language that's **appropriate** in one social group might not be appropriate in another. People **adapt** the way they speak depending on the **situation** they're in, and how they want to present themselves. For example:

1) **Politicians** tend to use **Standard English** when they're making a political speech, because they're in a formal situation. But when they're talking to individuals on the street they might use **non-standard** language and features of **regional dialect**, so that they seem down-to-earth.

2) Lots of people find that the way they speak to their **friends** is different from how they speak to their **parents**. They might use more **slang** with their friends, or speak in the same **regional dialect** as their parents when they're at home.

3) Some people have a **telephone voice** — a different voice that they use on the phone. Usually it involves using more **standard** forms and an accent that's closer to **Received Pronunciation**.

"Hello? Yes, I'd like to speak to a Mr Hugh Jass".

Sociolect and Idiolect

Idiolect is the Unique Language of an Individual

1)   The word choices that people make, and the way they form sentences, are specific to them.

2)   This means that the way you use language can **identify** you, like a **fingerprint**.

3)   Your **idiolect** is the result of a **unique combination** of **influences**.

Where you're from
- Where you're from affects how you speak. You might expect a person from Newcastle to have a Geordie **accent** and use **dialect** words like *gan* for *go*.
- But not everyone from the same **area** speaks in exactly the **same** way.
- A person could have **moved** from somewhere else and so **retained** aspects of **other** regional accents and dialects.

Social background
- The way you speak is also influenced by your **social background** (**sociolect** — see the previous page).
- Your sociolect is the **product** of lots of different **factors** such as socio-economic status, age, religious beliefs, education and gender.
- It's also affected by influences from **smaller** social groups, e.g. schools, sports teams and groups of friends.

"By 'eck, lad, this is a crackin' spread. Now pass us another pikelet."

Personal characteristics
- The language a person uses could be affected by aspects of their **personality**.
- For example, a **nervous** person might use sentences with lots of **fillers** (*um, like, sort of* etc.).

Practice Questions

Q1   What is a sociolect?

Q2   Give four examples of social groups that might have their own sociolect.

Q3   How might the situation you're in affect the way you speak?

Q4   What is an idiolect?

Q5   Give three factors that might influence a person's idiolect.

Essay Question

Q1   What can a person's use of language reveal about their identity?

You could comment on group influence, accent, dialect, slang, and social background.

Idiolect — the opposite of intellect...

You might have realised by now that language is a bit of a witch's brew — a foul concoction made up of dialect, sociolect and a pinch of accent, all stirred together and simmered gently under the light of the full moon. After twenty minutes take it off the heat, rinse around the gums, gargle, spit, and hey presto! A fun new voice to amaze your friends and family...

Slang

This is for everyone apart from AQA A. Here comes the final push before the end of the section, and we've saved the best till last. These pages are about slang. Cue embarrassing attempts at being cool and down with the kids...

Slang is Informal Vocabulary

1) **Slang** refers to **informal**, **non-standard** words and expressions that tend to be used in **casual speech**.

2) It's often **inventive** and **creative**, and enters the language in lots of different ways.

New meanings for existing words	Shortening existing words	New words
• *cool, wicked* — good	• *telly* — television	• *moolah* — money
• *sad* — pathetic	• *rents* — parents	• *yonks* — a long time, ages
• *chick* — girl	• *mare* — nightmare	• *snog* — kiss

Slang has Different Purposes

1) People tend to use slang to **identify** that they're part of a particular **social group** — it's part of their **sociolect** (see p.40). Using particular slang shows that you **fit in** and suggests **shared values**.

2) Slang can act as a code to **exclude outsiders**, e.g. groups of teenagers might use slang to establish a sense of identity which is separate from the adult world. It can be **exclusive** and **secretive**.

3) Two of the main **purposes** of using **slang** are to be **rebellious** or **entertaining**.

> **Slang and social taboos**
>
> • There's lots of slang for **taboo subjects** — things that are thought of as **inappropriate** or **unacceptable** to talk about in formal social situations, e.g. words for sex, sex organs and bodily functions.
>
> • Some of the most common and most offensive slang words are **swear words**.
>
> • It's seen as **taboo** to swear in some situations, e.g. in class at school. In this case the purpose of swearing is to be **rebellious**.
>
> • In other situations swearing is an **accepted** part of a group's **sociolect**, and people do it to **fit in** and be **entertaining**, e.g. when they're talking with a group of friends.
>
> • Not all **slang** is **taboo language**, but there's a lot **more** slang for **taboo subjects** than for any others.

Slang is Specific to Social and Regional Groups

1) Some slang words are **familiar** to **lots of speakers**, e.g. most people in the UK probably know that **tenner** is short for **ten pounds**.

2) However, slang also **varies** depending on which **region** speakers are from. Sometimes it's difficult to distinguish slang words from regional dialect variants.

3) One example of **regional slang** is Cockney rhyming slang, e.g. *butcher's hook* — **look**.

4) The slang a person uses also depends on **social factors**, e.g. a middle class speaker will probably speak something close to **Standard English** and use fewer slang words than a working class speaker.

5) Some slang is only used by very **small social groups**, like a particular school or group of friends.

6) Slang reflects **multiculturalism**, as slang terms can come from lots of different cultures, e.g. **tucker** — an Australian slang word for food.

7) The **media** also influences slang and gives people **access** to different subcultures.

> • British **youth** culture has been particularly influenced by **African American** slang, through popular music and TV.
>
> • **Hip hop culture** has introduced black American slang that lots of English speakers now recognise, e.g. *sick* — good, *bling* — flashy jewellery, *crib* — house.

Slang

Slang *is always* Changing

Slang changes very quickly as words go in and out of **fashion**.

1) Lots of slang words used to be popular, but you wouldn't hear them any more, e.g. *cove* — man, *beak* — magistrate, *viz* — face, *cits* — citizens.

2) Slang terms can quickly start to sound **dated**, e.g. *mega* — good, *dweeb* — someone who isn't cool. This happens especially with **teenage slang** that becomes more **mainstream** when adults and young children start using it, which causes teenagers to stop using it.

3) Sometimes slang terms become so widely used that they become part of **Standard English**, e.g. *okay*, *phone* and *bus*. These words were once considered **informal**, but now it would seem formal to say *telephone*, and very unusual to say *omnibus*.

4) The **opposite** can also happen — words can go from being formal or acceptable, to being classed as vulgar. An example of this is the word *arse*, which wasn't thought of as informal until the 17th century.

People have **Different Attitudes** towards **Slang**

Slang is sometimes seen as **low level**, **vulgar** language, which shouldn't be used in **writing** or in **formal situations**.

1) Some people think that if you use slang you're **undermining standards** by not using the language '**properly**'. They assume that people who use lots of slang are lower class and uneducated.

2) Slang is seen as the language of **informal speech**, so it's considered **inappropriate** to use it in a **formal context**, e.g. you'd lose marks if you wrote an essay using slang words and phrases.

3) This is because slang has a reputation for being **rebellious** and **subversive**, so it isn't formally accepted as a variety of English. Some people worry it doesn't follow the 'proper' **spelling** and **grammar rules** of **Standard English**.

4) However, most slang words and phrases **do** follow the rules of Standard English — they're just more flexible.

5) People who are interested in slang argue that it's an **intelligent** and **creative** variety of language, which **changes** and **develops** very quickly. It also serves an important **social purpose** — people use it to **identify** themselves as part of a **group**.

Practice Questions

Q1 Identify which word in each pair is slang, and which is Standard English:
Old Bill / police, upset / gutted, tired / knackered, quids in / wealthy, lucky / jammy

Q2 Give two reasons why people might use slang.

Q3 Explain two ways in which slang can change over time.

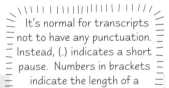

It's normal for transcripts not to have any punctuation. Instead, (.) indicates a short pause. Numbers in brackets indicate the length of a pause in seconds.

Essay Question

A: yeah I had a well good time (.) just really chilled (2.0) just sat on my arse all day

B: wish I had (.) Gemma was being a bitch again (.) I had to keep nipping off to phone her

A: it's not on

B: tell me about it (1.0) I wanna be like your attitude stinks but she'll just blank me till I cave in so what you gonna do

A: chuck her (.) she ain't worth it

Q1 Identify the different types of slang used in this extract and comment on the purpose it serves.

Cripes chums — learning about slang is smashingly wizard...

Good old Eng Lang — there aren't many subjects where you get the chance to discuss the ins and outs (oo-er) of swearing like this. Although I suppose the point of rude words is that they're not quite as fun if you're allowed to use them. Few things are likely to raise more of a snigger than slipping words like knockers into an exam answer...

Sources and Exam Questions

This is an exam-style question, based on sources like the ones you'll get in the real paper.

Text A is a conversation between three teenagers discussing some friends.
Text B is an extract from *Lady Windermere's Fan*, in which several friends discuss Mrs Erlynne.

1) Compare and contrast the extracts, commenting on the different varieties of English used. *[48 marks]*

Text A — a conversation between teenage friends

A: mate you can't be serious

B: do I look like I'm joking (.) seriously he is

A: oh he is really not

B: come on no right (.) right he is though cos he's like

A: // he's proper minging

C: he is he's minging he is

B: // ah come on though I mean it's not like he is like compared to some people

A: compared to some people even more minging than him

B: well obviously compared to that right

A: // well then

B: // but that don't even make sense

C: why not

B: thing is though he's (2) okay thing is he's well fit

C: // [inaud]

B: // but he can be he can be well horrid sometimes

A: yeah right like (.) like exactly right I mean it's not like he's ever tret anyone good is it really

B: well I dunno (.) I dunno like he tret amanda quite good till she chucked him

A: she didn't dump

C: // it was him what got rid right (.) it was him what like got rid of her that's why why erm why she's

A: that's why she's such a mardy cow with him innit though right

B: // mardy cow that's

A: // yeah don't jip me right (3) no stop your giggling right she's well mardy with him

C: it's not like you can go blaming her for that though though (.) I mean bless her though cos fact of the matter is (.) fact is that she didn't do nowt wrong and he he he was he went behind her back and proper messed with her head (.) cos it was when she was supposed to meet him at pub (.) right she was gonna meet him at pub but he said he were doing summat else right so like (.) so like she goes anyway with her sister and he were there just like completely shameless with another bird

A: // no way

C: // yeah I mean bless her right (.) like she just don't deserve that

B: // soz defending amanda all of a sudden (.) I knew I knew

A: // it's dead obvious now though

C: what you trying to say

B: you'll not admit (.) he'll not admit to it like but you well fancy her

A: yep

C: whatever right (2) like I clearly don't but whatever if you wanna (.) wanna say

B: // yeah you do you've proper got hots for her

C: no way though we're just just (.) just get on well and we just

B: // course yeah we're just good friends course (1) really good friends

A: yeah I don't (.) you'll not catch me snogging my friends (.) snogging

C: // what I ain't snogged her

Transcription Key

(.) *Micropause*

(2.0) *Pause in seconds*

// Interruptions / overlapping speech

[inaud] *An unidentified sound*

Sources and Exam Questions

Text B — from *Lady Windermere's Fan,* by Oscar Wilde

DUMBY	Clever woman, Mrs. Erlynne.
CECIL GRAHAM	Hallo, Dumby! I thought you were asleep.
DUMBY	I am, I usually am!
LORD AUGUSTUS	A very clever woman. Knows perfectly well what a demmed fool I am — knows it as well as I do myself.
[CECIL GRAHAM *comes towards him laughing*.]	
	Ah, you may laugh, my boy, but it is a great thing to come across a woman who thoroughly understands one.
DUMBY	It is an awfully dangerous thing. They always end by marrying one.
CECIL GRAHAM	But I thought, Tuppy, you were never going to see her again! Yes! you told me so yesterday evening at the club. You said you'd heard —
[*Whispering to him*.]	
LORD AUGUSTUS	Oh, she's explained that.
CECIL GRAHAM	And the Wiesbaden affair?
LORD AUGUSTUS	She's explained that too.
DUMBY	And her income, Tuppy? Has she explained that?
LORD AUGUSTUS	[*In a very serious voice*.] She's going to explain that to-morrow.
[CECIL GRAHAM *goes back to C. table*.]	
DUMBY	Awfully commercial, women nowadays. Our grandmothers threw their caps over the mills, of course, but, by Jove, their granddaughters only throw their caps over mills that can raise the wind for them.
LORD AUGUSTUS	You want to make her out a wicked woman. She is not!
CECIL GRAHAM	Oh! Wicked women bother one. Good women bore one. That is the only difference between them.
LORD AUGUSTUS	[*Puffing a cigar*.] Mrs. Erlynne has a future before her.
DUMBY	Mrs. Erlynne has a past before her.
LORD AUGUSTUS	I prefer women with a past. They're always so demmed amusing to talk to.
CECIL GRAHAM	Well, you'll have lots of topics of conversation with HER, Tuppy. [*Rising and going to him*.]
LORD AUGUSTUS	You're getting annoying, dear-boy; you're getting demmed annoying.
CECIL GRAHAM	[*Puts his hands on his shoulders*.] Now, Tuppy, you've lost your figure and you've lost your character. Don't lose your temper; you have only got one.
LORD AUGUSTUS	My dear boy, if I wasn't the most good-natured man in London —
CECIL GRAHAM	We'd treat you with more respect, wouldn't we, Tuppy? [*Strolls away*.]
DUMBY	The youth of the present day are quite monstrous. They have absolutely no respect for dyed hair. [LORD AUGUSTUS *looks round angrily*.]
CECIL GRAHAM	Mrs. Erlynne has a very great respect for dear Tuppy.
DUMBY	Then Mrs. Erlynne sets an admirable example to the rest of her sex. It is perfectly brutal the way most women nowadays behave to men who are not their husbands.

Language and Gender

This is for AQA B, OCR and Edexcel. Language and gender is a funny old game. There do seem to be differences between how men and women use language, but no-one seems to be sure exactly what they are or why they occur. Here goes...

Men and Women use Language Differently

Studies have shown that women tend to use **accents** from a **higher social class** than men.

Her parents disapproved of her bit of rough, but Ange couldn't keep her hands off him.

- **Trudgill (1983)** studied men and women's **social class accents** (see p.38-41). He found that women's pronunciation was closer to **Received Pronunciation (RP)**, the accent that's usually seen as the most **prestigious**.

- **Cheshire (1982)** studied the speech of adolescent girls and boys, and found that boys tended to use more **non-standard grammatical forms**, e.g. *ain't*, than girls.

1) Using **Standard English** and **RP** gives a person **overt prestige** — the prestige of being associated with a respectable, well-off section of society. **Women** tend to seek **overt prestige** more than men.

2) Using **non-standard** English gives a person **covert prestige** — they seem a bit rebellious and independent. **Men** are more likely to seek **covert prestige** than women.

Women may use more Prestigious Forms for Several Reasons

There are several **possible explanations** for why **women** use more **prestigious** language than **men**.

1) Women might be **less secure** than men in terms of their **social status**. If they feel that they have an **inferior position** in society, then they might use more **prestigious** language to **overcome** it.

2) Society generally expects **higher standards** of **behaviour** from **women** — they're expected to behave like 'ladies' and use 'ladylike' language. This includes things like not swearing or arguing.

3) Men already have a **higher social status** than women, so they don't need to use prestigious forms to improve it. Instead, they seek **covert prestige** by using non-standard language that seems tough and rebellious.

Remember — these explanations are based on studies of a few men and women. You can't generalise them to all men and women. There have also been changes in gender roles since the 1980s, when these studies were done.

4) **Non-standard language** is traditionally associated with **working-class** men, so men might use it to show that they share **traditionally masculine** qualities, like being '**tough**' and '**down-to-earth**'.

Women's language is usually More Polite than Men's

The researcher **Robin Lakoff (1975)** identified features that she felt were characteristic of women's language:

> **Hedges and fillers** — fragments of language like *sort of, kind of, maybe*.
> **Apologetic requests** — e.g. *I'm sorry, but would you mind closing the door?*
> **Tag questions** — e.g. *this is nice, isn't it?*
> **Indirect requests** — e.g. *It's very noisy out there* (meaning — *could you close the door?*)

1) **Lakoff** also pointed out that women tend to **speak less** than men, use **fewer expletives** (swear less), and use more **intensifiers** (words like **so** and **very**).

2) She argued that these features of women's language reflected women's **inferior social status**, and made it worse by making them seem **indecisive** and **needy**. She said that women's language is **weak** compared to men's language, and this **prevents** women from being **taken seriously**. This explanation is known as the **deficit model**.

3) **O'Barr and Atkins (1980)** suggested an alternative explanation to the **deficit model**. They analysed transcripts of **American courtroom trials**. They found that **male and female** witnesses who were of **low social status** and/or inexperienced with the courtroom practices, both showed many of the linguistic features that Lakoff labelled **female**.

4) This suggests that the kind of language **Lakoff** describes as female isn't only found in women, and might be more to do with individuals feeling **powerless**.

> **Lakoff's** research is quite **old**. More recently, researchers like **Holmes (1984)** have suggested that 'women's language' doesn't show **weakness**, but a desire to **co-operate**. Linguists like **Cameron (2007)** argue that there are actually very **few differences** between men and women's language, and **situation** affects how people speak much more than **gender**.

Language and Gender

Language can be Explained in terms of Dominance and Difference

Linguists have come up with other models to explain the **differences** between men and women's language.

1) Dominance model

- **Zimmerman and West (1975)** recorded interruptions in conversations between men and women.
- They found that **96%** of the interruptions were by men.
- This suggested that men are **dominant** in **male-female conversations**. They argued that this reflects male dominance in society.

2) Difference model

Tannen (1990) described male and female conversational style in terms of **difference**.

- **Men** are concerned with **status** and **independence**, e.g. they interrupt a lot.
- They give **direct orders**, e.g. *pass me that*, and don't mind **conflict**.
- Men are interested in gaining **factual information** and finding **solutions to problems**.

- **Women** are interested in **forming bonds** — they tend to talk less and agree more than men.
- They usually give polite, indirect orders, e.g. *would you mind passing me that*, and try to **avoid conflict**.
- **Women** aim to show **understanding** by **compromising**, and offering **support** rather than **solutions**.

The **reasons** for these **differences** in male and female interaction could be to do with the **topics** that they talk about in **single-sex groups**, e.g. traditionally **male** topics of conversation have focused on **work** and **sport**, where **factual information** and **status** are important. Traditionally **female** topics have centred on the **home** and **family**, where **emotions**, **support** and **compassion** are important.

There are Problems with these Explanations

Other researchers have cast **doubts** on some of these explanations of differences in **male** and **female language**.

1) **Beattie (1982)** questioned **Zimmerman and West's** idea that men **interrupting** women was a sign of **dominance**. He suggested that interruptions can be **supportive** and show that the person is listening, e.g. if they **repeat** what the speaker is saying, or say things like *yes* and *mm*.

2) **Cameron (2007)** argues that a lot of research is **biased** because there has been more focus on the **differences** between male and female language, which are actually quite small, rather than the **similarities**.

Practice Questions

Q1 What is meant by the terms overt prestige and covert prestige?
Q2 List the main features Lakoff attributed to female language.
Q3 Why might 'powerless language' be a better term to use than 'women's language'?
Q4 Explain the dominance model.
Q5 List the main features of Tannen's analysis of male and female language.

Essay Question

Q1 Outline the differences in the way that men and women use language. Explain some of the reasons for these differences.

To make your essay more balanced, you could focus on the different explanations that researchers have offered, as well as the problems with some of these explanations.

Try to avoid making genderalisations...

A lot of the stuff people believe about men and women's speech is based on stereotypes about what they think men and women are like. It's possible to think of loads of exceptions to any of these 'rules', and yet still assume that they must be true. Just remember, the way people speak is affected by loads of different factors, and gender is only one of them...

Language and Gender

This is for AQA B, OCR and Edexcel. These pages are about the different ways that men and women are spoken and written about. The basic idea is that the way they're represented shapes how men and women are perceived.

Men and Women are Represented Differently

1) **Sexist language** is language that **insults**, **patronises** or **ignores** people on the basis of their **gender**.

2) There is a lot **more** sexist language about **women** than men.

3) Some language implies that the **male** version is the **norm**, and the **female** version is **different** or **wrong**:

Marked terms
- These are words that reveal a person's **gender**, e.g. *policeman, wife*.
- **Unmarked terms** don't reveal the person's gender, e.g. *police officer, spouse*.
- Some words are **marked** by a **feminising suffix**, e.g. *actress, usherette, comedienne*.
  The suffix implies that the male version is the **original** or the **norm**, so it seems **superior** to the female version.

Generic terms
- This is when a **marked term** is used to refer both to men and women.
- It's nearly always **masculine terms** which are used to mean **people** in general, rather than just **men**.
- The most common example is the word *man*, e.g. the noun *mankind*, or the verb *to man the desk*.
- **Generic terms** refer to everybody, but using them can make **females** seem **invisible** by **ignoring** them. When this occurs, women are said to be occupying **negative semantic space**.

Lexical Asymmetry refers to **pairs of words** that appear to have a **similar meaning**, but aren't **equally balanced**, e.g. *bachelor* and *spinster* (unmarried man and unmarried woman).
- The connotations of *bachelor* are usually **positive** — it's associated with a man living a carefree, independent life.
- The connotations of *spinster* are usually **negative** — it implies that the woman has been unable to find a partner.

Patronising terms are words used by speakers that imply **superiority** over the person they're talking to.
- Terms that imply someone is **younger** than the speaker can be patronising, e.g. *girls, young lady*.
- **Terms of endearment** can be **patronising** in some circumstances, e.g. *love, dear, sweetheart*.
- Whether a word is **patronising** depends on the **context**, e.g. a male employee who addresses a female colleague as *love* could be seen as patronising, but boyfriends and girlfriends calling each other *love* might not.

Grammar can be Sexist

The idea that the **male** is the **norm** is also evident in English **grammar**.

1) **Pronouns** — the 3rd person masculine pronoun *he* or *his* is often used to refer both to men and women, e.g. ***an employee** who is absent for longer than five days must obtain a sick note from **his** doctor*.

2) **Syntax** — when one gender specific word is always placed before another, it's known as **order of preference**, e.g. *Mr and Mrs, men and women, Sir or Madam*. Usually the male term comes first.

There are More Insults for Women than Men

There are a lot **more insulting terms** for **women** than there are for **men**. This is known as **over-representation**.

1) Lots of insulting terms for **women** have an **animal** theme, e.g. *bitch, cow*.

2) There are lots of words to label women as **promiscuous**, e.g. *slag, slut, slapper*.

3) There are hardly any **equivalents** for men. Terms like *stud* tend to have **positive connotations**. Terms like *man whore* or *male slut* tend to be used **comically**, and imply that the **female** version is the **norm**.

4) The **lack** of an **equivalent term** for something — e.g. a male term for *slut* — is known as a **lexical gap**.

Language and Gender

Sexist Language can be Avoided and Changed

1) The **Sex Discrimination Act** was passed in **1975** to **protect** people from sexual discrimination and harassment, especially at work and at school.

2) It reflected the work of **feminist campaigners**, who wanted to promote **equality** between men and women.

3) Part of this campaign was a push to get rid of **sexist language**.

4) The idea is that language doesn't just **reflect** sexist **attitudes** — it helps to **keep them alive**.

5) So if you change **discriminatory language**, then people's **attitudes** might change too.

6) This is often called **political correctness** (more on this on p.53).

7) **Sexist terms** can be avoided by **replacing** them with **gender neutral** ones.

The only surefire way to remove gender issues... get everyone to dress like an idiot.

For example...

1) **Marked terms** can be replaced with **unmarked terms**, e.g. *head teacher* instead of *headmaster* or *headmistress*, *police officer* instead of *policeman* or *policewoman*.

2) **Feminising suffixes** can be **dropped**, e.g. a female manager is called a *manager*, not a *manageress*.

3) Instead of *Mrs* or *Miss*, the title *Ms* is often used, so you **can't tell** whether a woman is **married**.

4) The generic use of **man** can be replaced by gender neutral terms, e.g. *humankind* instead of *mankind*, *workforce* instead of *manpower*.

5) The **generic** use of the masculine 3rd person pronoun (*he*) can be replaced by *he/she*, *s/he*, or *they*. Sentences can be made **gender-neutral** by using the **plural** instead, e.g. ***Employees*** *who are absent for longer than five days must obtain a sick note from* **their** *doctor.*

People have Different Views about Avoiding Sexist Language

1) The point of encouraging people to avoid sexist language is to ensure people will be treated **equally**, and not feel they're being **singled out**, or **ignored**, because of their gender.

2) Sometimes there are **problems** with trying to **control language** in this way. People can feel that it's **controlling**, and find it frustrating because they feel they can't speak freely without getting into trouble. Some people argue that this can create **resentment** towards the group of people it's designed to protect.

3) It's hard to **enforce** the use of non-sexist language. Some people think that condemning all sexist language ignores **context** and **intent**, e.g. if everyone understands that a comment is a joke, and nobody is offended by it, then it's **pointless** to have laws that stop people from making it.

Practice Questions

Q1 Outline what is meant by the term negative semantic space.
Q2 Explain the term lexical asymmetry and provide two examples.
Q3 What is meant by the term lexical gap?
Q4 Outline three ways in which sexist language can be avoided.
Q5 Explain one argument for and one argument against changing language to avoid sexism.

Essay Question

Q1 How can language be used to suggest that women are inferior to men?

I'm not sexist — some of my best friends are men or women...

This is one of those topics where it can feel like you're stating the obvious some of the time, but at least it's not really complicated. And it's a good one for having a bit of a debate over as well. Just remember that you have to show you understand both sides of an argument before you start waving placards and holding a sit-in in the exam hall...

Language and Power

AQA B, OCR and Edexcel — this is for you. There are loads of ways to assert power over someone in a conversation — when stuffing your fist into the other person's mouth isn't an option, try some of these strategies instead...

The **Language** of **Power** is found in **Different Contexts**

The language of **power** tries to exert **influence** or **control**. It appears in various **contexts**, and in both spoken and written forms.

1) Political language

The purpose of political language is to **persuade**. To achieve this, politicians use **rhetorical devices** (**rhetoric** is the **art** of using language **persuasively**).

1) **Repetition** — *Those who **betray** their party **betray** themselves.*
2) **Three-part lists** — *He came, he saw, he conquered.*
3) **First person plural pronoun** (*we*) — ***We** must strive together for the better health of the nation.*
4) **Figurative language** — *Under our leadership, the **winter of discontent** has become a **summer of prosperity**.*
5) **Rhetorical questions** — *How much longer must our people endure this injustice?*
6) **Hyperbole** (exaggeration) — *Plague would be a better option than the health policies proposed.*

2) Legal language

1) **Legal language** is quite distinctive — it has its own **lexis**. The specific vocabulary used by an **occupational group** is know as **jargon** (see p.52 and p.62-63).
2) The syntax is often **complex**, with lots of **subordinate clauses**. It's also **repetitive**.
3) Because it's so complex, knowledge of this language gives **specialists** a distinct **advantage** over **non-specialists**. This means that lawyers have a lot of **power** — if their clients don't fully understand the difficult jargon, then they have to **trust** that their lawyers understand it and will deal with their case properly.

3) Education

1) The language of power is seen in schools, colleges and universities. The language of **education** reflects the **power structures** in schools.
2) Teachers often use **imperatives** — *open your books*, and direct questions — *what's the answer to question four?*
3) Students use **fewer imperatives** and ask more **indirect questions** — *is it okay if I go to the toilet?*
4) There's often an **imbalance** in **address terms** — students might use respectful address terms to the teacher like **Sir**, or **title + surname** constructions (Ms Smith), while teachers just use the student's **first name**. This shows an **understanding** that the teacher has **authority**.

4) Business

1) **Power structures** in the language of **business** are very similar to those in **education** — **managers** may speak more **directly** to their **employees**, while **employees** may use more **politeness strategies** (see p.31) and fewer **imperatives**.
2) The hierarchical structure of many businesses is shown in nouns such as **subordinate**, **superior**, **team leader** and **chief executive**.

Address Terms show Power Relationships

What people **call** each other can reveal **power relationships**. As with everything, they **vary** in different **contexts**.

Context	Form of Address
Politics	*Madam/Mr Speaker, Honourable Member*
Law	*Your Honour, Ladies and Gentlemen of the Jury*
Education	*Sir, Miss, Mr Briggs, Ms Briggs, Dr / Professor*
Business	*Madam Chair, Sir, Madam*

Look out for **imbalances** in address terms, because they can reveal **unequal power relationships**.

Language and Power

There are **Different Ways** to **Exert Power** in a **Conversation**

Power relationships are shown in the way people talk to each other. People **assert** power in different ways.

1) **Initiating a conversation** — this can be a means of **taking the lead** and establishing the **topic** of conversation.

2) **Holding the floor** — this is when one speaker gives little or no opportunity for other speakers to take a turn. Usually conversation involves **turn-taking**, so a speaker can show **dominance** by not letting anyone else in.

3) **Imperative sentences** — giving **orders** and **directions** can be a sign of **dominance**, e.g. *shut the door*.

4) **Interrupting** — some **interruptions** cut into the other person's turn. It shows that the person interrupting has **little interest** in what the speaker is saying.

5) **Unresponsiveness** — this a more **negative** way of asserting control. If the person speaking is ignored or if the **back-channel noises** (*mm* or *uh huh*) of the other participants are half-hearted or hesitant then the **status** of the speaker is **undermined**.

6) **Questioning** — questions direct the **topic** of conversation, and make it clear when the other person is **expected** to talk.

7) **Topic changing** — this can be a technique of **reasserting control**. Sometimes politicians do this when they're uncomfortable talking about a particular topic. By **diverting attention** to a **different topic**, where they may have something more positive to say, they're trying to **gain control** over the **direction** of the conversation.

8) **Closing down a conversation** — this asserts power by not allowing other speakers to carry on talking, e.g. saying *goodbye* or walking away.

Context is Important

It's important to pay attention to the **context** of a conversation when you're looking at **power**.

1) In a particular **situation**, the way power shows itself depends on how people are '**positioned**' in relation to each other.

2) These **relationships** between speakers can **shape** the **conversational strategies** and **type** of language they use, e.g. you'd **expect** a doctor to ask a patient lots of questions.

3) Depending on the context of the conversation, some of the above examples of **dominance** can actually be interpreted as ways of showing **support**.

4) For example, **interrupting** with words like *yes*, or cutting in to **repeat** what the speaker has said can show that you **agree** and you're **listening**. It doesn't necessarily mean that you're trying to assert power over the person speaking.

5) Similarly, **asking questions** can be a sign you want to **control** the topic of conversation, **or** it can be a way of **passing control** to somebody else to **encourage** them to **hold the floor**.

Practice Questions

Q1 What is rhetoric and what are rhetorical devices?

Q2 Why might a teacher prefer to be addressed by title + surname rather than by first name?

Q3 Outline three ways in which a speaker might try to dominate a conversation.

Essay Question

A: it's so funny isn't it darling (1) do you like it (.) it's really clever and //
B: // but it's so unrealistic turn it off
A: you can't say that (.) you've only just seen a bit of it
B: I don't need to realise (.) to see how bad it is (2) it's like //
A: // fine (1) just put something else on

Q1 How do the speakers in this extract exert power over each other?

Forget language — just get down the gym and show 'em who's boss...

This is a handy little topic — you can find evidence of language and power in pretty much any extract you'll have to look at. There are loads of different ways to exert power, so you shouldn't get too bored. Personally, when I want to dominate a conversation I go for the good old-fashioned fingers-in-ears-la-la-la-I'm-not-listening-to-you technique. Works every time...

Language and Power

This is for everyone apart from AQA A. *The language of power is about dominating your enemies and crushing your opponents, so they cower at your mighty presence and quiver in the face of your wrath. Mwahahaha...*

Power shows itself in Different Ways

The ways people **exert power** in a conversation aren't just about what they say.

1) **Non-verbal communication** (NVC) (see p.26-27) is using **posture, positioning, gestures, eye contact** and **facial expressions** to convey feelings and attitudes, e.g. crossing your legs away from someone can function as a **barrier** and appear **defensive**. Maintaining eye contact longer than normal can be an attempt to **assert dominance**. **Smiling** at someone and **pausing** as you walk past them can be a way of **initiating conversation**.

2) **Non-verbal aspects of speech** (**pitch, intonation, volume, pace** and **stress**) can also be used to assert control, e.g. when people **argue** they may try to dominate by **shouting**, raising the **pitch** of their voice or speaking more **quickly**.

3) **Standard English** and **Received Pronunciation** (RP) (see p.38-39) are the varieties of English that carry the most **prestige**. They're associated with **professional jobs** and a **good education**. Because of this, speakers who use Standard English and RP are often perceived to have more **authority** and **status** than people who speak in a regional dialect or accent.

Bruce didn't need words — he had raw animal strength.

Jargon can be used to Dominate

Jargon is the **specialist vocabulary** used in particular **fields** of **activity**, especially **occupations** (see p.62-63). For example

- The **medical world** uses terms like *adenovirus, meningococcal,* and *septum.*
- **Electrical engineers** use terms like *chrominance, phase jitter,* and *watchdog circuit.*
- Terms like these aren't generally understood by **non-specialists**.

1) **Jargon** is often **necessary** when **specialists** are talking to **other specialists** — it's a **precise** form of **labelling** objects, processes and conditions, so it means **technical information** can be communicated **quickly**.

2) People who **understand** the jargon have a sense of **inclusion** in a group, which often brings a **higher status**.

3) The **problem** with jargon is that when **specialists** use it to communicate with **non-specialists** it can become a **barrier** to **understanding**, e.g. doctors with patients, mechanics with car owners.

4) **Non-specialists** can feel **intimidated** by the **specialists** and **excluded** from the **high-status group**. In cases like this, the **specialists** have more power and can **dominate** the situation.

5) **Specialists** can exploit this by using jargon with **non-specialists** in order to **impress** them — it makes people feel that they want to be **part** of the high-status group that uses such specialist terms. It can also be used to hide what's really going on.

There are Alternatives to using Jargon

Jargon can cause real **problems** when it's used **inappropriately**, so different measures are taken to avoid it. For example:

1) Since 1999 some of the language used in the **civil courts** has been changed to make it easier for non-specialists to understand.

2) This includes **Latin** terms like *in camera* and *subpoena*, which have been replaced by *in private* and *witness summons*.

3) Using plainer language promotes **equality**, because it means that everyone has more chance of understanding what's being said, and specialists can't use jargon to **intimidate** non-specialists.

- The **Plain English Campaign** was set up in 1979 to **combat** the use of **confusing** and **unnecessary jargon**.
- It **advises organisations** on how they can use **plainer language**.
- Organisations can apply for the **Crystal Mark**, which shows that the **Plain English Campaign** has approved their documents.

Language and Power

Political Correctness aims to Promote Equality

1) Political correctness is a term to describe ways that language can be adapted to **minimise social inequality**.

2) It's politically correct to avoid language that **insults**, **marginalises** or seeks to **control** other people or groups of people — in particular language that is **sexist**, **racist**, **ageist** and **ableist** (discriminates against people with disabilities).

3) Political correctness is based on the idea that language doesn't just **reflect** social attitudes, but also helps to **shape** them. So if discriminatory language is changed or avoided, then people are less likely to discriminate against others.

There are always **reasons** for **why** terms are viewed as **politically incorrect**, e.g.

Original term	Alternative	Reason
half caste	mixed race	*half caste* suggests less than whole, incomplete.
stewardess	flight attendant	*stewardess* reveals the person's gender. The suffix -**ess** suggests that the male term (*steward*) is the original, so more important.
disabled person	person with disabilities	*disabled person* is a dehumanising label — it characterises people by their disability. The alternative version takes the focus away from the disability.

There's a lot of Debate about Political Correctness

Arguments for Political Correctness

- Language helps to **shape social attitudes**. Changing it sends a clear message about what is **acceptable**, which encourages people to change their attitudes.

- It acts as a **symbol** that society is committed to becoming more **equal** and **inclusive**.

- It's often **blown out of proportion** — people focus on **outrageous** examples of political correctness, when most actually have a **reasonable explanation**.

Arguments against Political Correctness

- People feel they're being **restricted**, and can't speak their minds without getting into trouble.

- It's pointless because language only **reflects** social **attitudes**, it **doesn't shape** them.

- Some feel it creates **resentment** towards the groups it tries to protect, so discrimination is just as likely.

- It's pointless because language **always changes** — words that **were** once politically correct eventually become **less acceptable**. For example, *Third World* was replaced by *Developing World*, but now *Majority World* or *Less Economically Developed Country* (*LEDC*) is seen as more politically correct.

Practice Questions

Q1 Give some examples of jargon associated with medicine.

Q2 In what ways can jargon be seen as a positive use of language?

Q3 How is jargon sometimes misused?

Q4 In what way might political correctness be a good thing?

Q5 Why do some people argue against political correctness?

Essay Question

Q1 Outline some of the ways that people can use communication to exert power over each other, and discuss whether it's important to change the language to avoid this.

You could focus especially on the use of jargon, and debates about political correctness.

It's political correctness gone mad...

This stuff is gold, and that's scientific fact. It might seem weird to have to talk about non-verbal communication, but it can be really useful — if you get an extract from some fiction, and it describes a speaker sighing or gesticulating, then just whack in something about NVC and the marks are yours. Gesticulate. Tee hee hee. Sounds a bit rude somehow...

Language and Technology

Just AQA B, AQA A and Edexcel. Technology has a huge impact on language, and it's always changing as new things are invented — proof if ever you need it that life without TV or the internet really would be boring and utterly pointless...

Radio Language is Different from TV Language

1) **TV language** has the support of **pictures**, **gestures** and **facial expressions**, and sometimes **text**.

2) On the **radio** there aren't any visual clues, so listeners have to rely on **what** speakers say and **how** they say it.

3) This affects the **type** of language used in each medium. For example:

Radio commentary of a football match
here's Burton making space along the left hand side (1.0) Peters in support to his right (1.0) cross hit hard and low (.) Oliver picks it up on the far right side by the corner flag (.) cuts inside (.) passes to Hilton

Linguistic features
- Lots of information.
- Mainly full sentences.
- Lots of adjectives (e.g. *hard*, *low*).
- Short pauses.

The numbers in brackets indicate the length of pauses in seconds. This symbol (.) indicates a shorter pause.

TV commentary of a football match
here's Burton (3.0) Burton's cross (2.0) Oliver (3.0)

Linguistic features
- Minimal information.
- Incomplete sentences.
- Long pauses.

Telephone Language is Dialogue

1) Telephone language shares many features with **face-to-face dialogue**. This includes **non-fluency features**, like **fillers** and **false starts**, and **non-verbal** aspects of speech, like **intonation** and **stress**.

2) The **opening sequence** is very formulaic, and generally involves the same **adjacency pairs** — the person answering says **hello**, and the person phoning says **who they are** or who they **wish to speak to**. Differences in this sequence usually depend on the **age** of the speaker — **older** people are more likely to answer with something like *Molesey 326*, while **younger** people tend to be **less formal**, e.g. *All right, Tyler*. How you answer can also depend on **context**, e.g. people tend to be more **formal** at **work** than at **home**.

3) **Mobile phones** are an exception to this. You can usually **see who's calling** before you answer, and the person phoning can be more certain of who's going to pick up, so the opening sequence is more **flexible** and **casual**.

4) The lack of **non-verbal communication** means that telephone language includes quite **strict turn-taking**, because there are no **visual clues** to indicate when a speaker has finished. There are also **few pauses**.

Mobile Phones have had a Big Impact on Language

Probably the biggest influence that mobile phones have had on language is **text speak**.

1) Text messaging is **creative** — it's not **standardised**, so everyone uses it slightly differently. It's a **mixed mode** of communication, because it's a **written** language that contains many features of **spoken** language (see p.35).

2) These distinctive features have come about because of a need to **communicate quickly**. Typing complete words into a mobile phone keypad is time-consuming, so text speak has evolved as a form of **shorthand**.

Feature	Example
acronyms	LOL (Laugh Out Loud)
numbers for words	2 (to)
numbers for phonemes (sounds)	gr8 (great)
symbols for words	@ (at)
phonetic spelling	coz (because)
incomplete clauses	home safe. speak soon
no punctuation	how u doin wana go out 2nite
simple sentences	went to the zoo. it was good.
smileys / emoticons	:-)

Roger hadn't quite got the hang of this texting lark.

Language and Technology

The *Internet* has affected language too

The language used over the internet, e.g. in **e-mail**, **live chat** and **forums,** shares some of the linguistic features of mobile text messaging.

1) E-mails are a **mixed mode**, containing **spoken** and **written** features. The mode that dominates depends on how **formal** the email is.

2) Internet language is dependent on **context**. An e-mail from one business to another business might be set out like a **formal letter** and use **Standard English** (p.38-39). But friends communicating in a chatroom might use **text speak**, and language normally associated with **informal spoken** English — e.g. **slang**, **non-standard grammar**.

3) Internet communication involves certain **conventions**, known as **netiquette**. This includes things like avoiding using all **capital letters**, because this is the equivalent of shouting.

New technology can be baffling.

New Technology has Created New Words and Meanings

Every piece of new technology needs **new words** to describe it. This can involve giving **existing** words **new meanings**, or **inventing** completely new terms.

Way of forming new words	Example
acronyms — the initial letters from a group of words form a new word	radar (**radio detection and ranging**)
affixation — adding a prefix or suffix to an existing word	**hyper**text
compounding — combining separate words	spyware
clipping — a shortened word becomes a word in its own right	fax (from facsimile)
blending — parts of two words are combined	netizen (internet + citizen)
conversion — an existing word changes its grammatical function	**the text** (noun) becomes **to text** (verb)

TV also increases people's knowledge of **specialist vocabulary** from **different fields**. Documentaries and the news do this to a certain extent, but programmes about specific occupations also have an impact, e.g. **medical dramas**, **courtroom dramas** and **cop shows**.

Practice Questions

Q1 What is the basic difference between TV and radio and what impact can this have on language use?

Q2 Outline one difference between telephone dialogue and face-to-face dialogue.

Q3 How does text speak differ from standard written English?

Q4 Define each of the following methods of forming new words: affixation, compounding, conversion.

Essay Question

Hey Sweetie!
hows you? what's my favourite sis been up2 — haven't heard from u in AGES, grrrr!! Anyway ive got some dead dead excitin news... I found a photo of you from when ur little in the bath and im gonna post it on the net for all to see... Nah not really lol! Actually, heard that Pat's comin back from australia next month! See, i knew ud be excited! Well, got to go, but see you really soon for a catch up — gimme a text next time ur free xxoxx

Q1 This is an extract of an email an 18 year old girl sent to her sister. Analyse it in terms of the impact that technology has had on the language.

This was all fields in my day...

If you get an extract from anything that's got even the merest sniff of technology about it, then throw in this stuff and you're laughing. See, it's not such a bad life really — pretty much everyone watches TV and knows about texting, but not everyone gets to talk about it in their exams. Just don't try to do any actual texting in your exams though, it won't go down well.

Language and the Media

These pages are for everyone. *Hurrah*. *'The media' basically means things like newspapers, magazines, TV, radio, the Internet and films. The language of the media can have a big influence on people's attitudes and values...*

The **Media** can be **Biased**

Bias is the tendency to **take sides** and view things **subjectively**, e.g. newspapers show political bias when they show preference for one political party over another.

1) **Newspaper reports** show bias through the writer's **word choices**. The **purpose** of particular word choices is to **shape** the reader's **perceptions** of an event.

2) Bias is shown in **different ways**. For example, **coverage** of a particular **news item** may be:
   * **selective** — e.g. only focus on the positive aspect of a new law.
   * present only **one viewpoint** — e.g. always present negative judgements of a particular political party.
   * use **loaded** and **emotive** language to present **factual information**, e.g. adjectives like *outrageous*, *tragic*.

The **Media** can show **Prejudice** towards **Social Groups**

1) **Prejudice** is a **preconceived** opinion of a person or a group, that isn't based on **experience** or **reason**.

2) It often includes **negative judgements** about different **ethnic**, **religious**, **gender** or **ability** groups.

3) The **language** used by the media can **create** and **reinforce** these negative opinions.

4) For example, if a newspaper consistently runs headlines about **asylum seekers** *scrounging from the taxpayer*, then it shows **prejudice** against this particular group. The **effect** of these headlines might be that readers start to **associate** asylum seekers with being dishonest or lazy.

> OCR only

The **Language** of **Children's Media** is **Distinctive**

Children's media has some **linguistic differences** from stuff for adults.

Lexis

1) The vocabulary used in children's media is quite **small**, so words are often **repeated**, e.g. *The birthday cake was **really** big and **really** nice.*

2) The language tends to be **simple**, e.g. there are few **polysyllabic** words (words with more than two syllables, like **antithesis** or **confabulation**).

3) It's generally **informal**, and often uses well-known **slang** words, e.g. **cool**.

Grammar

1) Media that **address** the audience, such as children's news programmes, use the third person plural pronouns **we** and **us** a lot. This **includes** and **engages** the target audience.

2) The **syntax** of sentences aimed at children tends to be **straightforward**. Sentences are usually short, and don't have many **conjunctions** or **subordinate clauses**. For example, instead of: *The Prime Minister, during his visit to a primary school today, promised more money for education,* you'd be likely to see: *The Prime Minister visited a primary school today. He's promised more money for education.*

Punctuation

1) Language aimed at children tends to be simple and informal, so it usually avoids **complex punctuation** like **semi-colons**.

2) It's also often quite **upbeat**, so you tend to see a lot more **exclamation marks** than you do in media for adults, e.g. *Take a look at these cool new pics!*

Language and the Media

Tabloid Newspapers use Different Language from Broadsheets

Every newspaper takes a slightly **different political viewpoint**, so their purpose is to **persuade** as well as to **inform**. Newspapers are in **competition** with each other, so they also need to **entertain** readers to keep them interested.

1) **Tabloid newspapers** are ones like *The Sun* and *The News of the World*. They tend to make their viewpoint on a story very clear, and use quite **straightforward language**.

2) **Broadsheets** are newspapers such as *The Guardian* and *The Daily Telegraph*. They're aimed at a **professional**, mostly **middle class readership**.

Features of tabloid newspapers	Features of broadsheet newspapers
Short paragraphs	**Longer** paragraphs
Large font, spread out	**Smaller font**, compact
Large print, sensational headlines (*May Day Massacre*)	**Smaller print**, factual headlines (*PM Defeat at Polls*)
Lots of **large photographs**	Fewer, **smaller photographs**
Short, Anglo-Saxon words (*think, dead*)	**Long, Latinate** words (*cogitate, deceased*)
Simple sentences with few clauses	**Complex sentences** with more **subordinate** clauses
Simple punctuation, exclamation marks	**Complex punctuation**, few exclamation marks
First names or **nicknames** (*Gordon, Macca*)	**Full names** or **surnames** (*Gordon Brown, McCartney*)
Sensationalised news stories, **one-sided** point of view	**Fact-based** news stories, often more **objective** stance
Emotive vocabulary (*Monster rapist gets off with five years*)	**Neutral** vocabulary (*Rapist gets five year sentence*)
Personal tone	**Impersonal** tone
Informal vocabulary (*pal, kids*)	More **formal** vocabulary (*friend, children*)
Use of **phonological features** like alliteration and rhyme. Also **phonetic spelling** (*No Bovver Says Becks*)	Fewer **phonological features** (*No Problem for Beckham*)
Use of **puns** (*Santa's Grotty*)	Few puns

1) Newspaper language also makes use of **modifier + headword** constructions.

2) In the case of **tabloids** this is often for **sensational effect**, e.g. emotive modifiers such as *tragic* hero, *incest* fiend, *heartbroken* midfielder, *chilling* image.

3) **Broadsheets** use these constructions less. When they do, they tend to be more factual e.g. — *experienced* manager, *Dublin-born* criminal. For a direct comparison, see p.14.

Practice Questions

Q1 Give an example of biased language.

Q2 What is prejudice? Give a linguistic example.

Q3 Explain how the language of children's media differs to adult media.

Q4 Outline three main differences between tabloid and broadsheet newspapers.

Q5 What is the effect of modifer + headword constructions?

Essay Question

Q1 Compare and contrast these two headlines:

More Cash For Single Mum Scroungers   Single Mothers Can Claim More Benefits

ENG LANG STUDENT IN NAP ON DESK SHOCKER...

It's at about this stage that the mind starts wandering — like, how many newspapers would it take to wrap up every surface you could see... Yes it might be a fire hazard, yes it might go soggy when it rains, yes the ink might rub off on your face when you go to bed (details, details). Don't listen to the naysayers. Join me, and together we shall paper the world with news.

Adverts

Everyone except Edexcel needs these pages. Adverts are everywhere. Well, not everywhere, that would be silly. They're not on kittens or your eyelids. But they are on lots of things, like the TV, the Internet, the radio and public transport...

Adverts are designed to Persuade

There are a few basic things you need to think about when you're looking at any advert:

1) **Subject matter** — the advert will focus on a **product**, **service**, or **cause**.

2) **Purpose** — adverts are designed to **persuade** the audience — usually to **buy** a **product** or **service**, **support** a **charity**, or join a **campaign**. They use different approaches to do this, e.g. they might show attractive people with luxurious lifestyles using a product to persuade the audience to buy it.

3) **Form** — written adverts come in different forms, e.g. in newspapers and magazines, appeal letters that come through your door, leaflets, posters and e-mails (spam). There are also the scripts for TV and radio adverts.

4) The **target audience** is the group the advert is aimed at. This could be very **broad** (food shoppers, drivers) or more **specific** (boys who like snowboarding).

5) The **hook** is the device advertisers use to get the audience's attention — it could be **verbal**, **visual** or **musical**.

6) In paper-based adverts the **text** is referred to as **copy**. People who **write** adverts are sometimes called **copywriters**.

Adverts use Language in Specific Ways to Achieve their Purpose

1) Lexis

- The lexis of an advert is designed to be **persuasive**. Copywriters use comparatives (*better, larger*) and superlatives (*best, largest*) to make their product or service seem better than their competitors'.
- Adverts often use **hi-tech jargon** to make a product seem **state-of-the-art**, e.g. *CBC* (cornering brake control).
- **Compound words** are common in lots of adverts, e.g. *farm-fresh*.

2) Grammar

- Adverts use different **sentence functions** as hooks — e.g. **exclamatives** *(it's your life!)*, **declaratives** *(it's all you'll ever need)*, **imperatives** *(come in from the cold)* and **interrogatives** *(why not have what you've always wanted?)*.
- **Imperatives** without **subjects** are common **hooks** because they're short and snappy, e.g. *unite, create, enjoy*.
- The **syntax** of most adverts is quite **simple**, with few subordinate clauses. Sentences are often **disjunctive** (they set up contrasts, e.g. *elegant but sturdy*), rather than **discursive**. This ensures the message is very **clear**.

3) Graphology

- Often the first thing that attracts you to an advert is the **immediate visual impression** it makes, e.g. **colour**, **visual images**, and the **size**, **type** and **colour** of the **typeface**.
- **Larger** text tends to be more **persuasive**. **Smaller** text tends to focus on **giving information** about the product or service.
- **Unconventional spelling** is sometimes used to make a product stand out or seem hi-tech, e.g. *frooty, pix, FX*.

4) Phonology

Phonetic features of language (what it **sounds** like) are often used to keep the audience interested:
- **alliteration**, e.g. *local, live and loud*
- **onomatopoeia**, e.g. *crash! bang!*
- **rhyme**, e.g. *try before you buy*

5) Pragmatics

- The **tone** of an advert varies, depending on **subject matter**, **audience** and **purpose**.
- Adverts often try to **engage** with the consumer by **addressing** them **directly**, e.g. by using the **second person pronoun** (you), **imperatives** (orders) and **interrogatives** (questions).

6) Discourse

Adverts have a discourse structure. This is made up of different elements:
- the **hook** (e.g. *Together We Can End Hunger*)
- further **persuasion** and/or **information** (e.g. *a child dies from starvation every 5 seconds*).
- **instruction** on what the reader should do next (e.g. *Simply donate £2 a month…*)

Adverts

Adverts need to Engage the Audience

Creative language is more likely to grab the audience's **attention**, and stick in their minds. For example:

- **Semantic puns**, e.g. *Fly with us, the sky's the limit.*
- **Phonetic puns**, e.g. *Hair today, gone tomorrow.*
- **Figurative language**, e.g. *Is there a black hole in your pocket? Start saving now!*

Adverts can Create and Reinforce Stereotypes

1) Adverts are usually very **short**, so they have a **limited** amount of **space** and **time** to get their message across.
2) Because of this, adverts often show **simplified** images of people and events — **stereotypes**.
3) For example, adverts can show **gender stereotypes** by casting men and women in **traditional social** and **occupational** roles. They might show men going out to work and women looking after children, or men working as plumbers and women as secretaries.
4) **TV** adverts often show a **woman** using a product, then have a **male** voiceover **explaining** how the product works. This **reinforces traditional gender roles** by implying that a man **invented** the product, **understands** how it works, and has more **authority** to explain it.
5) Some adverts **parody** the **stereotypes** of traditional adverts, often for **humorous** effect.

Intertextuality is the Relationship between Different Texts

Adverts often **make references** to other texts to create a particular effect.

1) References to well-known texts are **accessible** to lots of people, and will be **easily remembered**. E.g. a **hook** for a mattress advert — *and on the seventh day he rested*. This echoes words from the Bible, so a lot of people will recognise it.

2) Other adverts aim to appeal to a more **specific** audience. They reference lesser-known texts to 'stroke' the audience by assuming that they're knowledgeable. This suggests that the product will only appeal to an **elite few**. E.g. a **hook** for a luxury travel company advertising city breaks in London and Paris — *A Tale of Two Cities*. This references the title of a Charles Dickens novel, which not everyone would be familiar with.

Practice Questions

Q1 What function does a hook serve in an advert?
Q2 Which language frameworks can be used for analysing adverts?
Q3 Give an example of a semantic pun and phonetic pun.
Q4 What are stereotypes? Give an example of a gender stereotype.
Q5 What does the term intertextuality mean?

Essay Question

Q1 Explain the linguistic devices that might be used in an advert to persuade the audience.

If you'll excuse me — I've got a sofa sale to get to...

This stuff about the different ways adverts use language is really handy — you can use those headings for analysing any text you're faced with. Just don't dwell on graphology for too long. Talking about fonts and pretty colours can be a nice break from linguistic analysis, but it's more important to discuss how other language frameworks are used. Especially grammar.

Language and Occupational Groups

AQA B, OCR and Edexcel. Ever wondered why you never hear plumbers talking about PSHE or teachers talking about siphon-vortex water closets? No, me neither, but it's something to do with the specific language of occupational groups...

Different Occupations have their Own Sociolects

1) **Occupational sociolect** is the distinctive language used by particular occupational groups, e.g. lawyers or train drivers (see p.40).

2) It's found in **spoken** and **written** forms.

3) The **sociolect** develops to fit the group's **specific purposes** — it's not **everyday** language.

4) **Specialists** in a job use it to communicate **quickly** and **precisely** with other specialists in the **same job**. You wouldn't necessarily expect **non-specialists** to understand it.

5) Occupational language can be seen as **elitist** — **excluding** people who **don't understand** it.

Occupational Language has a Special Lexis

Occupational words are the **specialist terms** used in specific jobs — often called **jargon** (see p.52). They can refer to **concepts**, **processes**, **conditions**, **roles** or **objects**. For example:

- **Hairstylists** might say — *perm, feather, spritz, weave, layer, trim.*
- **Electricians** might say — *transformer, faceplate, fuse, amp, earth.*
- **Actors** might say — *role, script, agent, motivation, scene.*

These words might **not** be **familiar** to people **outside** the occupational group.

Police officers might say —
"you put your left leg in, your
left leg out..."

Occupational Language has Distinctive Grammatical Features

1) When you're analysing the grammatical features of occupational language, focus on elements like **word classes**, **syntax**, and **sentence functions**.

2) The example below is from a **medical report** written by specialists, to be read by other specialists:

> *A 27-year-old female **presented with** a pneumothorax, which progressed into **rapidly degenerative Bronchiolitis Obliterans Organising Pneumonia**.*

These aren't general features of all occupational language — the grammar used in different occupations varies.

- **Word classes** — the **past participle** *presented* is used in an unusual way. It's combined with the preposition **with** to create a **prepositional verb** which describes the **symptoms** the patient was showing.

  The **head word** *pneumonia* has **premodifiers** in front of it — the **adverb** *rapidly* and the **adjective** *degenerative*. This makes the sentence grammatically complex.

- **Syntax** — the long **noun phrase** '*Bronchiolitis Obliterans Organising Pneumonia*' is common in this type of medical writing. It packs as much complex information as possible into a small space.

- **Function** — the text's **function** is to **give information**, so it only contains **declarative sentences** (see p.15).

Occupational Language can have Distinctive Phonological Features

Some kinds of occupational language have **phonological** features like **repetition**, **alliteration** and **rhyme** (see p.25).

1) You usually find distinctive **phonological features** in the language of occupations where it's necessary to speak to **large groups** of people, e.g. **politician**, **religious leader**, **teacher**.

2) This example from a **political speech** uses **alliteration** and **phonological patterning** with a **three part list**, e.g. *we will bring you **peace**, **pride** and **prosperity** like you've never experienced before.*

3) Teachers' language might have some common **prosodic features** when they're addressing classes, e.g. they're more likely to raise their voices or say *shh*.

Language and Occupational Groups

Occupational Language Varies depending on its Form and Function

1) **Written** occupational discourse has lots of different **forms**, e.g. legal contracts and business letters.

2) **Spoken** occupational discourse also takes different **forms**, e.g. a counsellor might use gentle questioning, a sergeant major might shout out imperatives, and a politician might use rhetorical questions.

3) Occupational discourse also has a variety of **functions** depending on its **context**. For example:

> - **informative discourse** e.g. a manager explaining a task to an employee.
> - **persuasive discourse** e.g. a charity worker asking for donations.
> - **instructional discourse** e.g. an experienced plumber advising an apprentice.
> - **transactional discourse** e.g. a retailer buying from a wholesaler.

4) Some discourse has a **mixture** of functions, e.g. a factory's health and safety manual might be designed to **inform**, **instruct** and **persuade**.

Occupational Discourse can follow a Specific Structure

This sounds more complicated than it is — basically, it's just looking at the **order** the discourse takes, and how it can be separated by **discourse markers**. For example:

1) **Scientific reports** have a specific structure — **title**, **introduction**, **method**, **findings**, **conclusion**, **evaluation**. These **standard headings** act as **discourse markers** by organising it in a specific order.

2) A police officer arresting somebody follows a strict **verbal discourse structure**: *you do not have to say anything, but it may harm your defence if you do not mention when questioned something that you later rely on in court.*

> In this example of a teacher's report on a pupil, the discourse is structured in **four parts**:
>
> > *Ferdinand is doing well in Mathematics and has made significant progress. However, he really must apply himself next term if he is to fulfil his potential.*
>
> 1. Present performance — *is doing well* (**present continuous tense**).
> 2. Past to present performance — *has made significant progress* (**present perfect tense**).
> 3. What he has to do — *he really must apply himself* (**use of modal**).
> 4. Success depends on him doing this — *if he is to fulfil his potential* (**conditional clause**).
>
> Here the **adverb** *however* acts as a **discourse marker**. It gives the text an **order** by **linking** what's happened in the **past** with what needs to happen in the **future**.

Practice Questions

Q1 What is meant by the term occupational sociolect?
Q2 Give three examples of 'occupation-specific' lexis.
Q3 Give three types of grammatical features you should analyse in occupational language.
Q4 Name three kinds of phonological features that can sometimes be found in occupational language.
Q5 Give an example of one form and one function of occupational discourse.

Essay Question

Q1 Outline the main features of occupational language, and the specific purposes it serves.

You could focus on lexis, grammar, phonological features, form, function and structure.

At least all this revision will keep you occupied...

This is another topic where it can feel like you're stating the obvious quite a lot — you wouldn't really expect, say, doctors to spend much time talking about leather uppers and shoelaces. Well, not while they were at work. Unless someone had had a bizarre accident with a pair of brogues... But that's beside the point. This is all nice simple stuff, so fear not.

Language and Occupational Groups

AQA A, OCR and Edexcel here. Contrary to popular belief, jargon isn't a German boy's name. It actually refers to the specialist terms used by specific occupational groups. Bet you're glad to have cleared that one up, ja?

All Occupations use Jargon

OCR and Edexcel will have covered some of this on p.52, but it's new for AQA A.

1) All **occupational groups** have their own **specialist vocabulary**, known as **jargon** (see p.52).

2) The **purpose** of **jargon** is to allow members of an occupational group to **communicate** with each other **quickly**.

3) It's often **highly technical** and difficult for **non-specialists** to understand.

Jargon is Useful

Jargon allows people to exchange **specific**, **precise** information very **quickly**. This is important in lots of jobs, e.g.

1) **Air traffic controllers** use a wide range of technical terms to make sure aircraft land and take off safely. Terms like *taxi* (the movement of an aircraft on the ground) are much more **precise** and **quick to use** than **everyday English**.

2) **Legal language** contains lots of jargon because it has to be **unambiguous**. Because the legal system is very traditional, much of the jargon is **archaic**, e.g. *forthwith, hereby*. It has roots in **French** and **Latin**, so it contains terms like *ouster* and *tenant* from French, and *actus reus* and *ultra vires* from Latin. Jargon like this has been around for a long time and it hasn't changed much.

3) **New technology** needs **new words** to describe it, e.g. **webmasters** need to know a lot of **internet jargon** to do their jobs, like *dynamic RSS feed, fluid layout, box model*.

Jargon can be Confusing

1) **Jargon** can be **confusing** if people use **technical vocabulary** in situations where **everyday language** would be **more appropriate** (see p.52).

2) For example, a **doctor** might diagnose a **patient** with *acute viral nasopharyngitis*. The patient might be confused and worried if they don't know that it's just a **common cold**.

3) Sometimes **complex vocabulary** is used in place of **simple** language **on purpose**, because it sounds more **impressive**. This makes it **harder** for the audience to **understand**.

4) For example — *it is axiomatic that acquiring appropriate personnel bestows inestimable benefits* really just means — *it's obvious that there are lots of benefits to getting the right people*.

Jargon can be used to Hide Harsh Realities

Sometimes **jargon** is used to make out that things aren't as bad as they really are. Jargon that's used as a **substitute** for harsher-sounding words and phrases is **euphemistic**.

1) These **euphemisms** might be used in connection with **making people redundant**:

- decruit
- down-size
- workforce adjustment
- redeployment
- restructuring
- release

2) These **euphemisms** might be used by **politicians** to play down what happens in **wartime**:

- **collateral damage** — civilians killed by mistake
- **transfer tubes** — body bags for soldiers killed in action
- **friendly fire** — attack from allied forces

In this case the **purpose** of the **jargon** is to **soften** the real **meaning** of the language, to make it sound more **acceptable**.

Language and Occupational Groups

Occupational Language goes in and out of Fashion

1) Occupational language often **changes over time** — partly due to advances in **technology**, but also due to what's in fashion. Words that are **fashionable** in the workplace are known as **'buzz words'**, or **'management speak'**.

For example:

Nouns and noun phrases	
• solution	• ball-park figure
• feedback	• client focus

Verbs	
• incentivise	• facilitate
• coordinate	• touch base

2) **'Management speak'** is sometimes used as a **derogatory** term because some people think it's **overly complex**, **confusing** and **pretentious**.

3) The words might not be particularly complicated on their own, but the **problem** with **management speak** is the tendency to string lots of trendy words and phrases **together**.

4) You can end up with sentences that don't really **make sense**. For example:

> *In order to incentivise the optimum client focused solution,*
> *the coordination of the teams must be facilitated.*

5) This can cause problems at work because people might not really **understand** what they're being asked to do.

Management Speak has Distinctive Grammatical Features

The way people **form sentences** also follows **trends**. For example:

- Using **long noun phrases** instead of just **one word**. Lots of **job titles** are like this, e.g. *technical horticultural maintenance officer* instead of *gardener*. This affects the **syntax** of sentences — **clauses** become very **long**.

- Using **reflexive pronouns** instead of **non-reflexive pronouns**, e.g. *the presentation will be carried out by Najoud and myself*, instead of *Najoud and <u>me</u>*.

- Use of the **passive**, e.g. *the meeting will be chaired by Diane* instead of *Diane will chair the meeting*.

1) The aim of **management speak** is to **impress** people by sounding **up-to-date**, **formal** and **complex**.

2) However, it often ends up sounding **vague** and **confusing**.

3) Some people argue that **management speak** is **intentionally vague**, and that people use it to cover up the fact that they don't really know what they're talking about, or haven't done their jobs properly.

4) The **Plain English Campaign** (see p.52) was set up in 1979 to **combat** excessively complex language.

Practice Questions

Q1 Define jargon.

Q2 Give examples of jargon from four different occupational groups.

Q3 Give three examples of euphemistic jargon.

Q4 How has the use of jargon been criticised?

Essay Question

Q1 "If managers want their employees to understand them, they need to stop using jargon in the workplace."

Do you agree with this statement? Consider the positive and negative aspects of using jargon.

Time to facilitate some revisioneering management solutions...

If you really push the envelope, you should be able to incentivise some blue sky thinking strategies, vis-a-vis achieving exam success. Try to bring some 360 degree feedback to the table before rolling out your smart targets, because there's no 'I' in 'team'. At the end of the day, the most important thing is to use best practice and think outside the box — going forward...

Sources and Exam Questions

Here are some exam-style questions, with sources like the ones you'll get in the real paper.

1. The text below is a transcript of a conversation between the manager of a shoe shop and two trainees. It is their first day.

   What is the significance of gender in this interaction?   *[48 marks]*

M: right Josh I want you to work in the men's section (.) is that okay
J: cool
M: and you Susie erm I'd like you to man the customer service desk at first (.) that's on the lower floor (.) okay with that
S: yes (.) yes (.) that's fine
M: great (.) now then (.) let me tell what I'll (.) what I'll expect from you
S: mm mm
M: ok you need to be here by eight-thirty every morning (1.0) and I mean eight-thirty yes
J: sure
S: yes but erm er (1.0) sometimes (.) sorry I hope it's okay but my bus is late sometimes so (.) it should be fine
M: no that's okay (.) but if you can see about getting an earlier one if you can
S: mm mm no of course (.) sorry
M: there's not always much you can do about it though is there (.) don't worry sweetheart (2.0) now
J: // I live near yours Suzie
S: okay (.) erm
J: I'll give you a lift
S: oh are you sure (1.0) if you're sure that'd be great (.) thank you
M: brilliant (.) good lad (1.0) that's that sorted then (.) okay erm breaktimes for you two are erm ten forty-five to eleven (.) in the morning erm and two forty-five to three in the afternoon (2.0) finish at five
J: what about lunch-time
M: good question (1.0) lunchtime (1.0) we don't want a growing lad like you starving now do we (1.0) one till two (1.0) right (1.0) everything clear
S: yes thank you (.) although I just wondered
J: // fine (1.0) do we work every Saturday
M: no (.) alternate Saturdays erm we'll need to work out which ones I er want you in for later (2.0) but we'll do that later (.) now (1) the till
J: // don't worry about me (.) I were on the tills in me last job
M: great (.) okay what about you Suzie
S: yep no that's fine (.) I've worked in shops before
M: right (2.0) little miss efficient eh
S: mm
M: okay so we'll have Josh (.) you on the tills at first right (2.0) so Susie (1.0) polite at all times (2.0) and don't forget to smile (1.0) you going to be OK with that Susie
S: yep think so (1.0) thanks (.) can I ask for help if I need it
J: cool

Transcription Key

(.) — *brief pause*

(3.0) — *Numbers within brackets indicate length of pause in seconds*

// — *interruption or overlapping speech*

M — Manager
S — Female Trainee
J — Male Trainee

Sources and Exam Questions

2. The text below is a transcript of part of a Chemistry lesson.

What do you observe about the power relationships in this extract? *[48 marks]*

T — Teacher
A, **B**, **C**, **D** — Pupils

T: settle down now (.) we haven't got all day to get through this stuff (1.0) keep ties on please okay (.) yeah (.) okay and and top buttons done up James (2.0) so can we turn (.) can we turn to what we we were doing last week okay (.) ionic bonding page nine

A: page ten

T: what

A: page ten (.) it's on

B: // yeah it's on page ten

T: okay thanks page ten (.) fine okay now what do we remember (.) remember from last week about

C: // nothing

T: no not nothing (.) what about

B: // no it is nothing sir (.) we had sports day since then didn't we

T: well sports day doesn't wipe everything from (.) from your memory does it now (2.0) so what can you tell me about what happens to atoms (.) what is it that happens to atoms in ionic bonding (4.0) Melanie (1.0) what happens

A: erm (2.0) it's (.) they don't (.) they don't

T: // think about electrons

A: right yeah (.) well with electrons they like they like (.) have them when

B: // no-one remembers nothing about this

T: anything (.) remembers anything about this

B: right

A: // yeah

T: okay no (.) we do remember (.) let's just settle down and focus now right (1.0) if you don't get this it's you who has to do the exams so you really need to get this bit (2.0) in ionic bonding atoms lose or gain electrons to form (2.0) what do they form (3.0) James

B: ions (.) is it (.) ions yeah

T: yep ions (.) great okay (.) yes Tash erm (.) yes

D: sorry but erm (.) it's really hot in here sir (.) please may I (.) can I

B: // yeah

T: // okay well open the window (3.0) right so what are ions please

3. The text below is a chatroom conversation between two school friends.

What do you observe about the influence of technology on the language of this text? *[48 marks]*

hani_ani:	hey rosie hw u doin? havnt see u for time
Bubblicious:	i no! am cool chik hw u 2? how was tenerife?
hani_ani:	BRILL!!!!!! the guys are soooo hot there!!
Bubblicious:	naughty! u stil seein Billy?
hani_ani:	lol nah, he's weird man! dmped him
Bubblicious:	Ahhh! He wuz cool! Mite giv im a call lol!! nah fair enuff.Lookin fwd 2 going bak?
hani_ani:	Sort of. Gonna ave 2 do sum work this yr tho
Bubblicious:	yeh, cant wait :'-(
hani_ani:	newayz u wanna do somethin l8tr man? Catch up a bit?
Bubblicious:	love 2 bt no dosh :(u could cum round 2 mine?
hani_ani:	Cud do. Wot time?
Bubblicious:	Hw bout 8. cud watch a film or sommat....??
hani_ani:	Cool! I'll be ther @ 8
hani_ani:	bysie byes xxxx
Bubblicious:	XXXXXXXXX

Sources and Exam Questions

4. The text below is an online advert for a charity fundraising event.
In what ways does this text seek to influence the reader? *[48 marks]*

Tea Time

19 September
Whether it's lapsang souchong or a mug of builders', it's hard to beat a nice cup of tea. Unless it's a nice cup of tea that could help make a fairer world.

On 19 September, we're asking people across the world to get together, put the kettle on and help give poor communities the chance of a better future.

It's Tea Time. And this year absolutely everyone is invited.

- Order your free event pack
- Download free resources right now

What is Tea Time?

It's a unique fundraising event that puts the tea in the fight against poverty.

Last year, the first ever Christian Aid Tea Time saw more than 2,000 tea parties from Sheffield to Sri Lanka raise an incredible £195,000.

This year we'd love to beat that total. And all you have to do to help is invite your friends, family, colleagues or neighbours to join you for a cuppa on 19 September.

You can host your Tea Time anywhere you like – at home, in the office, your local hall, or somewhere more adventurous. Last year one TeaTime took place up a church tower.

It could be a posh do with hundreds of guests, or your best pals and a cracked old teapot. Just ask everyone to give a donation to Christian Aid in return for a refreshing brew and a tasty biscuit or two. Simple.

What's it all for?

The money you raise will help us in our mission to end poverty across the world.

Christian Aid works in around 50 countries, helping people, irrespective of religion, to tackle the problems they face and build the life they deserve. We can't think of a better reason to take a tea break.

Order your free event pack now

We have put everything you need – invitations, colourful posters, delicious cake recipes – into a handy event pack. Order yours now: complete our online registration form or call 0870 076 7766.

You can also download some of these resources right now - just click here.

And in the meantime, we're here to offer any advice, ideas or support you need along the way too. Just give us a call and we'll talk Tea Time – 020 7523 2248 or email events@christian-aid.org

christian aid We believe in life before death

http://www.christianaid.org.uk/getinvolved/events/fundraising/teatime/index.aspx

Sources and Exam Questions

> 5. The text below is a transcript of a conversation between two mechanics (A and B) and a customer (C). Identify and explain some of the features of occupational language they use.   *[30 marks]*

A: okay we've had a look and we couldn't pinpoint at first why it was (.) ah here's Greg actually it was Greg who was working on it mostly (.) erm I'll get him over (2.0) Greg

C: // okay

B: hiya (.) all right (1.0) back for the (.) er Range Rover is it (.) two point five diesel

C: yes that's right

A: I'm just saying it's you who was working on it really so do you (.) want to go through it and

B: // yeah yeah (.) no of course (.) great

C: great (.) thanks thank you

A: do you want to erm take him through to have a look at the v5 Greg

B: right yeah (.) yeah okay I'll get the get the v5 and we'll have a look

A: if you'd just like to come through here

C: // okay yes (.) okay

A: // we've had a bit of a problem with it really (.) the engine tone was changing slightly so we scanned it for any fault codes but we weren't getting anything from it

C: okay

A: so we thought it's like maybe (.) maybe your MAF playing up

C: // erm right (.) okay

A: // have you had any problems with that before

C: any problems with the (.) the sorry any problems with the (.) the erm (.) the (1.0) MAF

A: right no no (.) have you noticed any differences with your engine tone (2.0) sounds different (.) ever sound different

C: okay (.) erm no no (1.0) not re- (.) don't think I have really no

A: no problems in the past with that Greg

B: no (.) right no (.) I thought that but it can (.) it can just be it needs a clean (2.0) I mean I erm (.) I thought it was more that probably the injector was (.) yeah injector a bit blocked

A: // well yeah (.) that's what I'm thinking really (.) probably just your injector being a bit blocked up (.) happens a lot with these models so it's

C: // yes (.) right yes okay (2.0) so what do you need to do with that (.) how will you fix it

A: basically what I'm thinking is that it's probably not a big problem

B: right yeah (.) not major like is it really

A: nothing major

C: // okay

A: just keep it in a bit longer so we can (.) I'll get Greg on it when (1.0) Greg when you've finished with that coupe (.) with the rev limiter on that coupe

B: // yeah cool (.) okay

A: // so if we get some Forté* in the fuel system then we'll see if that (.) I mean that could sort it completely (1.0) is that okay then

C: is that okay for (.) is that (.) erm yes no that should be fine (1.0) what I mean is I mean when do you think I can come and collect it

A: well Greg's got to finish this coupe (.) but then erm (.) well well it could be tomorrow morning I reckon

C: okay great (.) that's great (.) as long as you think that'll fix it (.) I really don't want to have to be coming back and forth again really if that's (.) it's just a bit of a pain when

A: // oh no worries yeah (.) yeah no a bit of Forté will do it

*Forté™ is a brand of fuel treatment.

Spoken Language

Joy of untold joys, this section is for everyone — time to learn all about talking and stuff.
Spoken language refers to the patterns and styles of language you use to communicate things every time you open your mouth. Unless you're just doing your hilarious goldfish impression again.

Spoken language has **Two Main Purposes**

1) **To convey meaning** — when you need to **explain something** to someone, or **give orders** or **instructions**, you use language as a means of **clarification**, so that the listener will **understand** you.

2) **To demonstrate attitudes and values** — language lets you offer **opinions** on subjects, and get your **point of view across**.

Chris promised to give
conversation a chance next time.

The **Content** of spoken language **Depends** on its **Context**

Spoken language is usually the most **efficient** way for speakers to communicate with each other. As with written language, the way a spoken text is **constructed** can be affected by **external** features.

1) The **audience** or **person being addressed** — it could be someone the speaker has known for years, or thousands of people that they've never met before.

2) The speaker's **background** — this will affect their **word choices**, **grammatical constructions**, etc.

3) The **location** and **purpose** of the text — speakers use language differently depending on where the conversation is taking place, and what's being talked about.

Spoken language can be **Formal** or **Informal**

1) **Formal** speech is often used in situations when you **don't really know** the people you're talking to.

2) You might also use formal speech in a situation where you want to **show respect**, like a **job interview**.

3) It's most common in **prepared** speeches — the speaker is reading from **planned, written notes**.

4) Formal spoken language is more likely to use **complex** and mainly **complete grammatical structures**.

> 1) **Informal** speech is generally used **among friends** or in situations where there's **no need** for formality or preparation.
>
> 2) It includes mostly **colloquial language**, which is casual and familiar.
>
> 3) It has **simpler** and often **incomplete grammatical structures**, **simpler vocabulary**, more **slang** words and **dialect** features.

Speech can be **Individual** or involve **More Than One Person**

Individual speech is often known as a **monologue**. Monologues convey **internal thoughts**, **opinions** or **experiences**.

1) The term 'monologue' is usually used for a **scripted performance** (a dramatic monologue), but it can also include any **individual** speaking for a longer period of time than normal.

2) Monologues are directed at listeners who make **no spoken contribution**.

3) They can be **prepared** or **spontaneous**.

Dialogue is **spoken** language that involves **more than one** speaker.

1) A dialogue is a **conversation** involving two or more people — they use language to **interact** with each other.

2) Dialogue exchanges can be **short**, but in longer conversations one of the speakers may take the **major role**, with the others mainly listening and only **contributing occasionally**.

3) Dialogue can be prepared or spontaneous. Most conversations between characters on TV or in plays or films are **scripted** by a writer, but conversations between you and your friends are **unprepared** — in spontaneous dialogue speakers **respond** to the different **cues and contexts** that come up as the conversation goes on.

Spoken Language

Spoken Language Functions *in different ways*

There are **five** categories of **spoken language**, which are used in different situations.

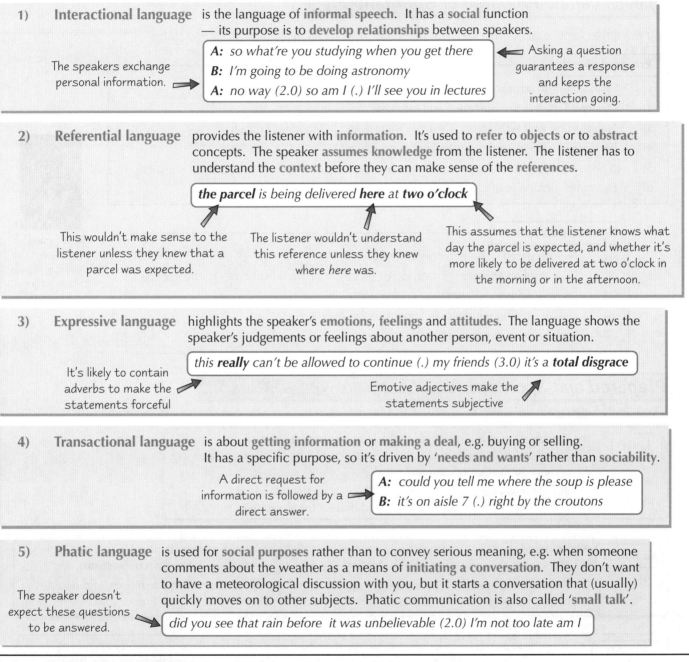

1) **Interactional language** is the language of **informal speech**. It has a **social** function — its purpose is to **develop relationships** between speakers.

The speakers exchange personal information. →

> **A:** *so what're you studying when you get there*
> **B:** *I'm going to be doing astronomy*
> **A:** *no way (2.0) so am I (.) I'll see you in lectures*

← Asking a question guarantees a response and keeps the interaction going.

2) **Referential language** provides the listener with **information**. It's used to **refer** to **objects** or to **abstract** concepts. The speaker **assumes knowledge** from the listener. The listener has to understand the **context** before they can make sense of the **references**.

> ***the parcel*** *is being delivered **here** at **two o'clock***

This wouldn't make sense to the listener unless they knew that a parcel was expected.

The listener wouldn't understand this reference unless they knew where *here* was.

This assumes that the listener knows what day the parcel is expected, and whether it's more likely to be delivered at two o'clock in the morning or in the afternoon.

3) **Expressive language** highlights the speaker's **emotions**, **feelings** and **attitudes**. The language shows the speaker's judgements or feelings about another person, event or situation.

> *this **really** can't be allowed to continue (.) my friends (3.0) it's a **total disgrace***

It's likely to contain adverbs to make the statements forceful

Emotive adjectives make the statements subjective

4) **Transactional language** is about **getting information** or **making a deal**, e.g. buying or selling. It has a specific purpose, so it's driven by '**needs and wants**' rather than **sociability**.

A direct request for information is followed by a direct answer.

> **A:** *could you tell me where the soup is please*
> **B:** *it's on aisle 7 (.) right by the croutons*

5) **Phatic language** is used for **social purposes** rather than to convey serious meaning, e.g. when someone comments about the weather as a means of **initiating a conversation**. They don't want to have a meteorological discussion with you, but it starts a conversation that (usually) quickly moves on to other subjects. Phatic communication is also called '**small talk**'.

The speaker doesn't expect these questions to be answered.

> *did you see that rain before it was unbelievable (2.0) I'm not too late am I*

Practice Questions

Q1   Explain in your own words the difference between formal and informal spoken language.
Q2   What's the difference between a monologue and dialogue?
Q3   Describe the features and function of referential spoken language.

Essay Question

Q1   Describe the different types of spoken language and suggest where each might be used.

What about people that actually want a meteorological discussion with you?

Just leg it. Pure and simple. It does sort of make me wonder what weathermen or weatherwomen talk about after they've had the small talk. Maybe they talk about things they're interested in, like... I don't know... jazz, or European cinema. I don't trust them though, with their funny laser-thumbs, always changing that map on the wall behind them... making it rain a lot.

Speech Features

Who are you calling speech features? Oh... oh right. These pages will give you some all-important features of spontaneous and prepared speech. These are pretty important — more building blocks for your analysis in the exam.

Speech can be *Prepared* or *Spontaneous*

You can either know exactly what you're about to say, or you can make it up as you go along.

Prepared speech

1) Worked out **in advance**.
2) Designed for specific **audience and purpose**.
3) Needs to be **well written** (so is usually **formal** and in Standard English).
4) **Performed** or **delivered** to try and make an impact.
5) Needs to **maintain the interest** of listeners (who may or may not be known to the speaker).
6) Examples include **political speeches** and **sermons**.

Spontaneous speech

1) **Not prepared** or written down beforehand.
2) Delivered **on the spot** as soon as, or shortly after, the idea comes to the speaker.
3) Usually **informal** (depending on context).
4) Usually shared with people **known to the speaker**.
5) Mainly **in response to** another speaker.

Ross probably should've put the vacuum appliance down before starting his speech.

Prepared and *Spontaneous* Speech are *Very Different*

If you apply **language frameworks** to prepared and spontaneous speech, you can see how different they are.

Lexis

* **Prepared speech** — the lexis is likely to be **standardised** and formal. Speakers have time to think about their word choices, so the vocabulary is more **sophisticated** and **technical**.
* **Spontaneous speech** — the lexis is likely to be **non-standard**. The informal context means **slang** and **dialect** forms are used more.

Grammar

* **Prepared speech** — the structure of sentences follows standard **grammatical rules** and pauses in the speech are controlled by **punctuation**. Speakers don't tend to use many **contractions**.
* **Spontaneous speech** — non-standard **agreements**, non-standard or **irregular tenses**, and **double negatives** are common in conversation, e.g. *I done it, We was planning to, I never told him nothing*.

Formality / Audience

* **Prepared speech** — speeches are aimed at an **audience**. The language is carefully chosen to persuade the audience in some way. Prepared speeches usually **address** the audience **directly** (the speaker uses *I* or *we*, and *you*). They're often **formal** to create a feeling of **prestige**.
* **Spontaneous speech** — most spontaneous speech is only meant for the speakers involved. Conversations that take place in **public places** (over a shop counter etc.) or between strangers are usually more **formal** than private ones.

Prepared and spontaneous speech also have some features in common:

1) **Discourse structure** — a prepared speech has a beginning, middle, and end. **Themes** and **ideas** are introduced at different points, and the whole thing is usually written to end on a **positive note**, so that the audience go away with a **lasting impression**. Spontaneous speech also has **formulaic** beginnings and endings (see p.72-73).

2) **Non-verbal communication** (p.26) — relates to body language, gestures and facial expressions. It **emphasises** certain words or phrases in both prepared and spontaneous speech, but can also be **disruptive** if it's overdone.

3) **Prosodic features** — include stress, rhythm, pitch, tempo and intonation. They're useful in prepared speech, where a speaker can use the devices to keep an audience **interested** over a long period of time.

Speech Features

Spontaneous Speech has many Unique Features

Even though **spontaneous speech** shares some features with prepared spoken English, it has lots of **specific features**. Look at the following **conversation** between two people:

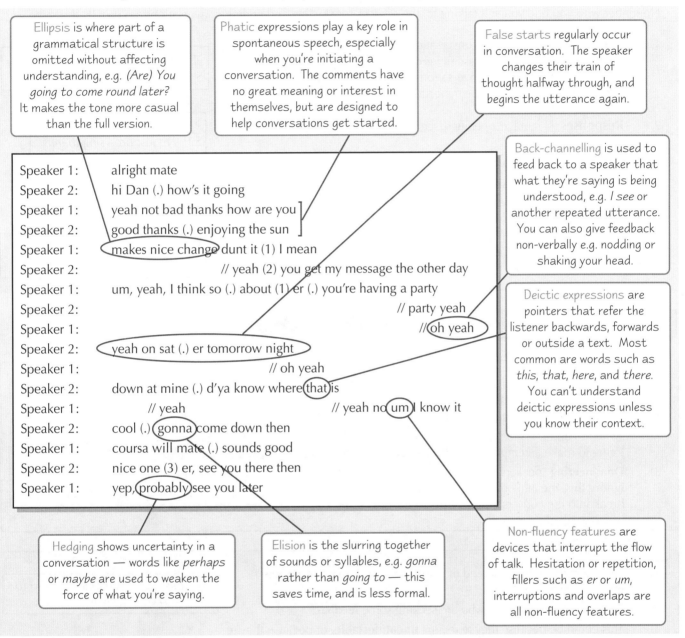

Ellipsis is where part of a grammatical structure is omitted without affecting understanding, e.g. *(Are) You going to come round later?* It makes the tone more casual than the full version.

Phatic expressions play a key role in spontaneous speech, especially when you're initiating a conversation. The comments have no great meaning or interest in themselves, but are designed to help conversations get started.

False starts regularly occur in conversation. The speaker changes their train of thought halfway through, and begins the utterance again.

Back-channelling is used to feed back to a speaker that what they're saying is being understood, e.g. *I see* or another repeated utterance. You can also give feedback non-verbally e.g. nodding or shaking your head.

Deictic expressions are pointers that refer the listener backwards, forwards or outside a text. Most common are words such as *this*, *that*, *here*, and *there*. You can't understand deictic expressions unless you know their context.

Speaker 1:	alright mate
Speaker 2:	hi Dan (.) how's it going
Speaker 1:	yeah not bad thanks how are you
Speaker 2:	good thanks (.) enjoying the sun
Speaker 1:	makes nice change dunt it (1) I mean
Speaker 2:	// yeah (2) you get my message the other day
Speaker 1:	um, yeah, I think so (.) about (1) er (.) you're having a party
Speaker 2:	// party yeah
Speaker 1:	// oh yeah
Speaker 2:	yeah on sat (.) er tomorrow night
Speaker 1:	// oh yeah
Speaker 2:	down at mine (.) d'ya know where that is
Speaker 1:	// yeah // yeah no um I know it
Speaker 2:	cool (.) gonna come down then
Speaker 1:	coursa will mate (.) sounds good
Speaker 2:	nice one (3) er, see you there then
Speaker 1:	yep, probably see you later

Hedging shows uncertainty in a conversation — words like *perhaps* or *maybe* are used to weaken the force of what you're saying.

Elision is the slurring together of sounds or syllables, e.g. *gonna* rather than *going to* — this saves time, and is less formal.

Non-fluency features are devices that interrupt the flow of talk. Hesitation or repetition, fillers such as *er* or *um*, interruptions and overlaps are all non-fluency features.

Practice Questions

Q1   Give a key difference in the use of grammar in prepared speech as opposed to spontaneous speech.

Q2   How can paralinguistic and prosodic features help speakers?

Q3   Give three examples of phatic expressions.

Essay Question

Q1   Discuss the differences between prepared and spontaneous speech, with reference to lexis, grammar and formality.

Everyone uses phatic expressions — even if they're not that phat...

Hopefully, you'll recognise some of these features from conversations you've had in the past with people you know (and probably people you don't). If you don't, good work. You're obviously the finest conversationalist since Talky McChatterlot, who never hedged, or false-started, or used phatic expressions or anything. He was dead dull though.

Conversation and Turn-taking

If you've ever had a conversation, you'll know that you can't just rabbit on all the way through... unless it's a conversation with yourself... in which case, sorry for interrupting. But if there are two people involved — learn the rules.

Some features occur in All Conversations

No matter who you find yourself talking to, the devices for **starting** and **ending** conversations are usually the same.

1) **Openings** — an informal conversation may begin with a simple **familiar starter**. These are usually **greetings**, such as *hello*, or *alright?* More formal conversations often include **inquiries** like *I wonder if you could help me?* to get someone's **attention**.

> Speaker 1: *good morning*
> Speaker 2: *hello (.) can I help you*

2) **Responses** — familiar openings (see above) invite a particular response.

> S1: *hello (.) can I help you*
> S2: *I'm just browsing thanks*

3) **Adjacency pairs** — **short, familiar exchanges** of conversation that follow **predictable** patterns.

> S1: *how are you*
> S2: *I'm fine thanks*

4) **Signalling closure** — speech indicators and other non-verbal signs can be used to show that a conversation is **drawing to a close**.

> S1: *he fell down a manhole once*
> S2: *really well (.) time I was off*

Some features depend on the Individual Speakers

Switching and turn-taking

1) The person speaking at any given time may be aware that **someone else** wants to speak.

2) In an orderly conversation they **invite** the switch to another speaker e.g. by **pausing**, or trying to make an **emphatic** final statement.

3) **Domineering** speakers sometimes choose to **ignore** this, meaning other speakers have to break into the conversation by **interrupting**, or just **stay silent**.

> S1: *I can't believe he didn't see it*
> S2: *why not (1) it wasn't a penalty (2) what do you think*
> S3: *I think it probably was*
> S2: *that's why you're not a referee*
> S1: *it's pretty hard to work out*
> S2:   *// maybe if you weren't watching*

Tag questions

1) These are attached to the **end of statements**, and **invite responses** from other speakers.

2) They're used by speakers who are seeking some **feedback**.

3) This could be because they're feeling **uncomfortable**, or because they're trying to **control** the conversation by bringing other people into it.

> S1: *this is an issue that we need to resolve quickly <u>isn't it</u>*

Topic Shifts

1) **Topic shifts** are when speakers **change** the **subject** of the conversation.

2) They move the conversation forward or **change** its **focus**.

3) They're usually started by the domineering speaker trying to control the **content** and **direction** of a conversation.

> S1: *so I said carbonara*
> S2: *right (2) did you ever hear back from Dave*

Feedback

1) When someone's speaking, people give **verbal** and **non-verbal** signs that they're **listening** to them

2) For example, brief comments, nodding or shaking your head, smiling, frowning, etc.

> S1: *no one told me it was a sponge*
> S2: *mm-hmm*

Conversation and Turn-taking

Different **Techniques** are involved at different **Stages** of a **Conversation**

Getting involved / Initiating conversation

1) Most participants in a conversation will offer a contribution **without waiting** to be asked — if you waited to be asked to speak in every conversation, you might **never** speak at all.

2) You might get a conversation started by showing an **interest** in the other people involved.

3) If you're talking to an **unfamiliar person**, appropriate **phatic expressions** and **questioning** can help get things started, e.g. you can use **tag questions** to initiate **responses**.

Sustaining conversation

1) Fluent speaking (following **adjacency patterns** and **turn-taking rules**), showing an interest (**feedback**) and generally enjoying talking are all factors that help people **sustain** conversation.

2) **Speaker empathy** is important — if people are exploring **shared interests** or **opinions** then the conversation is more likely to be sustained. Listeners might make it clear that they share the speaker's views by using feedback, e.g. *mm* and *yeah*.

Ending conversation

1) **Social convention** makes us not want to appear rude, cut people short or walk away when they're not ready — so **phatic expressions** are used to **signal closure** in a socially recognisable way e.g. *I should probably get going*.

2) There are also **non-verbal** cues that signal a speaker is about to end the conversation e.g. starting to **get up** from a seat, or increasing the **distance** between the speakers.

The conversation got heated as they tried to work out who'd thought of the fancy dress costume first.

Participants **Manage** and **Control** conversations

In an orderly conversation, you take **turns** speaking with other people. However, not all conversations are orderly and it's rare to find one where each speaker actually waits their turn — it depends on the **individuals** involved.

Prepared / Formal situations

1) These are the types of conversation where there is a defined power relationship between the participants, e.g. conducting an **interview** with someone or being interviewed yourself.

2) **Prepared situations** (like a tutorial, job interview or debate) have a **specific subject** or subject area on the agenda. You may not know precisely how the conversation will go, but you know what is **likely** to be discussed, and the level of **formality** you're expected to use.

3) There's usually a person **overtly** in charge of the exchanges, like a lecturer, interviewer or chairperson, whose **authority** to change the conversation at will is **already acknowledged** before it starts.

Unprepared / Informal situations

1) **Informal** social conversations are less likely to be prepared, and could involve any topic, but these still tend to be **controlled** by certain individuals.

2) People who are **louder**, **quicker** and more **forceful** than other speakers often **dominate informal conversations**.

3) It is easy for less confident and less assertive speakers to be **inhibited** or **intimidated**, and to end up contributing very little (for more on conversations and power, see p.50-53).

Practice Questions

Q1 Give an example of a tag question, and describe its purpose.

Q2 What are adjacency pairs, and how are they used in conversation?

Essay Question

Q1 Discuss the techniques speakers use to initiate, manage, control, sustain and end conversations.

You say potato, I say pipe down for ONE MINUTE so I can get a word in...

Is that too much to ask? Right then. You should now have all the tools you need for analysing spoken language, whether it's prepared speeches (when you need to think mainly about purpose and effect), or spontaneous conversation (where you need to think about features of interaction). And for once, eavesdropping would be really good practice.

Sources and Exam Questions

Now have a go at this practice exam question — don't forget to refer to all three texts in your answer.

> 1) Study the three texts below, **A**, **B** and **C**.
>
> Analyse and compare the use of language by the speakers in these texts.
>
> In your answer you should consider:
> - the features of spontaneous speech
> - the uses of standard and non-standard grammar
> - how the texts are controlled and managed   *[48 marks]*

Text A — Conversation between a customer and a newsagent.

A: now then Sam

B: now then (.) been sent to get the paper

A: yes here we are (.) bit late delivering today

B: oh yeah

A: yeah it's a right pain (1) here I saw your lad the other day (.) he back now from

B: // mm   // aye yeah (.) yeah back from university

A: comes round quick doesn't it

B: quick yeah (.) yeah he's back three months now

A: // three months

B: // aye (.) I er I wanted to ask actually (1) he's gonna need some er some work you see (.) while he's (.) but he doesn't drive so I mean you don't know anyone in the village who might need (.) need a bit of work done do you

A: oh aye yeah (.) I see (.) long time to go with no work is three months (2) I'll have a think

B: // mm I mean I think he's willing for most things (.) odd jobs and

A: // odd jobs like (.) mm (2) tell you what (.) some of the older people might need a hand in their gardens (.) you know mowing the lawn and that

B: // yeah that'll be

A: tell you what (.) write his name and a contact number on a card (.) I can put it up there with the others on the board over there

B: oh cheers yeah (.) oh that'll be great yeah thanks (1) if you hear anyone mentioning needing help in the meantime give us a nod will you

A: no problem mate

Text B — Extract from a job interview.

X: *(the interviewer)* you must be Matthew (2.0) come in and have a seat

Y: *(the candidate)* yep that's ri- (2.0) oh right (.) thanks

X: you found the office alright then did you?

Y: er (.) yep it was fine (.) I had a map so

X: // good good (.) we'll get started then (1.0) I don't want to keep you too long (.) basically what's going to happen is I'll ask you a few questions about your suitability for the role (1.0) and then we'll have a little chat about the company so you can see if you like us (.) and we can see if we like you (2.0) that sound ok?

Y: yeah grea- (1.0) um (.) yeah that sounds fine

X: excellent (.) so (2.0) I see from your CV and application that you've worked in radio before?

Y: Yep (1.0) yes I

Sources and Exam Questions

(Text B contd.)

X:　　　　　　　// why don't you tell me a little bit about that

Y:　OK (3.0) well basically (.) um (.) it was a hospital radio station and (1.0) er I had to go round wards and get requests from people that were going to listen to the show (.) and (2.0) um (.) sort of put it together you know

X:　mmm-hmm (1.0) right OK (1.0) and did you get a chance to do any work behind the desks?

Y:　Yeah (.) yeah I did (.) er (2.0) at first I was only really allowed to speak on air (1.0) you know, probably a good thing (2.0) but then I started to learn a bit about the presenting and I got

X:　　　　　　　　　　　　　　　　　　　// and then you got a shot at DJ-ing?

Y:　er (.) yeah (1.0) they let me loose after that

X:　good (.) great (1.0) so did you enjoy that or did you prefer producing the shows you were working on?

Text C — Speech by a company director to the company's employees.

ladies and gentlemen (1.0) err ladies and gentlemen (2.0) can (.) can you hear me OK at the back there?

(*indistinct responses*)

err (.) ladies and gentlemen thank you all very (.) very much for coming today (2.0) I (.) I know some of you were only given very short notice of this meeting (.) and I apologise for that but thanks for making the effort to be here (2.0) I wish I had better news to share with you (1.0) but as some of you will already know (1.0) I'm afraid I don't

it's difficult to know how best to put this (2.0) but here goes (.)

many of you will already be aware that the company has been struggling of late to break even (1.0) what with the increasing costs of production (.) the high cost of borrowing (1.0) and so on (2.0) and so (.) management has been forced into the kind of decision that we hoped that we were never going to have to make

(*murmuring from the floor*)

the branch is going to have to close down in order to keep alive the chances of us keeping going elsewhere (5.0) we aim to find work elsewhere for as many of you as possible (.) especially our younger workers (1.0) but we simply can't provide enough for everyone (1.0) so with the greatest regret (1.0) and I assure it is with the greatest regret and we're not smiling behind your backs (2.0) we are going to have to offer redundancy packages to some of you (.)

I want you all to be aware that a redundancy package in no way suggests that we think that you are no longer valued by us (1.0) but we simply can't avoid doing this if we're to have any chance of continuing to hold our place in the market in the future (3.0) we have to be pragmatic about this — we have no choice (3.0)

Les (.) the branch manager (.) will be speaking to each of you individually within the next few days (1.0) I don't envy him this for one moment (1.0) so that you're all in the picture as quickly as possible.

I can't really say very much more (2.0) other than to emphasise once again how much it hurts me to have to stand up and do this (2.0) thank you all very (.) very much

Transcription Key

(.) *Micropause*

(2.0) *Pause in seconds*

// *Interruption / overlapping speech*

Purpose

These two pages are for everyone except OCR. All the texts that you see have a purpose. You identify the main reason a text was written by analysing the language it uses. This is known as writing a commentary on the text.

Texts usually have one of *Four Main Purposes*

1) Written texts usually try to achieve one of the following purposes.

> 1. **Inform** e.g. newspaper   2. **Instruct** e.g. cookbook   3. **Persuade** e.g. advert   4. **Entertain** e.g. comic

Not all texts slot neatly into these categories, e.g. a film review might be informative, entertaining and persuasive.

2) Despite this, you can usually work out the primary function of a text by looking at its language and presentation. To find out the **purpose** of a text you need to apply these **frameworks**:

> • **Lexis** — vocabulary / specific words   • **Grammar** — sentence length and structure
> • **Graphology** — how the text is arranged   • **Semantics** — meaning (actual or hidden)

Informative Texts are Factual

1) There are many different types of informative text. Informative writing needs to contain **knowledge** or **facts** that readers want to know, like the latest news in a newspaper.

2) Informative texts are **structured clearly** so they're easy to **understand**.
They might include presentational features such as headings / subheadings, bullet points, boxes and illustrations.

3) The information is presented in a way that's **suitable** for the **intended audience**. If it's intended for children, the language is **simple** and **less detailed**. An informative text for an older audience might use more **complex** language — assuming that the reader has some **previous knowledge**.

4) The text may include **specialist** or **technical terms**, and explain them.

5) The tone is usually **serious**. Informative texts don't generally include **opinions** or **comments**.
Some informative texts simply consist of times and dates, e.g. a train timetable.

6) Informative texts are usually written in the **third person**, using *he*, *she*, or *it*.

Instructional Texts tell you How to do something

These texts are similar to informative texts because they include **information**. However, the main function of an instructional text is to show the reader **how** to do something **practical**. They have a **clear**, **structured** style:

> 1) Instructional texts usually include **chronological**, **numbered** sections.
> 2) They use graphological devices such as **bullet points** and **headings**.
> 3) The instructions are often given as **imperative** sentences e.g. *Add the butter, sugar and flour to the mixture.*
> 4) The text may use **second person** forms (e.g. *you do this*) to address the reader directly.
> 5) The lexis is **straightforward** and **uncomplicated**, but can be **subject-specific** (e.g. *beat*, *whisk*, *fold* in cooking).

Persuasive Texts aim to Change Your Mind

1) Persuasive texts try to either **influence** the reader's opinions or **persuade** them to do something.

2) They often use **first person address** (*I* and *we*) to communicate the writer's **feelings** and include the readers. Possessive pronouns like *our* and *your* also **personally** involve the reader in the views expressed in the text.

3) They often use **emotive adjectives** and **subjective judgements** to provoke emotional and intellectual responses.

4) They use facts, statistics and other **evidence** to support the main argument, linked together with connectives such as *therefore*, *because*, and *however* to create a **logical route** to a conclusion.

5) They might use eye-catching **graphology** (p.32-33), such as **logos**, **capitalization** and **colour**, to attract the reader's attention and **stress** the importance of a particular point or argument.

Purpose

There are many **Different Types** of **Entertainment** texts

1) **Entertainment texts** include novels, stories, articles, verses, songs, poetry, plays, biographies and autobiographies.

2) Even though there's a big **range** of entertainment texts, they tend to have **several features in common**:

- **Sophisticated** language
- **Extensive** vocabulary
- Varied **sentence types**
- **Figurative** language
- Often **complex structure**
- Eye-catching **layout**

3) These techniques help the writers of entertainment texts to express personal **feelings** and produce **poetic** thoughts and ideas.

4) Writers also use these features to influence how the audience **experiences** the text. Entertainment texts can help audiences **escape** from reality, **frighten** and **shock** them, affect them **emotionally** or make them **think**.

5) Some writers might choose to **change** or **ignore** these **expected conventions** to achieve **different effects**.

Texts that **Analyse Language** are called **Commentaries**

A **commentary** or **language analysis** (which you'll be asked to produce in your exam) needs to focus on the following areas:

1) The **linguistic choices** made by the writer.
2) **Distinctive features** of the style or genre chosen by the writer.
3) The influence of the **context** upon the language choices.
4) What **effects** were **intended** or **achieved** in the text.

Linguistic terminology is all very well, but sometimes the only appropriate medium is contemporary dance.

As a writer, commentaries enable you to do the following things:

There's more on writing commentaries in the Do Well in the Exam section, on p.105.

1) Communicate your **knowledge** and **understanding** of how language works by applying it to a particular piece of writing or speech.
2) Use appropriate **linguistic terminology** to explain your points.
3) Demonstrate your knowledge of appropriate **frameworks of language**.

Practice Questions

Q1 How can you tell if the purpose of a text is to inform?

Q2 Which type of text (informative, instructive, persuasive or entertaining) is more likely to use sophisticated language and a variety of sentence structures?

Q3 In persuasive texts, why is the reader often directly addressed in the second person *you*?

Essay Questions

Q1 What sort of language would writers use to make their purpose obvious to an audience in the following types of text: reference book, feature article for a magazine and an advertisement for a charity.

Revision guide texts aim to make you really really really smart...

And that's just the start. I also aim to solve the world's climate problems, but I've yet to work out how to do it using only a handful of verbs and some prepositions. I imagine the eventual solution will be glorious and I'll be hailed as a genius. For now, I'll just advise you to try and be a better student by learning everything there is to know about purpose.

Audience

These pages are for everyone. When you're analysing texts, you need to be able to identify the target audience.

The **Audience** is the group of people that the **Text** is **Aimed At**

Intended audiences can vary from the very **general** (e.g. 'adults'), to the very **specific** (e.g. 'females over 30 with young children').

1) Writers tailor their texts for different audiences and purposes.

2) To work out the audience of a text, you need to be able to recognise and describe how a text suits a particular kind of reader.

3) You can find clues about the audience, their age and relative status, and how the writer feels about them in the language of a text, e.g. if a text contains simple sentences and basic lexis, it's likely to be for a young audience.

A writer may or may not **Know Their Audience**

A lot depends on **how familiar** the writer or speaker is with their audience:

Known audience

1) The writer might use **personal pronouns** like *I* and *you*. This writing is most often found in memos, personal letters, diaries and stories.

2) The writer may use language that expresses **emotion**, **feelings** or **opinions**.

3) A writer might also have a **target audience** they know quite a lot about e.g. science fiction fans, or film buffs, or supporters of a particular political party. The writer will choose language that they **expect** will be understood and have an effect on members of the target audience.

Unknown audience

Sometimes the text is for an audience that is **unfamiliar**. This type of writing is often found in **academic** or **instructive texts**. The main characteristics are:

1) The writer doesn't **acknowledge** the reader directly as it's usually written in the third person.

2) There is no expression of **personal feeling** and no use of first or second person **pronouns** (*I* or *you*).

3) The text is quite **formal** — it may use formal vocabulary, imperative sentences (in instructive texts) or the **passive voice**. Texts for unknown audiences deal with **serious** subject matter rather than entertainment.

You can **Work Out** the **Intended Audience** of a text

To **identify** the intended **audience** of a text, you need to look at the **style** of the text, its **content**, the choice of **vocabulary** and the **tone**.

1) **Style** — formal and serious writing is usually for an **older audience**. If the text is informal and more **light-hearted** it's often aimed at a **younger audience**. To narrow down the audience further, you need to look at the content of the text.

2) **Content** — the text might be about a **general topic** like global warming, or it might be something **very specific** like the writer's new trainers. The first would have a very **broad** audience, but the second would be aimed at a much smaller audience.

3) **Lexis** — if there are any **complex**, **specialist** or **technical** words, the audience are probably experts — they will already be **familiar** with the jargon. If there are no specialist words, and the lexis is **uncomplicated** and easy to follow, this suggests a **younger** or **less specialist** audience.

4) **Tone** — the tone reflects the purpose of a text, e.g. an informative text would have a serious tone. The tone can also say something about the audience, e.g. a **serious** tone suggests a **mature** or **interested** audience.

5) **Formality** — formal texts (e.g. reports, articles) are usually aimed at **older**, **professional** audiences (with the exception of textbooks, which are aimed at students). Other texts, e.g. e-mails, are more **informal** and **friendly** as the audience is a **known person** or **group**.

Audience

Texts need to **Suit** their **Readership**

Texts are more **accessible** if they are tailored to suit their readership.

1) The text needs to be **tailored** depending on whether it's aimed at children or adults, e.g. different language is used on a **newspaper front page** compared to a **children's comic**.

2) Texts can sometimes be **gender-specific**, aimed at male or female audiences, e.g. the style and content of *Cosmopolitan* is different to that of *FHM*.

3) The **expertise** of the audience is also an important factor — if the audience are experts then the lexis can be more **specialised** than if the text is for a general readership.

Texts can have **Multiple Audiences**

1) Texts may have **more** than one audience, each of which may respond **differently** to it.

2) For example, a children's story is principally aimed at a **young audience**. However it is an **adult** who will decide whether to buy the book — so it needs to **appeal** to the adult as well.

3) If you've ever seen the film **Shrek**® (2001), you'll have seen how a text can appeal to **lots of different** audiences. It's designed to work on **different levels**, with plenty for kids but also jokes that only adults will understand.

Audiences of **Spoken Discourse** vary too

1) The **content** of a spoken discourse can **reveal** the audience, e.g. the **content** of a **university lecture** reveals that it's intended for students specialising in a subject.

2) The talk could be **formal**, like a public speech, or **colloquial**, like a conversation. The level of formality shows the **relationship** of the listener to the speaker, e.g. you speak **respectfully** and **politely** to someone in a position of **authority**, but **casually** with friends.

3) In the same way, **long complex** sentences would be appropriate in an academic lecture or formal context. **Shorter sentences** and the use of **contractions** (like *won't* or *can't*) as well as **interruptions** and **non-fluency** features are more frequently found in informal conversations.

4) Use of a **regional dialect**, or words and grammatical constructions not considered to be **'correct'** English, can help place a target audience **geographically**, **socially** or **ethnically**.

"We've been talking for 3 days now — I should probably get back to work."

Practice Questions

Q1 What are the main differences between a text that is written for a known audience and a text that is written for an unknown audience?

Q2 Name at least two elements of a text that you need to analyse in order to work out the intended audience.

Q3 Explain how analysing the lexis of a text can help you understand the audience.

Essay Question

Q1 What differences would you expect to see between an instruction text for children and an instruction text for adults? Explain your answer with reference to style, content, lexis, tone and formality.

If you're aiming for a target audience, make sure you don't miss...

For some reason people get really uppity about texts pinging around and hitting them in the chops when they're not expecting it. But on a serious note, don't forget that writers identify audiences through the attitudes, beliefs and needs they think a group might have or want. Then they can tailor texts specifically to attract the audience (more on this later).

Genre

These pages are for everyone. *Genre is one way of classifying and organising texts into different categories.*

Genre *groups texts that have* Similar Features

Similar types of texts often seem to follow a **distinctive pattern**. A group of texts with the same features is called a **genre**.

1) **Genre conventions** make **written** and **spoken** communication more **efficient**.

2) When you read a text from a particular **genre**, you have certain **expectations** about it.

3) Knowing **what kind of text** you're reading lets you **predict** what form it will take.

Knowing about genres means you can **classify** language. It allows a reader to form **expectations** about the text based on their **experience** of the **genre**.

There are Many Different Genres *of* Written Text

Examples of **written genres** include: letters, reports, poems, stories, advertisements, postcards, recipes, e-mails, cartoons, text-messages etc. Each genre has a different **writing style** associated with it. For example:

Letters

Formal convention:

1) Sender's address at the top
2) Date and *Dear Sir/Madam*
3) Concludes *Yours sincerely/faithfully*
4) Followed by a signature

Postcards

Abbreviated format:

1) Very informal
2) Contractions common (e.g. *won't, can't*)
3) Dashes and exclamation marks

Recipes

Step-by-step instructions:

1) Start with list of ingredients
2) Followed by numbered instructions
3) Short instructive sentences
4) May include some technical words (like *braise, simmer* or *baste*)

Text messages

Extremely informal:

1) Highly contracted language (*lol* or *btw*)
2) Emoticons (e.g. :-))
3) Language based on sound (e.g. *gr8* or *neway*)

Spoken Texts *also follow* Conventions

Spoken text also has its own genres with **distinctive patterns**. Spoken language is broken down into two main areas — **monologue or dialogue** (see p.68). Each spoken genre has different **conventions** associated with it. Some examples are:

Genre	Conventions
Answer-phone message	The message often begins with *"Sorry, I'm not around at the moment"* (or something similar), and is likely to end with *"Please leave a message after the beep"*.
Interview	An interviewer will often ask typical questions such as *"Why are you interested in this company / college?"*, or *"What are your strengths and weaknesses?"*.
Lesson	A lesson might begin with some questions to recap a topic, and may end with the teacher giving out homework to the class.
Radio show	A radio presenter would normally begin a show with *"Hello, and welcome to..."* and then give the name of the show and their own name. They'd typically refer to the listener directly as *you*, and refer to the audience and themselves collectively as *we*.

Genre

You can also Group Genres

1) As well as classifying texts into genres, you can group **similar genres** together according to how they use **language**.

2) Each group of genres is called a **field**, e.g. music, literature and conversation.

3) Each field has **field-specific lexis**, or vocabulary, that is used within that particular topic, for example:

Music
Genres — jazz, rock, classical, folk
Field-specific lexis — *CD, album, single, artist, band.*

Henry and Jonny couldn't believe they were the only ones in their field.

Literature
Genres — plays, poetry, short stories, novels
Field-specific lexis — *metaphor, stanza, chapter, stage directions*

TV
Genres — game shows, soap operas, dramas, sitcoms
Field-specific lexis — *studio, script, lighting, boom, presenter*

Genres can be Broken Down into Sub-genres

As if that's not enough, you can divide genres into smaller groups of texts, called **sub-genres**:

Field	Literature
Genre	Poems Novel Plays
Sub-genre	*Ghost Horror*
	Love
	Science Fiction Detective

Field	Journalism
Genre	Newspapers Magazines TV/Radio
Sub-genre	*Women's Cookery*
	Car
	Puzzle Men's

Each of these sub-genres has developed its own **specific lexis** that relates to that sub-genre in particular. For example, the word *autocue* is specific to the **sub-genre** of **TV presenting**, and *blog* relates to the **sub-genre** of **online publishing**.

Practice Questions

Q1 Why are texts categorised into different genres?
Q2 Give three examples of spoken genres.
Q3 What is a field? Give an example and list some of its field-specific lexis.

Essay Question

Q1 Choose three examples of written genres. Explain the differences between them, focusing in particular on graphology and lexis.

That's where my answerphone message has been going wrong then...

I've been using Hello, *by Lionel Richie. Which I suppose is pretty unconventional, and might be the reason no one leaves me any messages. Or maybe they're not actually looking for me. Make sure you've got your head around the field / genre / sub-genre distinctions here, and learn some written and spoken examples. Then make like a new leaf and turn over.*

Literary Texts

These pages are for AQA A and WJEC only. Literary texts are mainly written to entertain, and people read or listen to them for pleasure. They usually contain imaginative uses of language, e.g. experimentation with vocabulary and grammar.

Authors of Literary Texts can be very Creative

Literary texts are part of the very broad entertainment field. People read literary texts because they can:

1) **Entertain** or **amuse** the reader.
2) Affect the reader's **emotions**, e.g. make them scared, excited or sympathetic.
3) Describe the **atmosphere** of a place or setting.
4) Examine the **personality** of a **character**.
5) Influence how the reader **looks at the world**.

His wife's shopping list evoked an atmosphere o mild panic.

There are Three Main Types of literary texts

The most common types of literary texts are prose (like books), poetry (like poems), and plays (er... like plays).

PROSE

- For example, novels, short stories, biography, autobiography.
- It's structured as **running text**, and divided into paragraphs and chapters (for novels).
- There are often no subsections, charts, or lists, and **usually no illustrations**.
- It has a **beginning** and usually a **definite ending**.
- The narrative is told from a certain **point of view**.

POETRY

- Poems **vary** in content, structure, style and intention.
- Some present **narrative stories**, some are written to be **performed**, others explore **emotional issues**.
- Poems are organised into **stanzas** (verses) of varying sizes.
- **Line length** can vary considerably and the poem may or may not **rhyme**.
- There are some **traditional forms** poems can take, e.g. sonnet or villanelle.
- There are also traditional **metres** (rhythms) e.g. pentameters.

PLAYS

- Plays consist of **dialogue** between characters, or (if it's a monologue) a character talking **directly** to the audience.
- They also include **stage directions** to instruct the actors and describe actions etc.
- The speech is very important, as it's the main way for the audience to **understand** the **action** and the **characters**.

All literary texts use a Narrative Voice

Writers use different **narrative voices** within literary texts.

1) A **first-person narrator** in a text tells the reader directly about their **feelings and experiences**. The text is viewed through the character's eyes.

> The moment I woke up that morning I just knew that something wasn't right. I was utterly exhausted and Ryan wouldn't stop talking...

2) A **third-person narrator** tells the story from a detached viewpoint, as a voice separate from the characters.

3) A **third-person omniscient narrator** lets the reader see into the **minds** and **thoughts** of **all** the characters.

> Kit explained it to her as gently as he could, there was no point upsetting her even more. But still, poor Sarah was devastated. As soon as she got home she flung herself on the bed and was overcome with sorrow...

Literary texts use lots of Figurative Language

Figurative language adds layers of meaning to texts. There's loads more on this on p.22.

1) **Imagery** creates a scene in the reader's mind e.g. *the sea was wild and stormy*.
2) A **simile** is when something is described in **comparison** to something else, e.g. *The sea is like a savage beast*.
3) A **metaphor** creates a **comparison**, like a simile, but it implies the subject and the thing it's being compared to are the **same**, e.g. *the sea is a savage beast*, rather than comparing them.
4) **Personification** is a kind of metaphor, in which the **attributes** of a person are given to abstract or non-human things, for example *the sea shrieked and roared*.
5) **Symbolism** is where a word or phrase **represents something else**, e.g. the colour *red* could represent danger.

Literary Texts

Rhetorical Language *is used to provide* Extra Effects *or* Meanings

There are **two categories** of rhetorical language.

Phonological — manipulates sound. Words or phrases might be used because they sound good.

1) **Rhyme** is particularly effective in poetry because it can contribute to the **musical quality** of a verse. It unifies the poem and can **add emphasis** to certain words. There are different kinds of rhyme, including **half rhyme** — where the vowel or consonant may vary (e.g. *roll* and *tell*) and **internal rhyme** — where rhymes occur within a line itself (e.g. *in mist or cloud, on mast or shroud*).

2) **Alliteration** is the repetition of the **same sound**, usually at the beginning of each word, over **two or more words together**, e.g. <u>s</u>ink <u>s</u>lowly into a <u>s</u>oothing <u>s</u>leep.

3) **Assonance** is a similar repetition, but of **vowel sounds** in the middle of words e.g. *a hoover manoeuvre*.

4) **Onomatopoeia** refers to words that sound like the noise they describe, e.g. *buzz, pop, bang*.

Structural — affects the overall meaning of a text by manipulating its structural features.

1) **Repetition** is often used to add **emphasis or persuasiveness** to a text. It can add **power** to a subject, or help a text lead to a **dramatic climax**.

2) **Parallelism** repeats **structural features**, like the construction of a **phrase**, e.g. *She jumped from the bed, and raced to the window,* which repeatedly uses the **past tense** form of the verb with a preposition and noun. An example of **non-parallelism** is something like *He loves films and to eat* — the construction of the phrases *loves film* and *to eat* are different and seem awkward to the reader.

3) **Antithesis** is when contrasting ideas or words are balanced against each other, e.g. *when there is need of silence, you speak, and when there is need of speech, you are silent*.

Dialogue *can also be* Very Effective

Dialogue is an especially effective device in **plays**.

1) Different characters may speak in **different ways** to influence the audience's opinions of them.

2) Dialogue helps to show the **relationships** between characters — whether they get on, or if there's **tension** between them. It also tells you about a character's **personality** through their **interactions** with other characters, e.g. if they're assertive, nervous, thoughtful, domineering, etc.

3) There are differences between dialogue in **literary texts** and **natural conversation**. In plays and novels, the dialogue tends to be **organised** and **fluent**, e.g. there is strict **turn-taking** and not much **interruption** or **hesitation**. In real-life conversations there are a lot of **non-fluency features** because the dialogue is **spontaneous**.

4) **Dramatic writing** relies on **dialogue** to create and develop **characters**. In **fictional texts**, the writer can **experiment** with **language** to describe these features.

Practice Questions

Q1 What are the main purposes of literary texts?

Q2 Why might a writer choose to use a third-person narrator instead of a first-person narrator?

Q3 What is the importance of rhyme in poetry?

Essay Question

Q1 Read the opening page of a novel that you already know. How does the author use language to convey the setting, characterisation and atmosphere effectively? You should consider:

1) the ways in which the writer's attitudes and values are conveyed to the reader.

2) features of the language such as figurative and rhetorical devices, and dialogue.

Even the simplest texts are still just one thing after an author...

Well it's not like there's a good pun for "symbolism", is it? These pages are all about ways of manipulating language, and the effect this has on the audience of a literary text. They've got some great terms to have at your disposal in the exam — being able to pick out these sorts of features and describe their purposes in different texts will get you tonnes of marks.

Ideology and Representation

These pages are for everyone. This basically covers what people think about different texts. Both writers and readers approach texts with their own attitudes, which affect what the writers write, and how the readers interpret it.

Writers show their Attitudes in their Texts

An ideology is a set of beliefs and ideas.

You can often get a sense of a writer's **opinions** and **ideology** through **how** they write and the **topics** they choose.

1) The **values** and **morals** in a text will probably depend on those held by the writer or speaker, e.g. a politician might speak about their attitude to marriage, based on the views of their particular political party or religion. This is often the case in **fictional** texts too, but not always.

2) Texts can show **prejudice** and **bias**, e.g. a writer might portray British characters sympathetically, and make their foreign characters all appear rather shady. This is an **implicit** meaning — it's not immediately obvious.

3) A writer might also show their **attitudes** quite **explicitly**, e.g. a journalist writing for a liberal newspaper might express their dislike for conservative politics.

4) Writers sometimes draw on **personal experience**, because it's easier to write about what you know, e.g. because he's been through the experience himself, a writer might describe a young gay man struggling to come out to his parents.

5) Writers' attitudes are also influenced by the social or political **environment** they're in. This is often evident in the **representation** of their **characters**, **narrator**, and the **themes** and **issues** that the text tries to deal with.

Social and historical context

- Texts often **reflect** the **concerns** of a **society** at a particular **time**.

- For example — the James Bond books often feature Soviet villains being thwarted by Bond, a British spy. They were written during the **Cold War** period of the 1950s and 60s, so they reflect the fear that countries like Britain and America had of the communist USSR.

- A text is a **product** of the **culture** and **time** it's written or set in — you wouldn't expect a spy novel written in the UK today to feature Russian Communist villains.

Writers can show their Attitudes through their Characters

1) Writers might draw on **stereotypes** when they're **constructing characters**, e.g. they might present a character who is an MP as a middle-aged man with grey hair who wears a suit.

2) A writer may create characters based on how the **media** represents groups of people (see p.56-59). This includes **stereotypes** like portraying a group of young people as a *gang of hoodies*.

3) The writer might **unconsciously** reflect the views or values of **wider society**. Someone from a Western culture, writing nowadays, might refer to a character as '*lovely and slim*'. This would reflect the **broader** attitude in Western society that being slim is beautiful.

4) You can also get an idea of a writer's values and beliefs from how they **subvert stereotypes**, e.g. a feminist author might write about workplaces and homes dominated by women.

A writer's Language Choices can Influence the Reader

The language of a text is often **manipulated** to create certain emotions or reactions in the reader. The **manipulation** of the reader is a frequent tool that writers use to **increase** the **impact** of their texts or even to **subvert conventions**.

1) Politicians delivering speeches about social problems want listeners to feel like they **share** their desire to solve the problem. They use **inclusive pronouns** like *we* and *us* to position the listener as a **confidant** and therefore a potential **supporter**.

2) A charity leaflet might use emotive words like *cruelty* to **represent** the **treatment** of people or groups, or *desperate* to convey the **seriousness** of their situation.

3) Writers can use **different viewpoints** in novels and articles. First person narrators can bring readers **close** to the text and they can get **emotionally involved**. Third person omniscient narratives give **insights** into characters and allow the reader to step back and be **objective**.

4) Writers can also **subvert** these conventions to manipulate the reader, e.g. using a first person narrator that turns out to be **completely unreliable**.

Ideology and Representation

Writers still have to Appeal to Readers

Writers know that audiences **approach** texts in different ways so they have to represent ideas and characters that readers can identify with.

1) Members of an audience bring their own **experience**, personality, background, prejudices, beliefs and values to their interpretation of any text. These factors shape how a reader **views** a situation or **feels** about a character.

2) Writers might aim to **appeal** to audiences by writing things that they know they'll **agree** with — e.g. most people buy a particular newspaper because they know it will express **similar views** to theirs. Journalists for that paper know what views will appeal to the audience and make them want to keep reading.

3) Writers might know their readership and try to **influence** or **change** their views in some way, e.g. charity adverts.

4) The meaning of a text can be **ambiguous**. Often the meaning expressed on a **literal** or **explicit level** is different to the one on a **figurative** or **implicit level** (see p.22). Writers can challenge readers to provide their **own** meanings.

5) For example, writers are sometimes **ambiguous** on **purpose**. They leave things **open** for the audience to **interpret**, e.g. in the film *Lost in Translation* (2003), a character whispers something to another character at the end. The audience never find out what he says, and it's left up to them to come to their own conclusion.

Readers Interpret Texts in different ways

Readers **draw on** their own **values** and **experiences** when they **approach** texts.

1) Just like writers, readers bring their individual **backgrounds** and **biases** to texts — each reader's interpretation will be slightly different.

2) A reader's response to a text depends on the influences of social factors like **education**, **religion**, **family** and **the media**. These factors create the reader's **ideological position**.

3) Interpretations of texts are also a **product** of the readers' **historical context**, e.g.

- *Dr Jekyll and Mr Hyde* is a **Victorian** novel about a man who appears to have two sides to his personality.
- The way it was **interpreted** by Victorian readers is quite **different** to the meanings that it's given now.
- When readers at the time first saw the words *shame* and *sin* in the novel, some of them assumed that Mr Hyde was Dr Jekyll's **homosexual lover**.
- This is because **Victorian readers** would have **viewed** such a relationship as shameful and sinful.
- Other readers associated the character with **Jack the Ripper**, a **murderer** who was plaguing London **at the time**.
- Modern readers might see the novel as exploring issues related to the **self**, e.g. good and evil, and are less likely to think of the Victorian interpretations.

"No Hyde — I don't know what's wrong with her, but I don't think that's helping."

Practice Questions

Q1 Give two examples of how a writer might express their personal opinions in a text.

Q2 Explain the different effects created by using a first person narrative or a third person narrative.

Q3 What factors can influence a reader's interpretation of a text?

Essay Question

Q1 Outline the main factors that can influence a writer producing a text.

Apparently, "Lost in Translation" was actually lost in translation...

I kid you not. When the title was translated into Hebrew, Chinese and Spanish (in South America), it turned up as Lost in Tokyo *instead. So there you go... little bit of Hollywood trivia for you there. And you thought English Language was going to be all about spelling, grammar and babies learning to talk. Well it's not. It's actually cool and ultra-glamorous.*

Sources and Exam Questions

These pages show you what to expect from an exam question on analysing written language. It's important to apply the different parts of analysis that you've learnt in this section methodically to get the best marks.

> 1) Study the following texts A - E. The texts illustrate different varieties of language use.
> Analyse and compare the language in these texts and discuss the various ways in which these texts could be grouped, giving linguistic reasons for your choice.
>
> *[48 marks]*

Text A — An extract from the novel *The Way of All Flesh* (1903), by Samuel Butler

Old Mr. Pontifex had married in the year 1750, but for fifteen years his wife bore no children. At the end of that time, Mrs. Pontifex astonished the whole village by showing unmistakeable signs of a disposition to present her husband with an heir or heiress. Hers had long ago been considered a hopeless case, and when on consulting the doctor concerning the meaning of certain symptoms she was informed of their significance, she became very angry and abused the doctor roundly for talking nonsense. She refused to put so much as a piece of thread into a needle in anticipation of her confinement and would have been absolutely unprepared, if her neighbours had not been better judges of her condition than she was, and got things ready without telling her anything about it. Perhaps she feared Nemesis, though assuredly she knew not who or what Nemesis was; perhaps she feared the doctor had made a mistake and she should be laughed at; for whatever cause, however, her refusal to recognise the obvious arose, she certainly refused to recognise it, until one snowy night in January the doctor was sent for with all urgent speed across the rough country roads. When he arrived he found two patients, not one, in need of his assistance. For a boy had been born who was in due time christened George, in honour of his then reigning majesty.

To the best of my belief George Pontifex got the greater part of his nature from this obstinate old lady, his mother - a mother who though she loved no one else in the world except her husband (and him only after a fashion) was most tenderly attached to the unexpected child of her old age; nevertheless she showed it little.

Text B — A film review of the *Sex And The City* movie, By Celia Walden

"Everything that happens tonight must stay in this room," said Sarah Jessica Parker to the several hundred guests at last night's world premiere of Sex And The City the movie.

But with the girlish excitement filling the cinema it seemed unlikely anyone would heed her plea.

Just in case none of us remember, the producers of the much-awaited film version of the hit TV series remind fans with a quick recap at the start of the film where the four characters were at the point we left them when the series ended.

Three years on, the two Ls are still carrying the storyline along: labels and love. In the first half-hour we're bombarded by so much brand placement that one might as well be witnessing an extended Vogue photo shoot brought to life.

While love scenes between the happy characters brought not so much as a murmur from the audience, a Vivienne Westwood dress and a Louis Vuitton handbag provoked coos of heartfelt admiration.

The triumph of capitalism is as unabashed as it always was but given, if possible, a greater ironic twist.

In 20 years, Carrie Bradshaw, the lovelorn journalist, has come a long way: she is engaged to a billionaire, who can offer her a walk-in wardrobe and more Manolos than she can ever dream of - but the consumer Cinderella has a crash heading her way.

And as the film progresses, the seemingly adult and perfect lives of the four fortysomethings start to show cracks.

Miranda's husband Steve commits an act she may never be able to forgive him for while Samantha's ego threatens to derail her relationship with Smith Jerrod.

Just Charlotte seems to have escaped the New York clique's curse.

It is only in the last 10 minutes that we find out whether the fairytale has the happy ending the audience so desperately seemed to crave. But one thing's for sure: fans of the series will lap this film up.

It was coarse, sentimental, and outrageously materialistic - just as we hoped and expected it would be.

The Daily Telegraph, 2008

Sources and Exam Questions

Text C — A web page for an educational children's club

| Who are We? | Teaching | Case Studies | Contact Us |

Why fish?
Instructors
Lessons
Links
Gallery

Welcome to Carp-ey Diem

Carp-ey Diem helps children master the ancient art of carp fishing, whilst building strong learning skills, boosting their confidence, and teaching them respect for nature.

We give your child:

* an opportunity to learn at their own pace
* a positive attitude
* confidence to meet new challenges
* invaluable experience

Realise your child's potential — Join in Now

Carp-ey
Diem

Carp-ey Diem - teaching kids to fish since 1947

Text D — A competition entry form

CAPTION COMPETITION ENTRY FORM

Name

Address Line 1

Address Line 2

Town

Postcode

D.O.B

Please note — this competition closes at midnight on 25/08/2008

Your Caption

I declare that this caption has not been published elsewhere and that I am the original author

You may use my caption in advertising should it be declared the winner of the caption competition

*Please inform me if my caption is **not** successful (see over for Terms and Conditions)*

Send your entries to:
Caption Competition,
P.O. Box 4653,
Sheepy Parva,
Nuntonshire,
NU88 9UN

Signed:

Text E — A self-diagnosis booklet

Insomnia is best known as the inability to get to sleep, but sufferers are also affected by being unable to stay asleep, or by waking up too early. Experiencing these effects for an extended period of time is called chronic insomnia, whilst short-term sufferers experience what's called transient insomnia.

Chronic Insomnia

You can take some measures to try and alleviate chronic insomnia (see page 17). If these fail to have the desired effect then it may be best to seek medical advice to try and isolate the causes of the sleeping disruptions. On occasions, chronic insomnia is one of the symptoms of depression, but there are also many other potential causes.

Transient Insomnia

Short term insomnia often remedies itself in the space of a few days. Usually it is nothing to worry about but if you start to experience excessive worry about not being able to sleep, and if this in turn keeps you awake, then you might want to seek medical advice. Ultimately though, transient insomnia is fairly common and could be caused by bereavement or stress in your professional or personal life.

Early Language Development

This section is ONLY for the lucky souls doing AQA A and OCR, except p.98-99 and 103 (only AQA A) and p.100-2 (OCR).
None of us remember exactly how we learnt to speak — it just sort of happened. But now, many years later, you're
going to learn how you did it. It's pretty amazing, so pay your best attention, grown-up you.

Language Development may Begin in the Womb

There is some evidence that suggests language development starts **before** birth.

1) **DeCasper and Spence (1986)** found that babies sucked on their dummies more when their mothers read them the **same story** that they'd also read aloud during the last six months of the pregnancy.

2) **Mehler et al (1988)** found that four-day-old French babies increased their sucking rate on a dummy, showing interest or recognition, when they heard French as opposed to Italian or English. This suggested that they had acquired some awareness of the **sounds** of **French** before they were born.

3) **Fitzpatrick (2002)** found that the heart rate of an unborn baby **slowed** when it heard its **mother's voice**.

> All this suggests that even in the womb, babies become familiar
> with the **sounds**, **rhythms** and **intonations** of language.

Babies start to use their Vocal Chords Straight Away

1) The period between birth and the first word being spoken is known as the **pre-verbal** or **pre-language** stage.

2) **Crying** is the first main vocal expression a baby makes. It makes the **caregiver** (e.g. parents, sibling, or baby-sitter) aware that the baby needs something. Crying can indicate **hunger**, **discomfort** or **pain**.

3) This isn't really a **conscious act** on the baby's part. It's more an **instinctive response** to how it feels.

Babies then start to Form Sounds — the Cooing Stage

1) At the **cooing** stage (which starts when they're **six to eight weeks old**), babies start making a **small range** of sounds — they get used to moving their lips and tongue.

2) This starts with **vowels** like /u/ and /a/. Then they start linking these to produce **extended vowel combinations** like *ooo* and *aaah*. They start to use **velar consonants** (ones made using the back part of the tongue) like /k/ and /g/ to form sounds like *coo* and *ga*.

3) These sounds don't carry any **meaning** — the baby is just **experimenting** with sounds.

4) Gradually these sounds become more **defined** and are strung together. This **vocal play** is the start of babbling.

Babbling is the next significant stage

1) Babies usually start to babble when they're about **six months** old.

2) At this stage, they start producing repeated consonant / vowel combinations like *ma-ma-ma*, *ba-ba-ba*, *ga-ga-ga*. These sounds are common in babies from many different nationalities. Repeating sounds like this is known as **reduplicated** or **canonical babbling**.

3) Sometimes these sounds are not repeated, e.g. *goo-gi-goo-ga* or *da-di-da*. This is called **variegated babbling**.

4) The **consonants** that you usually get in **reduplicated** or **variegated** babbling are: *h, w, j, p, b, m, t, d, n, k, g*.

5) Research has shown that **deaf** babies who've had some exposure to **sign language** will **babble** with their **hands** — producing consonant and vowel combinations in sign language. This suggests that babbling is an **innate activity**, which is **preprogrammed** to happen in the process of language development.

6) Most people argue that babbling is a **continuation** of the baby's experimentation with **sound creation** (cooing) rather than the production of sounds which carry **meaning**. For example, the infant may produce *dadadada* but they're not actually saying anything referring to *Dad* or *Daddy* at this stage.

7) Some people argue that babbling is the **beginning of speech**:

> **Petitto and Holowka (2002)** videoed infants and noted that most babbling came more from the **right side** of the mouth, which is controlled by the **left side** of the brain. This side of the brain is **responsible for speech production**. Their findings suggest that babbling is a form of **preliminary speech**.

Early Language Development

The **Babbling Stage** can be divided into **Two Parts**

1) When babies start to babble, the number of different **phonemes** (see p.24) they produce **increases**.

2) This is called **phonemic expansion**.

3) Later in the babbling stage, they **reduce** the number of phonemes they use (**phonemic contraction**).

4) This is the period when the baby starts to concentrate on **reproducing** the phonemes it hears in its **native language**. It **stops using** the sounds that it doesn't hear from its carers.

5) It's at this stage (about **ten months old**) that children of **different nationalities** start to sound different.

> A study at **Bristol University** in **2008** showed that babies who are exposed to different languages in the first nine months of their life are more able to pick out the sounds of these languages as they get older. This is because **phonemic contraction** has occurred less than it would if the baby had been exposed to one language only.

Infants start to show **Intonation Patterns** at the babbling stage

1) Even in the early stages of babbling (at six months) some babies will use **rhythms** that resemble the **speech patterns of adults**. There will be recognisable **intonation** in the strings of phonemes they put together.

2) For example, at the end of a babbling sequence the intonation may **rise**, mirroring the kind of intonation adults use when **asking a question**. Babies can also accompany these sounds with **gestures**, like pointing.

Babbling leads to the production of a **Child's First Words**

1) Eventually, certain **combinations** of **consonants** and **vowels** start to carry meaning. For example, a child might say *Mmm* to show that they want some more food. This is not a word in itself but it **functions** like one. These are called **proto-words**, and sometimes they're accompanied by **gestures** as well.

2) Another example of a proto-word is when a child refers to a cat as /da/. This is still just a **sound** rather than a recognisable word, but it **refers** to an **object** and is not just a random utterance.

3) In the later stages of babbling, sound and meaning start to **come together**. At this stage, *ma-ma* does indicate *Mum* and *ka-ka* does mean *car*. This usually happens by the time the baby is **ten months old**.

"AUDREY! Get this checked monstrosity off of me!"

Practice Questions

Q1 What evidence is there to suggest that language develops before birth?

Q2 What's the difference between reduplicated babbling and variegated babbling?

Q3 Explain the terms phonemic expansion and phonemic contraction.

Q4 What is meant by the term proto-word?

Essay Question

Q1 Describe how very young children develop sounds and communication, from before they are born up to the point when they are able to produce their first words.

Stop babbling and get on with some revision...

This stuff about how children learn language is pretty interesting... and it should be fairly straightforward to learn if you can remember at what age everything happens. I can guarantee that if you discuss this with your mates some annoying person will say "I learnt to speak fluently in 3 languages by the time I was 6 months old..." Prepare a sarcastic reply in advance.

Phonological and Pragmatic Development

After cooing and babbling, children learn to master vowels and consonants to form words. As well as phonological development, children also learn the skills and rules they need to hold conversations and interact with others.

Phonological Development depends on the Individual

1) Children learn **vowels** and **consonants** at different speeds. Children will master some phonemes earlier than others.

2) Most children will be able to use all the **vowels** in English by the time they're two-and-a-half years old.

3) They might not use all the **consonants** confidently until they're **six** or **seven** years old. The earliest consonants that they master tend to be *m, n, p, h, t,* and *k*. The latest tend to be the */th/* sounds in words like *thing, thimble* and *thought* (the */θ/* **phoneme**), and *this, those* and *them* (the */ð/* **phoneme**).

4) Children find using consonants at the **beginning** of words (**word-initial**) easier than consonants at the end of words (**word-final**). For example, they'll find it easier to say the */t/* in *teddy* than the one at the end of *sit*.

Simplification helps children Communicate

1) Learning to **pronounce** things properly is difficult, but children can still **communicate** — if they can't pronounce a word as adults do, they use a simpler version. Simplification mainly applies to **consonants**.

2) There are three main kinds of phonological simplification — **deletion**, **substitution**, and **cluster reduction**:

> **Deletion** Sometimes a child **drops** a consonant altogether, particularly at the **end** of a word. For example, a child might say *ca* rather than *cat*.

> **Substitution** Instead of dropping a consonant, a child might **replace it** with one that's easier to say. For example, they might say *wegs* rather than *legs,* or *tup* rather than *cup*.

> **Cluster Reduction** Where there are **consonant clusters** (two or more consonants together in a word), a child may **drop one** of the consonants. For example, the child will say *geen* rather than *green*.

> **Berko and Brown (1960)** reported what they referred to as the *fis phenomenon*. A child referred to his plastic fish as a *fis*. When an adult asked *Is this your fis?*, the child said no, stating instead that it was his *fis*. When the adult then asked *Is this your fish?*, the child replied *Yes, my fis*.
> This suggests that children can **recognise** and **understand** a **wider range** of phonemes than they can **produce**.

Other Features are common in phonological development

1) **Addition** is when a vowel is added to the end of a word, e.g. *dog* is pronounced *dogu*.

2) **Assimilation** is when one consonant in a word is changed because of the influence of another in the same word, e.g. *tub* becomes *bub* because of the influence of the final */b/*.

3) **Reduplication** is when a phoneme is repeated, like *moo-moo* (for *cow*), or *bik-bik* (for *biscuit*).

4) **Voicing** is when voiceless consonants like *p, t, f, s* (sounds produced without using the vocal chords) are replaced by their voiced equivalents *b, d, v, z*, so instead of saying *sock*, a child might say *zok*.

5) **De-voicing** is when voiced consonants (sounds produced using the vocal chords as well as the mouth / tongue / lips), are replaced by their voiceless equivalents, so instead of saying *bag* a child might say *pag*.

It takes longer to Develop Intonation

1) Even at the babbling stage, babies begin to demonstrate **intonation** patterns. When they start to put words together, it becomes even more obvious, e.g. they put stress on certain words, e.g. *that's <u>mine</u>*.

2) It takes a long time for children to understand the complexities of intonation and stress. For example, **Cruttenden (1985)** found that ten-year-olds had difficulty distinguishing between:

> a) *She <u>dressed</u>, and fed the <u>baby</u>* (she dressed *herself*, and fed the *baby*), **and**
>
> b) *She dressed and fed the <u>baby</u>* (she dressed the *baby* and fed it too).

Phonological and Pragmatic Development

Children's Language has a range of Different Functions

1) At first, a child can get responses or reactions by using **proto-words**. After a while they start to use **recognisable** words, which have **different functions** depending on their context. For example, the word *dummy* could be an order (*get my dummy*), or a question (*where's my dummy?*).

2) **Halliday (1975)** states that the early language of children has **seven functions**:

Instrumental	to get something (e.g. 'go toily' meaning 'I want to go to the toilet').	These four are about the child satisfying their social, emotional and physical needs.
Regulatory	to make requests or give orders (e.g. 'Not your teddy' meaning 'Leave my teddy alone').	
Interactional	to relate to others (e.g. 'Nice Mummy').	
Personal	to convey a sense of personal identity and to express views and feelings (e.g. 'naughty doggy').	
Heuristic	to find out about the immediate environment (e.g. 'What boy doing?').	These three are about the child coming to terms with their environment and their place within it.
Imaginative	to be creative through language that relates to imaginative play, storytelling, rhymes and humour (e.g. 'One day my Daddy came home and he said...').	
Representational	to convey information (e.g. 'I'm three').	

Children quickly learn to Interact With Others

1) Babies learn about **social conventions** even before they can speak. For example, the game of "peek-a-boo" familiarises the baby with **turn-taking** and is an early form of social interaction.

2) Even at the babbling stage, a child's carer might respond to their babbling as if they were having a **conversation** — so there's some basic **interaction** between child and caregiver.

3) As children develop they can interact in more **sophisticated** ways. They will **start conversations**, use a full range of **speech functions** and show **politeness features**. They start to use more adult forms of interaction like **turn-taking**, **adjacency pairs**, and **opening and closing sequences**.

4) **Non-verbal communication** (like hand gestures and facial expressions) and **non-verbal aspects of speech** (like pitch, volume, intonation and pace) also become increasingly **sophisticated** as children grow up.

Practice Questions

Q1 What do babies acquire first, vowels or consonants?

Q2 Explain the terms deletion, substitution and cluster reduction.

Q3 What can you deduce about phonological development from the *fis* phenomenon?

Q4 According to Halliday, what are the four functions of language that relate to a child's social, emotional and physical needs?

Q5 What are the three functions of language that relate to the way a child comes to terms with its environment?

Essay Question

Q1 Children use certain phonological features to communicate when they are not fully capable of pronouncing every word they know.
1. Describe these phonological features.
2. Discuss the evidence that even though the child cannot pronounce a word, they can understand and recognise it.

Revision — only marginally better than a slap in the face with a wet fis...

Obviously, I'm going to leave my extensive back-catalogue of fish / fis jokes out of this particular section — it's neither the time nor the plaice. Alright... I'm sorry. That one even upset me. I'll scale them down from now on. Time to get learning how baby-you got from crying like a little... well, like a little baby, to conversing and stressing and questioning as a child.

Lexis, Grammar and Semantics

At the ripe old age of one, most children have spoken their first words. As their vocabulary grows, they start to use grammatical structures. This — like everything in language acquisition — is a stage-by-stage process.

Children acquire vocabulary **Very Quickly**

1) This table gives you an idea of how your **vocabulary grows** as you get older:

Age	Number of Words Used
18 months	50 +
2 years	300 +
5 years	approx. 3000
7 years	approx. 4000

A child's ability to **understand words** will always develop quicker than their ability to **use** them. At 18 months old, a child can **actively** use 50 words, but can **understand** around 250.

The **increase** in vocabulary between age 2 to 7 is so big that these figures can only ever be an **estimation**.

2) Children's first words relate to their **immediate surroundings**. They're connected to things that children can see, hear, taste, smell and touch, or that have a **social function**. Words that express concepts and more abstract ideas start to appear as the child becomes more **self-aware** and **experiences** more of the world.

First Words can be put into Categories

Nelson (1973) studied the first fifty words produced by eighteen children and grouped them into **five categories**:

1) **Classes of Objects** — *dog, shoe, ball, car*
2) **Specific Objects** — *Mummy, Daddy*
3) **Actions / Events** — *give, stop, go, up, where*
4) **Modifying things** — *dirty, nice, allgone*
5) **Personal / Social** — *hi, bye-bye, yes, no*

Don't tell me... don't tell me... Dog... No? Table?

Classes of **objects** formed the largest group — it's easier for children to identify things that they can actually **touch**.

Children soon learn to Use Words Creatively

When they're between 12 and 18 months old children will **improvise** if they don't know the word for something. This takes **two** main forms — **underextension** and **overextension**:

1) **Underextension** is when a child uses a word in a very **restricted way**. For example, when a child says *hat*, but means only the hat that she wears rather than any hat.

2) **Overextension** is when a child uses a word to refer to several **different** but **related** things. For example, she might use the word *cat* to refer to anything with four legs, like foxes, dogs, etc.

Rescorla (1980) said there were two types of overextension — **categorical** and **analogical**:

- **Categorical** is when a word is used to refer to things in a similar category, e.g. the word *car* is used to refer to buses, trucks and other forms of four-wheeled vehicle. This kind of overextension is most common.

- **Analogical** is when a word is used to refer to things that aren't clearly in the same category but have some **physical** or **functional relation** to each other, e.g. the word *hat* is used for anything near or connected with the head.

Aitchison (1987) suggested three other Development Processes

1) **Labelling** is when a child links a **sound** to an **object** — they are able to call something by its **correct name**.

2) **Packaging** is when a child begins to understand the **range of meaning** a word might have. They recognise that the word *bottle* can cover different shapes and sizes, but that they all have a similar **function**.

3) **Network building** is when a child starts to make **connections** between words, e.g. they understand that words have **opposites** like *big* and *small*, or know that *little* and *small* are **synonyms**.

Lexis, Grammar and Semantics

Most first words function as Holophrases

1) The stage where a child says their first words is known as the **holophrastic** or **one-word stage**. **Holophrases** are **single words** that express a **complete idea** — an individual word performs the same function as a sentence would.

2) For example, when a child says *teddy*, the **meaning** of this utterance isn't obvious straight away. It could be *here's my teddy* (like a **declarative** sentence), *where's my teddy?* (an **interrogative**), *get my teddy* (**imperative**), or *here's my teddy, excellent!* (**exclamative**).

3) Caregivers often need **contextual clues** (e.g. being able to see the objects surrounding the child, intonation and stress) and the child's **non-verbal communication** to interpret holophrases.

The two-word stage is the Beginning of Syntax

At around **eighteen months** children start to use **two words** in **conjunction**. When they do this they automatically begin to create **grammatical relationships** between words — the start of **syntax**.

There are some common combinations:

baby crying	**subject + verb**
catch ball	**verb + object**
daddy dinner (daddy is cooking dinner)	**subject + object**
dolly dirty	**subject + complement**

- These combinations show **similar patterns** to more complex grammatical constructions.
- The phrases use the **basic blocks of meaning** needed for sentences (subject, verb, object and complement).

complement — gives more information about the subject or object.

The Telegraphic Stage combines three or more words

At around **two years old**, children start to use three or four word combinations — the **telegraphic stage**.

These utterances are also formed according to **grammatical rules**:

doggy is naughty	**subject + verb + complement**
Jodie want cup	**subject + verb + object**
give mummy spoon	**verb + object + object**

- Children still focus on the words that carry **most meaning**.
- They **omit functional words** e.g. prepositions (*from, to*), auxiliary verbs (*has, is*) and determiners (*a, the*).

By **age five**, children will be able to use a **range** of **grammatical constructions** which include:

1) **Coordinating conjunctions** (like *and* and *but*) to link separate utterances.

2) **Negatives** involving the auxiliary *do* (e.g. *don't like it*).

3) **Questions** formed with *Who, Where* and *What*.

4) **Inflections** like *-ed* for past tense, *-ing* for present participles and *-s* for plurals.

Practice Questions

Q1 Explain the terms overextension and underextension.

Q2 Explain Rescorla's categorical and analogical overextension.

Q3 What does Aitchison mean by the terms labelling, packaging and network building?

Q4 What three major stages do children go through in terms of their grammatical development?

Essay Question

Q1 How does a child's lexical and semantic understanding develop as it gets older?
Discuss the process with reference to vocabulary, categorising words, extension and any other developmental processes or stages you think might be important.

I got grounded for stealing a ball when I was two — apparently it was Lexis...

I don't know why I got in trouble, he wasn't even playing with it at the time. But this is no time for snatching a break or cutting corners — you need to understand how you eventually build up meaningful sentences from all those words you've been so busy learning. So, make sure you've grasped all of this page. Oh, and stealing toys = wrong. Learn that too.

More Grammar Acquisition

So this is where it gets interesting — in Section 1, you learnt about grammar. But now you're going to learn about how you learnt about grammar in the first place. I know, I cursed my lousy grammar memory when I found out too.

Inflections seem to be *Acquired* in a *Set Order*

1) Children start to **add inflections** to their words as early as **20 months old**.

2) Studies have shown that inflections are acquired in a certain order. A study by **Brown (1973)** of children aged between 20 and 36 months suggested that the **order** in which children learn inflections is as follows:

If you're a little rusty on inflections and affixation, have a look at p.16 in Section 1.

	Inflections	A Child Will Say (e.g.)
1	present participle -ing	I go<u>ing</u> (although am will still be missing)
2	plural -s	cup<u>s</u>
3	possessive 's	Teddy<u>'s</u> chair
4	articles (a, the)	get <u>the</u> ball
5	past tense -ed	I kick<u>ed</u> it
6	third person singular verb ending -s	She love<u>s</u> me
7	auxiliary be	It <u>is</u> raining (or, more likely, It's raining)

3) **Katamba (1996)** found that there was **little connection** between the **frequency** with which these inflections are used by parents and the **order** in which children acquire them.

4) *A* and *the* are used **most frequently**, and *-ed* **least frequently**, but they're fourth and fifth in terms of acquisition. This suggests that **imitation** doesn't have a strong influence on how children acquire inflections.

5) The *-ing* inflection is acquired the **earliest** — probably because it represents the **present tense**, and the child will relate more to things happening 'now', than in the past or the future.

Inflections are *Learnt* in *Three Stages*

Cruttenden (1979) identified **three stages** in the acquisition of inflections:

Stage 1 — Inconsistent Usage
A child will use an inflection correctly **some of the time**, but this is because they've learnt the **word**, not the **grammatical rule**, e.g. they might say *I play outside* one day and *I played outside* the next.

Stage 2 — Consistent Usage but sometimes misapplied
For example, applying the regular past tense inflection -ed to irregular verbs. A child will say something like *I drinked it*, rather than *I drank it*. This is called an **overgeneralisation** or a '**virtuous error**' — they understand how past tense verbs are formed but **mistakenly apply** the construction to an irregular verb.

Stage 3 — Consistent Usage
This is when children are able to cope with **irregular forms successfully**, e.g. they say *mice* rather than *mouses* and *ran* rather than *runned*.

Children use grammatical rules *Without Being Taught Them*

1) Children seem to acquire the grammatical rules of language just by being in an environment where language is spoken and where they can **interact with others**:

Berko's (1958) 'Wug' Test

Children were shown a picture of a strange creature and told it was a *Wug*. They were then shown a drawing of **two of the creatures** and told 'Now there is another one. There are two of them — there are two...', encouraging the children to complete the sentence. Three-to-four-year-old children said there were *two Wug<u>s</u>*.

2) The test showed that children hadn't used the -s because they were **imitating someone**, as they'd **never heard** of a *Wug* before. They'd **automatically** used the **rule** that states -s is added to a noun to form a plural.

3) This is called **internalisation** — they'd heard the rule so often that it was second nature to **apply** it to make a plural.

More Grammar Acquisition

Learning to Ask Questions is a three-stage process

In the first **three** years, children develop the ability to construct **questions**.

> **Stage 1 — around 18 months**
>
> During the two-word stage, children start to use **rising intonation** to indicate a question, e.g. *Sit me?*, or *Go walk?*

> **Stage 2 — between the ages of two and three**
>
> In telegraphic talk, children continue to use rising intonation but now **include *Wh-* words** in the utterances, e.g. *Where tractor?* or *What Mummy doing?* As they continue to develop, they use a wider range of **interrogative pronouns**, such as *why*, *when*, and *how*.

> **Stage 3 — From the age of three upwards**
>
> Children will use what's called a **subject-verb inversion**, e.g. *Can I see it?*, or *Did she break it?*, instead of constructions like *I can see it?* They also use **auxiliary verbs** for the first time, e.g. *What is Mummy doing?*

Oscar the Grouch was never that intimidating before he went into make-up.

Negatives follow a Similar Pattern

At the same time as they start using **interrogatives** (questions), children learn to use **negatives**.

> **Stage 1 — around eighteen months**
>
> Children use *no* or *not* to make things negative, normally at the **beginning of the phrase** rather than at the end, e.g. *no juice*, *not baby's bed*.

> **Stage 2 — between two and three years**
>
> Children start to use *no* and *not* in front of **verbs** too, like *I no want juice* and *I not like teddy's bed*. They also develop the use of **contracted negatives** like *can't* and *don't*, e.g. *I can't drink it* and *I don't like it*. These two forms can sometimes get **mixed up**, e.g. *I can't like it*.

> **Stage 3 — from three years upwards**
>
> Children stop using *no* and *not* in the way they did in stage 1. They **standardise** their use of *can't* and *don't*, and start using other **negative contractions** like *didn't* and *won't*, e.g. *she didn't catch it* and *he won't build it*. The use of *isn't* develops **slightly later** (e.g. *Mummy isn't here*).

Practice Questions

Q1 Which inflection is normally acquired first and which is acquired last?

Q2 Why is the *-ing* inflection usually among the first to be acquired?

Q3 Explain the term overgeneralisation.

Q4 What is internalisation?

Q5 What three stages do children go through when acquiring questions?

Q6 What three stages do children go through when acquiring negatives?

Essay Question

Q1 Describe how children acquire the grammatical rules of their native language, with reference to appropriate research

This is for your exam, remember — you can't just sweep it under the wug...

...even if it is dusty and boring. Still, it's pretty amazing that once, approximately 17 or 18 years ago, you couldn't speak a single word. Even if you'd wanted to say 'There's absolutely nothing weird about Bert and Ernie sharing a bed on Sesame Street', you couldn't have. Whereas now, older and wiser, you can bandy that particular gem around all you want.

Theories of Language Development

Are you paying attention? Because here comes the science. Well... sort of. There are a few theories knocking around about how children acquire language. So take a deep breath and prepare for imitation, cognition, and friends.

Behaviourists *argue that language is* Acquired *by* Imitation

Imitation Theory

1) **Skinner (1957)** suggested that language is acquired through **imitation** and **reinforcement**:
   - Children **repeat** what they hear (imitation).
   - Caregivers **reward** a child's efforts with **praise**.
   - They also reinforce what the child says by **repeating** words and phrases back and **correcting mistakes**.

2) This approach says that children learn all the **specific pronunciations** of individual words by copying an adult — therefore in theory it explains an important part of their **phonological development**.

Problems with Imitation

1) There are some problems with imitation theory:
   - Children can construct new sentences they've **never heard before**, so they aren't always directly **imitating**.
   - They don't **memorise** thousands of sentences to use later, so their development can't be **exclusively based** on repeating what they've heard their parents or other people saying.
   - Imitation can't explain **overgeneralisations**, like *he runned away* (see p.94).
     Children can't **copy** these errors because adults don't make them.
   - Imitation theory also **can't explain** things like the *fis* phenomenon (see p.90) — the fact that children can **recognise** a much larger range of words than they are actually able to **use**.

Other people argue that Language Acquisition *is* Innate

1) **Chomsky (1965)** argued that a child's ability to acquire language was **inbuilt**. He said that language isn't taught, but it's a **natural development** that occurs when children are **exposed to language**.

2) He suggested that each child has a **Language Acquisition Device (LAD)**, which allows them to take in and **use** the grammatical rules of the language that's spoken where they live.

3) Chomsky's approach seems to explain **how** children end up making overgeneralisations and **why** they acquire inflections in a **certain order** — it's as if the brain is **preprogrammed** to make this happen.

4) Therefore children might learn language quickly because they are **predisposed** to learn it.

5) More evidence for Chomsky's theory is that **all children** pass through the same early stages of language acquisition, before **refining** their range of sounds to their native language (see p.88-89).

6) There are some **common features** of language known as **linguistic universals**, e.g. everyone uses a combination of regular and irregular verbs. This suggests that all speakers acquire language in a similar way, so it supports the idea that children have an **LAD**.

7) One criticism of Chomsky's theory is that the innate approach **underestimates** the **significance** of Skinner's argument that **interaction**, **imitation** and **reinforcement** are important in language development.

Piaget *developed the* Cognitive Approach

The **cognitive approach** focuses on the importance of **mental processes**. **Piaget (1896-1980)** stated that a child needs to have developed certain **mental abilities** before it can acquire particular aspects of language:

1) At first a child can't mentally process the concept that something can exist **outside** their **immediate surroundings**. This is called being **egocentric**.

2) By the time they're 18 months old, children realise that things have **object permanence** — they can exist all the time, even if the child can't see them. This coincides with a big increase in vocabulary (see p.92).

3) The child is then mentally better equipped to understand **abstract** concepts like **past**, **present** and **future**.

4) One **criticism** of this approach is that it doesn't explain how some people with **learning difficulties** are still **linguistically fluent**. This suggests that **cognitive** development and **language** development aren't as **closely connected** as the cognitive approach suggests.

Theories of Language Development

Language Development needs Input from Others

The **input approach** argues that in order for language to develop there has to be **linguistic interaction** with **caregivers**.

1) **Bruner (1983)** suggests that there is a **Language Acquisition Support System (LASS)** — a system where caregivers **support** their child's linguistic development in **social situations**.

2) There are clear **patterns** of **interaction** between child and caregiver in **everyday social situations**, like meal times, bath-time and when playing. The caregiver talks to the child and encourages them to talk back by pointing things out and asking questions, e.g. *what's that there, is it a doggy?* As a result of this **linguistic support** the child gradually learns to play a more **active part** in social situations, e.g. asking the caregiver questions.

3) Children who are **deprived** of language early on don't seem able to acquire it easily later. **Lenneberg (1967)** proposed the **Critical Period Hypothesis**, which states that without linguistic interaction **before** ages 5-6, language development is **severely limited**.

4) This view is supported by some rare cases where children **without** any exposure to language in the first five years of life (e.g. cases of extreme **child abuse**) subsequently fail to develop **normal speech**.

Vygotsky presented a Socio-cultural theory of Language Development

This theory suggests that **social interaction** and experiencing different **social and cultural contexts** are very important for language development. **Vygotsky (1978)** identified two significant factors that contribute to language development — **private speech** and the **Zone of Proximal Development (ZPD)**.

1) **Private Speech** — when a child **talks aloud** to itself. Vygotsky saw this as a major step forward in a child's mental development — this is evidence the child is **thinking for itself**.

2) **The ZPD** — when a child needs a caregiver's help in order to **interact**, e.g. if a doctor asks *Where does it hurt?*, the child might not answer. The caregiver either responds for the child or tries to encourage a response. This gives the child a **model** to apply to **similar situations** in the future when it might respond without help.

This kind of support is known as **scaffolding**. Children require it less and less once they become more able to deal with different social and cultural situations on their own.

Language Acquisition can't be explained by Just One Theory

Unfortunately, there isn't one model of language acquisition that can **fully explain** how a child learns to speak.

1) Theories of **innate acquisition** and **cognitive developments** do not take into account the role of **interaction** in the development of a child's language.

2) Theories of **imitation** and **reinforcement** can't explain the fact that some features of language apply to **everyone**, and that all babies show similar cooing and babbling features, **regardless** of their native language.

3) The most likely explanation is that language development involves **all** of these different influences to some degree.

Practice Questions

Q1 What is the behaviourist approach to language acquisition?
Q2 What does Chomsky mean by a language acquisition device (LAD)?
Q3 What does it mean for a child to be egocentric?
Q4 What did Bruner mean by LASS?
Q5 Explain Lenneberg's critical period hypothesis.
Q6 What is meant by Vygotsky's zone of proximal development (ZPD)?

Essay Question

Q1 Describe and evaluate the various theories of language acquisition, stating which one you think is the most viable. Your answer should refer to specific linguistic theories, benefits and drawbacks of specific theories, and present a clear line of argument.

Is it me, or does the "zone of proximal development" sound a bit weird...

...like something the government doesn't want you to know about, or part of a secret evil laboratory... or, better still, a rollercoaster. That'd be brilliant. Of course, it's nothing nearly as sinister (as the first two). It's a tiny part of a much bigger jigsaw that attempts to explain the different influences upon children as they grow up. They all contribute, so learn 'em all.

Reading and Writing

These two pages are only for AQA A. *Once your brain's done its bit, and you've acquired some basics of spoken language, you get whisked off to school. Yay school, with its teachers and detentions and PE in the rain. Yay indeed.*

There are **Different Approaches** to **Teaching Children** to **Read**

There are three major approaches to the teaching of reading: **phonics**, **look and say**, and **psycholinguistics**.

1) The **phonics approach** — looking at letters and letter combinations in terms of **sounds**. It's useful for words like *latch* that are pronounced as they appear (**phonetically**), but is less useful with words like *through*.

2) The **look and say** or **whole word** approach — recognising a word by **sight** alone. Relying on this method requires the child to **memorise** a large number of words.

3) The **psycholinguistics** approach — sees reading as a **natural development** that comes from being in an **environment** where books are read, valued and available. Relying on this method alone can leave a lot to **chance**.

Over the past sixty years, there has been a great deal of debate about which method is best. Teachers tend to use a **combination** of approaches rather than just rely on one — some children respond better to one method than another.

Reading **Develops** in **Stages** as you go through school

Obviously, everyone progresses at different rates, but there are some **general stages** that **most children** pass through.

Pre-school (up to age 5)	• Kids take part in activities that **prepare** them for reading e.g. playing with bricks, jigsaws, and matching pictures. This helps them distinguish between **different sizes**, **shapes** and **patterns**. In turn this prepares them for identifying **letters** and **combinations of letters**. • They can turn pages in books themselves and verbally **create** their own **stories**. • They begin to identify some **individual letters**, such as the first letter of their name, and also begin to match some **sounds** to letters.
Between five and six years old	• They **increase** the number of **letter-sound** matches that they know. • They realise that in English, letters on a page move from **left** to **right** and **top** to **bottom**. • They begin to **recognise** frequently used words.
Between six and seven years old	• They can read stories they're **familiar** with. • They use a range of **reading strategies** — when they're stuck on a word they may use the context to guess what it is, or guess what word comes next in a **sequence** of words. • They recognise more and more words just **by sight**. • They **break down** words into individual **sounds** to read an unfamiliar word. • They start to read with some **fluency**.
Between seven and eight years old	• They read more **fluently**, and their **vocabulary** continues to increase. • They use reading strategies **accurately** (such as **predicting** what words might come next). • They're better at working through **individual sounds** to read unfamiliar words.

Techniques for **Developing Reading Skills** depend on the **Child's Age**

1) Up to age **five**, caregivers may **read** stories and nursery rhymes to children, and help children enjoy the **physical experience** of books e.g. turning pages, pointing to letters and saying the sounds out loud.

2) Between **five** and **six**, caregivers / teachers will read them fiction and non-fiction, get them to **break down** words into individual sounds (**phonemes**), and get them to **match sounds** to **letters**.

3) Between six and seven, they'll get children to **read aloud**, set classroom tasks involving speaking, interacting reading, and encourage them to **talk** about what they've read.

4) Between seven and eight, they may introduce children to **different genres** and provide them with the chance to **discuss** different aspects of what they've read.

Or, here's an idea. How about you TURN YOUR OWN PAGE AND STOP BEING SO LAZY.

Reading and Writing

Writing also develops in Stages

1) When young children do **drawings** they're actually starting to learn skills they'll need when they learn to **write**.
2) Between **five** and **six** years old, most children can write **some** letters of the **alphabet** and some **words**.
3) Between six and seven, children will start using simple **punctuation** and write in short sentences (similar to how they speak) about things of **personal interest**, e.g. their family, or what they did at the weekend or on holiday.
4) Between seven and eight years old, children start to write for **different purposes** and **audiences**. They will be able to write and punctuate more complex sentences and check their work for **errors**.

Learning to Write and Spell Complete Words is a gradual process

Children go through **stages** of **development** before they can write and spell entire words.
The following stages **overlap** with each another.

1) First, children start **creating letters**, or symbols that look like letters (called pseudo-letters). There's **no particular pattern** to how the shapes are combined.
2) Following this, they might start to use **consonants** from the start of the word they want to write, e.g. *w* for *want*.
3) They may move on to combine **initial** and **final** consonants, e.g. *sm* to represent the sounds of *some*.
4) Children then start combining vowels and consonants in more **recognisable ways**, e.g. *bes* for *best*.
5) The next development is writing words that contain all the **right syllables**, e.g. *sleping* for *sleeping*.
6) Finally children start to get to grips with various **spelling patterns**, e.g. *creeping, weeping, long, strong*.

Teachers and Caregivers also help develop writing skills

1) In pre-school years caregivers encourage children to draw **lines** and **shapes** to build their **coordination skills** and imitate letters, e.g. a child can copy their own **name** if it's been written out for them by an adult.
2) When children are between **five** and **six** years old, caregivers and teachers usually get them to experiment with **different writing activities**, e.g. filling in gaps in sentences, or writing a shopping list.
3) When children are six and seven years old, caregivers and teachers can get them to write **personal information**, such as short letters to relatives.
4) When children are between seven and eight years old, caregivers and teachers teach them to experiment with **different kinds** of writing and about **different genres**, e.g. short stories, poetry, and non-fiction forms.

Practice Questions

Q1 What do children do in pre-school years that prepares them for reading?
Q2 Give three examples of how caregivers or teachers can help children's reading skills to develop.
Q3 Explain the phonics, whole word, and psycholinguistic approaches to reading.
Q4 Outline the stages that children go through in the development of spelling.
Q5 Give three examples of how caregivers or teachers could help children developing writing skills.

Essay Question

Q1 Describe the techniques used to develop children's reading and writing skills when they are between pre-school age and eight years old.

Learning to read and write takes stages...

Compared to all that babbling and telegraphic stuff... unless you're a real smart cookie that is, in which case you can do it in double-quick time. Although sometimes that can be interpreted as showing off, and that's not a great idea if you want to hold on to your dinner money. Similarly, if you want to hold on to a good mark, learn these pages. Or I'll nick yer crisps.

Language for Children

These two pages are only for OCR. In Western culture, caregivers tend to adopt particular linguistic features when they are talking to children, especially in the pre-school years. The media changes tone for children's programmes, too.

Caregivers talk to children in a *Particular Way*

1) This kind of language is referred to as **child-directed speech** (CDS), **caretaker speech**, or even **motherese**.

2) The language features of CDS are often **simplified** or **exaggerated** and often have the purpose of **encouraging** a child to **interact** as they are easier to understand.

Child-directed speech has *Distinctive Linguistic Features*

Phonology and Prosody

1) **Intonation** is exaggerated and words are **stressed** more strongly than they are in adult conversation, e.g. stress on *good* in *What a <u>good</u> girl you are Annie*. The **pitch** is usually **higher**.

2) Words and phrases are **repeated**, e.g. *Get the ball, Annie, get the ball*.

3) The **pace** is often much **slower**, with **longer pauses** than in adult speech.

Lexis

1) **Vocabulary** is often **simplified**, so instead of saying e.g. *banana*, a parent might say *nana* instead.

2) Caregivers use **reduplication** (see p.88) — constructions like *choo-choo*, *din-din*, or *moo-moo*.

3) They also use **diminutives** — like *birdie*, *doggie* or *fishy*.

4) A high proportion of words will refer to objects that the child can **see** and **touch** e.g. *Look at the pussy-cat, Annie, it's playing with the ball*.

Grammar

1) **Sentence structures** are simplified, and **function words** (e.g. auxiliary verbs) are often **omitted**. E.g. instead of saying *Annie, shall we go for a walk?*, a caregiver might say *Annie go for walk?*

2) **Proper nouns** (including frequent **repetition** of the child's name) are often used instead of pronouns, e.g. instead of *Are you making a sandcastle?* a parent will say *Is Annie making a sandcastle?* A higher proportion of nouns will be **concrete nouns** (e.g. *cup*, *apple*, *bottle*).

3) The **present tense** will be used more than the past tense. The caregiver will talk more about what's **happening 'now'** e.g. *Are you singing?* rather than in the past e.g. *Were you singing yesterday?*

Caregivers use *Techniques* to *Encourage Language Development*

1) They **repeat** certain **structures**, e.g. *Annie get the tractor, Annie wash the baby, Annie find the bottle*.

2) They ask lots of **questions**, e.g. *Annie, where's doggie gone?*, *Have you got a poorly hand?*, *Is Sally crying, Annie?* This **encourages** the child to **respond**.

3) They use lots of **imperatives**, e.g. *pick up dolly, eat din-dins, drink milk*.

4) Caregivers often **recast** what a child has said, re-presenting information in a **different way**:

Mother:	*What you doing, Annie?*
Child:	*Playing with my car.*
Mother:	*Yes, that's your car, isn't it?*

5) Caregivers also **expand** on what children say:

Mother:	*What you doing, Annie?*
Child:	*Playing.*
Mother:	*Yes, you're playing with your car.*

No one really knows if *CDS* has any *Impact* on *Development*

1) Child-directed speech isn't used by parents in **every culture**, but speakers of all cultures grow up to be **fluent**.

2) There's **nothing conclusive** to suggest that CDS does or doesn't work — research has produced conflicting results.

3) It could be that CDS is more about **building a relationship** than about language development in particular.

Language for Children

Media Texts for children make Specific language choices

The way that children are addressed in **print media** and on the **Internet** varies according to the **age** of the intended reader, and the **purpose** of the discourse. There's more on this on p.56.

1) Generally speaking, typeface for children is **larger** and might **vary** in **size** and **colour**.

2) The tone is **upbeat** and there are usually lots of **exclamation marks**.

2) The vocabulary is **simple**, and the language **informal**. The text will probably include some **slang** or **colloquialisms** to keep it as similar to spoken language as possible.

3) You often see lots of **phonological features** in this kind of discourse, like **alliteration** and **repetition**. There might also be some spellings based on phonetics such as *gotcha* rather than *got you*.

4) The texts often **address** the reader **directly** (using *you* and *we*). It might also include lots of **imperatives** to make children feel more **involved** and **stimulate** them, e.g. *Take a look / create your own / learn how to*.

Television Programmes show lots of examples of CDS

1) TV and radio discourses that are aimed at children normally use **phonological features** found in child-directed speech. **Presenters** of children's programmes will use features similar to those used by the caregiver.

2) They have a **slower pace**, **exaggerated intonation** and probably **increased volume** as well as **stronger stress** on important words than there would be in adult speech.

3) There are plenty of **interactive features**, like questions and **inclusive direct address** (e.g. *we*).

4) They use **deictic words** (see p.71) like *here* in conjunction with the action that's taking place on the screen. This extract involves dialogue between two children's TV presenters:

"Felix... move man, you're totally in my shot..."

A:	*do you know what a kangaroo is? (3)*
B:	*shall we see? (3)*
A:	*here's one! (2)*
B:	*can you see its (1) little pouch? (3) I wonder what's in it?*

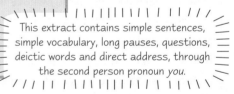

This extract contains simple sentences, simple vocabulary, long pauses, questions, deictic words and direct address, through the second person pronoun *you*.

Practice Questions

Q1 Name two other terms for child-directed speech?

Q2 List three phonological features of child-directed speech.

Q3 List three grammatical features of child-directed speech.

Q4 How do caregivers get children to interact?

Q5 What features of child-directed speech do television and radio presenters use?

Essay Question

Q1 Discuss the linguistic features of language aimed at children, focusing on lexis, grammar and phonology.

How appropriate that the end of this section is the end of the book...

... because, my friends, just as our hypothetical children of section seven are now language-proficient, so indeed are you. All that remains are some practice exam questions for section seven — excellent — and then some really handy advice about your exam, and your coursework. So one last effort on this page, and then you're on to the good stuff. Oh yes.

Sources and Exam Questions

Now have a go at these practice exam questions.

This is an OCR style exam question	1) Study Text A below — Helen is Reuben's babysitter. She's helping him to complete a jigsaw puzzle. Write about the way Helen and Reuben use language to complete the task. *[30 marks]*

Text A — Conversation between Reuben (aged 3 years 4 months) and Helen (his babysitter)

Helen: Reuben (.) shall we do this puzzle

Reuben: yeh

Helen: what you gonna start with

Reuben: these (2) those

Helen: start with the piggy

Reuben: yeh picgi *(snorts)* can't get right size here

Helen: why not

Reuben: cos it's stuck together (2) look hahaha (1) I know where it can go (1) there (.) that (.) yeh

Helen: well done (.) Reuben (.) that's GREAT

Reuben: going great at this (1) brilliant (2) this is going to be great when (3) can't (1) which way (1) can't do it

Helen: shall I help you

Reuben: but

Helen: no (.) it goes like this (3) that's it (1) you're very GOOD aren't you

Reuben: the thing is missing (.) for (.) it look (1) something's missing

Helen: here it is (2) what is it

Reuben: cockadoodledoo (2) this getting harder this (2) is it too hard (1) I'm tired

Helen: let's try this one (1) what's this one Reuben

Reuben: tiger (3) you gotta do dat and then you dat

Helen: that's it

Reuben: it's gonna be finished when grandma's here

Helen: what's your favourite animal

Reuben: I don't know (2) a cat

Helen: have you got a cat Reuben

Reuben: yeh

Helen: what you doing now Reuben

Reuben: bear

Helen: what kind of bear is it

Reuben: panda bear

Helen: what's this one

Reuben: birdie (2) tickie bird (2) *(sings)* two little tickie birds sitting on a waw (.) one called Reuben (1) one called mummy (1) and one called (2) granma

Transcription Key

(.) *Micropause*

(2) *Pause in seconds*

UPPER CASE *indicates stress / increased volume*

Sources and Exam Questions

EITHER

This is an AQA A style exam question

1) a)   Study Text A below — comment on five features of the language used that you find interesting   *[10 marks]*

1) b)   To what extent do children acquire language skills by imitation? In your answer you should:
   - discuss relevant linguistic theories and studies
   - provide evidence to support your suggestions
   - present a clear line of argument   *[35 marks]*

Text A — Conversation between Annie (2-and-a-half years old) and her grandfather

Grandfather:	d'you want to go for a walk Annie
Annie:	yeh (1) like walk
Grandfather:	come on then (1) get yer wellies on
Annie:	welli on
Grandfather:	ooo (2) they're nice wellies aren't they
Annie:	yeh (.) nice welli
Grandfather:	what colour are they Annie (3) they're red wellies aren't they (2) say red
Annie:	wed
Grandfather:	that's right (1) RED wellies (3) shall we take Simon and Costa
Annie:	yeh (1) take Simee and Co'a
Grandfather:	you like Simon and Costa don't you
Annie:	yeh (2) they naugh'y
Grandfather:	naughty (2) yes (1) they're very naughty doggies aren't they
Annie:	barky
Grandfather:	yes you're right (1) they're always barking aren't they
Annie:	yeh noisy

OR

2) a)   Study Text B below — comment on five features of the language used that you find interesting.   *[10 marks]*

2) b)   Explore the language development processes involved when a child begins to develop reading and writing skills, referring to:
   - particular developmental periods and processes.
   - the role of caregivers and teachers.   *[35 marks]*

Text B — the writer is six years old

I was goin down a really darc lan**e**. Iwas all aloan. It was realy scary. sudenly I herd a noise comin from behine a **b**ush. It was makin lots of moning noises I nearly jumpd up in the air. I whanted to run for help but nufin cam**e** out. Sumfin was russling the Bushes and I didn no wot it was. I ran and ran and ran. Wen I got hom**e** I tole my brother what had happend. He laughed. He said it wuz him inthe bushes.

Key

Letters in bold were reversed in the original

General Exam Advice

For your AS exam, you'll need to understand language frameworks and linguistic concepts, know how to analyse different types of discourse, organise your answers, and write clearly and precisely. If that's all Greek to you, panic ye not. For here is a helpful little page, with some exam tips neatly crowbarred into a nutshell.

Make sure you know your **Language Frameworks**

Language frameworks can be thought of as **headings** to help you to **structure** your **analysis**. You need to be able to **identify them** in different kinds of texts and explain how the features are used to **create meaning**. So here they are:

Language Frameworks

- **Lexis** (vocabulary)
- **Semantics** (meanings that words convey)
- **Grammar** (word classes and syntax)
- **Phonology** (sounds)
- **Pragmatics** (social conventions surrounding language use)
- **Graphology** (visual appearance and arrangement of the text)
- **Discourse** (how segments of language are developed and structured)

1) You need to refer to as many of these as possible, as long as they're **appropriate**.

2) Don't focus on just **one framework** and **ignore** the rest.

3) Don't just be descriptive. You have to relate the frameworks to **meaning** and **purpose**, e.g. *The adjective 'unique' is persuasive [**purpose**], suggesting that the product is special [**meaning**].*

Think about how you're going to **Approach the Questions**

When you're analysing **non-topic-based discourse** in the exam (e.g. in questions that ask you to group texts etc.), think about the points on this checklist:

1) Read the texts **quickly**, just to get a feel for what they're generally about. Then read them again **more carefully**, noting down what the **subject matter** is.

2) For **written** texts, identify genre, register, likely audience and purpose.

3) For **spoken** texts, identify context, role of participants, register, pragmatics and conversational theory.

4) Find **examples** of the language frameworks — be selective and **link** linguistic features to purpose and meaning.

Topic-based questions still give you a **text** to **analyse**, but your analysis has to focus upon a certain aspect of the text.

1) Look for features that **specifically relate** to the topic (e.g. power, gender, occupation, technology, etc.).

2) The best way to prepare is to **underline key features** in the texts you're given.

3) You also need to think about the **assessment objectives** for both types of question — these are the **criteria** the examiners use to mark your answers:

For short questions at the start of the exam you just get A01 or A02 marks. For long essay questions, you can get A01, A02, A03 and A04 marks.

AO1	You get **AO1** marks for using linguistic terminology correctly and writing accurately.
AO2	You get **AO2** marks for applying linguistic approaches to questions, and showing that you understand issues related to the construction and analysis of meaning in texts.
AO3	You get **AO3** marks for analysing and evaluating the influence of context on the language used.
AO4	You get **AO4** marks for using linguistic concepts to show expertise and creativity.

Think about how to **Organise Your Answers**

These are **general guidelines** for how to best cover everything in your answers — if you're asked about something **specific**, you'll have to **tailor** what you say to the particular areas the question asks you to focus on.

Written Discourse	Spoken Discourse
Write a **couple of paragraphs** on:	Write a **couple of paragraphs** on:
Genre, purpose, register, formality, likely audience.	Context, content, function, participants.
Write in **more detail** about:	Write in **more detail** about:
Graphology (layout, fonts, use of visual stimuli)	**Phonology** (pronunciation features)
Phonology (alliteration, assonance, repetition)	**Non-fluency features** (pauses, false starts, fillers)
Lexis (lexical fields, figurative language)	**Non-verbal** aspects of speech (stress)
Grammar (word classes, e.g. modals, types of adverb)	**Pragmatics** (conversational theory)
Discourse structure (beginning, how it's developed, end)	**Lexis**, **grammar** and **discourse structure**

Commentaries

*Commentaries are where you get the chance to **explain** the language choices you made in your **coursework**. There's more detail on what you need to do in your coursework on the pages for your specific exam board.*

Writing a **Commentary** shows your choices were **Intentional**

1) The commentary shows the examiner that you knew what you were doing in the **writing process**, and that you've thought about the effect that your **language choices** have had on the piece of writing you produced.

> **Your commentary is a review of what you've done and how you did it.**
> It will refer to all or some of the following frameworks, depending on the kind of text.
> **Lexis, semantics, grammar, phonology, pragmatics, graphology** and **discourse structure**.

2) You need to keep to the point and make sure you discuss all the features **equally**.

3) Your commentary should explain how your language choices in your coursework **match** the genre, mode, purpose, audience and subject matter of your text.

4) Commentaries should be **400-500** words.

Check the coursework tasks with your teacher — there's a chance they might change.

Your commentary should be *Concise and Well-Organised*

Start by stating what **kind of text** you've written, who it's **aimed at**, and what its **purpose** is. For example:

> I chose to write the kind of unsolicited letter that charitable organisations send out to the public. The purpose of this letter is to persuade adults to donate money to a good cause; in this case, a campaign to end forced child labour in developing countries.

Now describe some of the **specific language choices** you made, making sure that you always refer back to how they helped you **identify with** and get your **message across** to the audience. Here are a few examples of the kind of things you should be aiming to write about:

Mentioning narrative voice is a good way to describe how you're treating the reader.

> Throughout the letter I used the second person pronoun *you* to address the reader directly. By doing this, I aimed to involve the reader by making it seem I was talking to them personally...

Try to describe how you've attempted to manipulate the reader's response to the text.

> Another technique I used for involving the reader was incorporating a number of rhetorical questions, e.g. *Can we stand by and let this happen?*, and *Would you let this happen to your own child?*. My purpose here was to further personalise the issue and involve the reader by projecting the situation onto their lives...

Discuss the lexis you've used, and why you've chosen certain words (e.g. for their connotative meaning).

> To further the personal impact of the text, some of the lexis I used was deliberately emotive as I wanted the reader to be shocked by what they read. For this reason, I gave a short case study of a six-year-old boy called Arjit. I used adjectives such as *fatherless*, *unloved* and *malnourished* to give a sense of his vulnerability, loneliness and frailty. I also used the metaphor *dungeon* to describe the factory where Arjit works to emphasise that his workplace is a dark, harsh and restricted environment...

Grammar can be just as influential as lexis on the tone and style of a text, so make sure you discuss it. Also think about how the complexity of the sentences and words make your text accessible to your reader.

> I mainly used simple sentences because it gives the text a shorter, more dynamic tone, making it more assertive and therefore more persuasive. As this is a letter that someone might easily throw away without reading, it was important that the opening sentences in particular were short and to the point, e.g. the very first sentence, which simply states that *Two hundred children died last year*. This is a stark fact and grabs the reader's attention straight away...

Describe how you've organised your text.

> The letter has a clear structure. First I paint a picture of the situation focusing on Arjit, then broaden the text to show how forced labour is a worldwide issue which affects thousands of children. Finally, having hopefully influenced the reader, I have urged them to donate money, using modals and adverbs of time to give a sense of urgency: *You <u>must</u> do something <u>now</u>!*

You might want to talk about how the structure reflects or subverts the conventions of the genre you've chosen to write in.

There are **two** important things to remember.
1) **Support** every point you make with **examples**.
2) For every linguistic choice you discuss, say how it **affects** the **audience** or contributes to the **effect** of the text.

AQA A Exam

*If you're doing **AQA A**, the AS exam is called* **Seeing Through Language**.

The exam has Two Sections

The **AQA A** paper lasts **two hours** and is split into **two sections**:

Section A — Language and Mode

1) You'll be given **two texts** to analyse, which could be **spoken**, **written** or **multimodal**.

2) You'll need to think about the main **mode characteristics** of the texts (e.g. the formality of a text in written mode compared to spoken) and how the language used in each relates to **purpose** and **meaning**.

3) There are **45 marks** available for this question.

Section B — Language Development

1) This section consists of two questions — but you only need to answer **one**. One question will be on **initial language acquisition** and the other will be on a piece of **children's writing**.

2) Each question will be based around a piece of **spoken** or **written** data.

3) Both questions have **two parts**:

   • The first part will ask you to **comment** on a short piece of child's **speech** or **writing**.

   • The second part is more of an essay-style question. You have to discuss a **particular issue** relating to **initial language acquisition** or **children's writing** (depending on which question you choose).

4) There are **45 marks** available for this question.

Here's an Example Question and Answer to give you some tips:

> **2 b)** To what extent do you think children acquire language through imitation?

There has been a good deal of debate about how children acquire language. This debate has explained the development of language skills from different perspectives such as imitation, innateness and cognition.

The introduction gets straight to the point, identifying different approaches

Some argue that language skills are acquired through imitation. This is imitation theory, which is associated with Skinner (1957). According to this view, language is acquired though a process of imitation, reward and reinforcement. When a child says something right, the adult will praise the child and ask him or her to repeat what has just been said.

Clear explanation of the imitation theory, with key terms and key figures identified

This gives a critique of imitation theory, supported by key terms

The problem with this theory is that children have the capacity to create sentences that they have never heard before. If acquiring language was just about imitation, this would not be possible. Moreover, children over-generalise and commit what are known as virtuous errors. This is where they appear to be making a mistake but are in fact showing an understanding of the rules of language. For example, a child may say *I runned down the road*, an utterance unlikely to be copied from an adult. What a child is doing here is adding the suffix *–ed* to the end of a verb, something that we do with all regular verbs. Here, however, the child has applied it to an irregular verb.

Examples explained using key grammatical terms

Shows evidence of personal 'research' / experience

It has also been shown that children don't always respond to correction. I have a younger brother who is three years old. When I ask him if he would like some spaghetti he replies, *can't like it*. When I say to him, *you mean you don't like it* he replies, *no, I can't like it*. All this shows that children do not rely just on imitation in the development of their language skills.

This answer is quite good. It's **to-the-point**, well written and well organised. It **explains** imitation theory but also states that there are **problems** with it. It mentions **key terms** and gives **relevant examples**. When explaining the examples the writer shows a **clear understanding** of grammar.

The writer uses **relevant personal experience** to make an extra point, but an example of a study or part of the **AS course** would be better. The essay would get at least **29 marks** out of **45** if it kept up this standard all the way through.

AQA A Coursework

What the Exam Board Wants

You have to produce **two** pieces of work for the **coursework** part of the AS level:

	Type of Writing	Description
Piece 1	Investigation (**1000-1500 words**)	Analyse between three and five texts with some kind of temporal relationship (see below).
Piece 2	Production (**600 words**) plus commentary (**400 words**)	In a genre of your choice, produce a text that creates or challenges the representation of a social group, individual, event or institution.

See Section 2 (terminology and framework for analysis, p.18-35).

See Section 6 (written language, purpose, genre and representation, p.76-85).

1) For the **Production** piece you also need to produce a **400 word** commentary (see p.105). This should state **what kind** of text it is, its **intended purpose,** and the **techniques** used to achieve it.

2) In both pieces of coursework, you need to show **how language** is used to **create impressions** of people or groups, and how the writer aims to **position themselves** and **the reader** in relation to the text.

Analytical Investigations need a lot of Planning

Check the coursework tasks with your teacher — there's a chance they might change.

You need to analyse **3-5 texts** that are about a particular **social group**, **individual**, **event** or **institution**. For example, they could be about teenagers, a celebrity or religion.

Understanding the question

When the exam board says *texts with a temporal relationship*, they mean things like:

- Texts that are produced at **different times**, e.g. newspaper articles from the 1940s, 1960s and 1990s.
- Newspaper articles that are all from the **same day**, whether about the **same story** or from the **same paper**. They might show **divided** or **shared opinions**, or reflect the **political** or **ideological issues** of the time.

You also have to make sure you select a set of texts that will give you **enough to talk about**.

Analysing the texts

You need to focus on these points when you're analysing the texts:

1) **Genre** — what **conventions** and **features** you should expect to find in the text.
2) **Purpose** — what the text tells you (or doesn't), how the text **represents** its subject, and what it aims to **achieve**.
3) **The Writer** — or narrative voice, and how their **identity** comes across in relation to the **content** and the **reader**.
4) **The Audience** — who the **target audience** is and how they might interpret the text.
5) **Representation** — how the group, issue, event or person is **portrayed**. To do this you should look at the **language frameworks** — lexis, grammar, semantics, phonology and pragmatics.

1500 words might seem like a lot, but when you've got up to **five texts** to talk about, it really isn't.
Try to be as **concise** as possible, and **back up your points** with **examples** from the texts. It also pays to be **methodical** — don't go **jumping around** from point to point. Cover one area thoroughly, then move on.

The Production task gives you a bit more Freedom

For this part you're **creating** the text rather than **analysing** it, but you need to use **linguistic techniques** to produce a good piece of **original writing**. The text you write can be **literary** or **non-literary**.

Production

1) Like your investigation, this piece of writing should be about a particular **social group**, **individual**, **event** or **institution**.
2) Deciding **what** to write about can be tricky — the best thing to do is write about what you **know**. This way you'll have a better idea of how your subject is **normally represented**, and a better idea of how to change or reproduce this representation in your own text.
3) Then you need to decide **how** to write it — think about what you want to say, and the best way to say it in only **600 words**.
4) Concentrate on who your **audience** are, **what** you want to say, and using **appropriate techniques** to say it.

AQA B Exam

If you're doing **AQA B**, the AS exam is called **Categorising Texts**.

The exam has **Two Sections**

The **AQA B** paper lasts **two hours** and is split into **two sections**.

Section A — Text Varieties

1) This section contains **one** compulsory question.

2) You'll get about six texts from **everyday sources**.

3) You'll have to discuss the various ways in which these texts can be **grouped together**.

4) You'll need to write about things like: **purpose**, **genre**, level of **formality**, **mode** (spoken, written, multimodal), **representation** and linguistic features (**lexis**, **grammar**, **phonology** and so on).

5) There are **48 marks** available for this question.

Section B — Language and Social Contexts

1) In this section you have to choose **one** question out of three.

2) The three questions are on **language and gender**, **language and power**, and **language and technology**.

3) There'll be **one text** to analyse for each question.

4) There are **48 marks** available for this question.

Here's an **Example Question** and **Answer** to give you some tips:

> 4) Read Text 1. How has the language of the text been influenced by technology?

Straight to the point, focusing on the impact of technology.

These text messages show some of the distinctive qualities of text messaging language. The language used is influenced by the need for participants to respond quickly with a limited set of buttons to work with.

Good range of examples, supporting the idea of simplification.

For this reason, words are abbreviated, as in *sis*, and spelling is simplified, as in *nite*. Another form of simplification occurs with the omission of vowels (*wkd, Lndn*) and with the dropping of final consonants (the final *g* is dropped in *goin, doin*, and *hangin*). There is one example where a single consonant is used to replace a consonant cluster (*athletix* rather than *athletics*). Silent vowels at the end of words are also omitted (*els*). In addition to simplified spelling, there are also examples of phonological spelling: *bin, wiv, nuffin, strick*.

Text 1 — text messages from the mobile phones of a 17-year-old boy and his 14-year-old sister.

Simon:	*hi sis,ows it goin down in Lndn?*
Trish:	*its cool.bin on the EYE*
Simon:	*wow bet that was wkd. wot els?*
Trish:	*nuffin much.bin hangin round wiv billy*
Simon:	*BILLY? aw billy, hes well cool.*
Trish:	*yeh*
Simon:	*he still doin athletix?*
Trish:	*yeh,really into it.trains every nite almos*
Simon:	*hows auntie Bett? lol.*
Trish:	*lol shes really strick. we don't get away wiv nuffin not even Billy n hes nearly 16*

Colloquial expressions such as *ows it goin?*, *wkd* (wicked), *hangin round*, and *well cool* suggest an informal conversation between two people who are comfortable with each other. Grammatical structures are incomplete, especially with the omission of personal pronouns: *[I] bet that was wkd*, or subject-verb combinations: *[I've] bin on the EYE*.

The text conversation mirrors some features found in actual spoken conversation. There is an opening sequence with Simon addressing his sister with *hi* and her responding. Brother and sister take turns with Simon driving the conversation forward by asking questions. However, there are also declaratives, particularly from Trish, who tells her brother about Billy's athletics training and the strictness of her aunt.

Comments on lexical / grammatical frameworks with examples.

Comments on conversational features of text messaging.

This is quite a good answer. It **focuses** on the **question**, identifies a **range** of **features** and gives some **good examples**. It explores how text messaging has some of the same features as **spoken conversation** and shows that the student is aware of the **context**.

The student could **improve** the answer by writing about the **function** of the **interaction**, and how the exchanges might fit in with **conversational theory**. If it carried on like this, the essay would get at least **32 marks** out of **48**.

AQA B Coursework

What the Exam Board Wants

For your AQA B coursework, you have to do **two** different pieces of **original writing**. They have to be from **different genres** and written for a **different purpose** and **audience**.

The total length for the two pieces together is 1500 - 2500 words. You can pick a type of text from any of the following areas:	
A text to entertain	• an extract from an interview • part of a script from a TV show • a parody or piece of satirical writing
A text to inform	• news coverage of an important event • a piece of travel writing • a press release from a football club
A text to instruct	• a step-by-step fitness regime • a manual for a computer game • a novice's guide to email (or similar)
A text to persuade	• a film, music, car or restaurant review • a political speech • a piece of motivational speaking

Check the coursework tasks with your teacher — there's a chance they might change.

For help with this, see Section 2 (terminology and useful language features, p.18-35), Section 4 (language in different contexts, e.g. the media and exerting power, p.46-63), Section 5 (e.g. if you're doing a script, refer to features of spoken language, p.68-73), and Section 6 (written language, purpose, genre and representation, p.76-85).

You also have to submit **two commentaries** in total — one for **each** piece of writing (see p.105). The **total** word count for the **two** commentaries together is **1000 words**.

Each type of text shares some Common Features

Here are some hints on the main features to include. For more on these features, see Section 6.

1) Entertainment Texts

You can write in several different styles if you pick an entertainment text, but they all share some features:

- **Structure** — Most entertainment texts have a **fairly complex** structure. For example, a novel usually has a **sophisticated plot line**, and plays need **stage directions** as well as lines for the characters.
- **Language** — a written entertainment text usually has quite complex language and lots of **figurative devices**. Spoken and written entertainment texts sometimes use **non-standard** language to **subvert convention**.

2) Informative Texts

Informative texts may be **factually based**. Make sure your **facts** are right and the language is **appropriate**.

- **Structure** — the bulk of the facts you want to get across should be in the **middle** of the **text**. Have a more general introduction and conclusion to **frame** what you're talking about.
- **Language** — it's important that your language **suits** your **target audience**. If you're writing to inform **children**, you'll have to use quite different language to what you'd use in a text written for your friends or parents.

3) Instructional texts

If you write a set of instructions, you need to guide a reader through the text, step by step.

- **Structure** — you'll probably need to use numbered or bullet-pointed **lists**. The reader can't go on to the next one until they've **completed** everything the former one tells them to do — they're very **linear**.
- **Language** — instructions are usually **imperative sentences** (see p.15). Sometimes the word choices are **specific** to the type of task or process that the reader is doing.

4) Persuasive texts

The best persuasive texts manage to get the reader to 'buy into' the idea they're promoting.

1) **Structure** — it's best to steadily **build** your **argument** as you go along and end with an **emphatic conclusion**.
2) **Language** — persuasive texts are meant to be **emotive**, so use lots of **direct address** and **inclusive pronouns**, as well as **emotive adjectives** to promote your subjective judgements.

Edexcel Exam

*If you're doing **Edexcel**, the AS exam is called **Language Today**.*

The exam has *Two Sections*

The Edexcel paper lasts **two hours 15 minutes** and is split into **two sections**.

Section A — Language and Context

1) You'll have to answer some **short questions** in response to the source texts.
2) Think about the **genre features** of the texts, their **context**, **mode**, and the **identity** of the speaker or writer, as well as the **relationship** that they form with the **audience**.
3) There are **50 marks** for this section.

Section B — Presenting Self

1) For this section you have to write an **extended** answer based on **new data**.
2) Think about **contextual features** and the way the speakers or writer **present themselves**.
3) There are **50 marks** for this question.

Here's an *Example Question* and *Answer* to give you some tips:

5) Read texts A and B. Analyse and compare the ways in which the writers of the two texts present themselves.

Text A is an extract from a weblog, in which a young woman writes about her struggles with drug addiction.

My addiction has ruined my life. Most people of my age – I'm only thirty-two – have had what you call a normal upbringing. They've rebelled a little bit against their parents, that's normal. They've had boyfriends, they've gone to college and then they've settled down. Got a job maybe, got married, had a couple of kids, got their own house, got a car. It's been different for me. I got into stuff early. And there was sort of no going back. I had nice parents, a nice home. But after I started to get into it – you know, there are whole months, maybe YEARS, of my life that I just CAN'T remember. I was so OUT of it. Living in derelict buildings. Living in shop doorways. On the streets. Begging. Totally focused on one thing and nothing else. You don't know how it gets you. In the end, you don't care about anything – friends, family… they just mean nothing. I mean NOTHING. You don't care. It's only later, when you come out of it, when you get off it, that you start to realise what you've done.

Neatly summarises the speaker's perception of others

In this extract, the writer addresses herself directly to the reader with the use of the second person pronoun *you*. She compares herself with other people of the same age who have taken a better pathway through life. She describes what this consists of: a little rebellion, then boyfriends, college, a career and perhaps marriage.

In contrast, she presents her life as *ruined* by drugs. She can't remember long stretches of time and she has been homeless. She describes how addiction takes over a person's life so that no one else matters, no matter how close. It is only after someone is free of drugs that there is an understanding of just what effect this has had on others.

Gives good examples from the text to describe speaker's perception of herself

Discusses language features such as level of formality, prosody and sentence structure

She uses colloquial expressions such as *bit* and *stuff*, and contractions such as *you've* which are characteristic of spoken language. She stresses certain words such as *years* and *nothing* for emotional effect. Her sentences are often fragmentary, presenting her life in a series of separate images.

This answer picks out some good points such as the **informal delivery**, the **direct address** to the audience and examples of **colloquial features**.

The essay needs to mention the **purpose** of the text (almost confessional), its **spontaneous**, **unscripted nature**, its **genre** and **audience**. It also needs to explore a **wider range of language frameworks**. It should go on to discuss text B [not shown] and offer **comparisons** with text A. If it carried on at this standard the essay would get at least **30** marks out of **50**.

Edexcel Coursework

What the **Exam Board Wants**

For your coursework assignment you'll have to choose **one task** from each of the lists:

Task List 1 — 1000 - 1500 words		Task List 2 — 500 - 1000 words	
Journalism Interview	• Conduct an **interview** and **transcribe** sections of it word for word. • Write up your work so your **interviewee** is **presented** in a **particular** way to your audience.	**Scripted Presentation**	• Write a **presentation script** on an **issue** of language you've already studied on the course. • **Research** the topic and **aim** the presentation at a **specific audience**.
Narrative Writing	• Research different **audiences** and **narrative techniques** and **styles**. • Produce a piece of writing in a style **suitable** for your **target audience**.	**Dramatic Monologue**	• Write a **script** from the **point of view** of an **individual character**. • Look at features of **spoken language** and how **meaning** can be conveyed.

- To help you with this, see **Section 2** (terminology and useful language features, p.18-35), and **Section 6** (written language, purpose, genre and representation, p.76-85).

- Your entire coursework folder for both tasks (not including commentaries) should be **no more** than **2500 words**. Your commentaries should be no more than **500 words** each (see p.105).

Check the coursework tasks with your teacher — there's a chance they might change.

In **Task One** you're producing **Writing** to be **Read**

Remember that an audience of a written text only have the words on the page and their own personal perceptions to help them **interpret** the **meaning**. You have to make sure you **communicate clearly**.

Journalism Interview

1) Make sure the interview gives you enough **material**. When you write the text you have to use your **interviewee's** own **words**. Make sure you ask the **right questions**, and that they're **cohesive** — even though you're not doing much of the talking, you can still **control** the conversation (see p.72-73).

2) You need to use **linguistic devices** to **represent** the interviewee in the way you want to, for the **audience** you decide to **target**. See p.78-79 and p.84-85 for help with this.

OR

Narrative Writing

1) This is a text that recounts a **story** or sequence of events from a certain **point of view**, so you need to be clear what kind of **narrative voice** to use (p.82), and what sort of **audience** you're addressing.

2) Look at **language** and **semantics** (p.20-23) and remember your text must be **accessible** for your **target audience**.

In **Task Two** you're writing for a **Live Audience**

This means you can also use **phonological features** to develop meaning and reach your audience.

Scripted Presentation

1) Your presentation should **inform** or **persuade** the audience. Think about the audience that you're producing the presentation for, and change the **complexity** of your text to suit them. For example, you might use **formal** and **standard language** for an **adult** audience and **less formal** language if you were addressing **children**.

2) You need to make sure you research any **talking points** (e.g. controversial issues or opinions) in your subject.

3) Remember that you might need to produce **handouts** for this task.

Dramatic Monologue

1) You can change how **formal** your language is depending on what **kind** of **character** you want to create. You could also use a particular **non-standard** accent or dialect to **imply** things about the character (section 3).

2) Try p.20-23 for some tips on **figurative and emotive language** and p.30-31 on **pragmatics**.

OCR Exam

If you're doing **OCR**, *the AS exam is called* **The Dynamics of Speech**.

The exam has Two Sections

The OCR paper lasts **two hours** and is split into **two sections**.

1) Section A focuses on **Speech** and **Children**.
2) Section B focuses on **Speech Varieties** and **Social Groups**.
3) Both sections have **two** questions but you only have to answer **one** from each section.
4) Each question asks you to analyse a piece of **discourse**, which could be **scripted** (like an extract from a play or speech) or **unscripted** (like a transcript of a conversation).
5) There are **30 marks** for each question.

Here's an Example Question and Answer to give you some tips:

4) Read the following transcript of two footballers talking about their team after a match. Write about some of the features of their language and explain why some occupational groups have their own variety of language.

A:	'ow bad was that Steve
B:	FOUR nil (3.0) mind you (.) that third goal was WAY offside
A:	just a bit (1.0) still (.) it's excuses (.) we really GOT to defend our set-pieces better
B:	yeah (.) take our chances (1) how many how many chances did we just BLOW
A:	we need a new striker (.) it's as simple as that (2.0) Ratters just can't do it (1.0)
B:	// Billy was a bit useless too (2.0) that winger 'ad 'im every time
A:	trouble is (.) there's no money
B:	no (1.0) seems to me though right seems like if we don't invest in the future (.) mate (.) we don't have no future
A:	mm (.) not sure the manager's got it right neither (1.0) WHY WHY WHY (.) Steve (.) are we playin' four three three given the players we've got it's suicidal (1.0) we need to go for a four five one (1.0) 'specially 'gainst the good side
B:	// yeah

(.) brief pauses
(2) number indicates pause in seconds
// interruption

Briefly describes level of formality and neatly summarises the content →

This is an informal conversation showing two players' disappointment at their team's performance. They criticise the referee (one goal was offside), other players and the manager.

Give a good range of examples to support the point about informality →

The informal nature of their conversation is seen through their use of colloquial phrases such as *that winger 'ad 'im every time*, contractions such as *don't* and in lexis such as *mate*. Non-standard grammar is evident, in particular when A uses the non-standard adverb *neither* for *either* and B uses the non-standard double negative *we don't have no future*. Non-verbal aspects of speech are shown where words are capitalised, showing strength of feeling. For example, A stresses the verb when he says *we really GOT to defend our set-pieces*, and also the interrogative adverb *WHY*, which is also repeated three times for impact.

Explains non-verbal features

General point about cooperative features supported by a specific example →

There are a number of cooperative features in the way the two speakers relate to each other. B uses positive feedback, agreeing with A's opinion on set-pieces by saying *yeah*, and then, at the end of the conversation, he says *yeah*. Another cooperative feature is when one speaker develops a topic that the other has started. A says *there's no money* and B makes the point that without investment there's no future.

Applies the analysis of the text to answer the second part of the question →

The dialogue consists of many occupationally specific words such as: *set-piece, striker, winger, offside* and *goal*. Occupational dialects are a means by which individuals interact within a specific occupational group. First, it enables those who are in the group to communicate more efficiently with each other by using specialist language. Second, the use of such language creates a sense of group identity. The repeated use of the first person plural pronoun *we* shows the sense of solidarity that teams often have.

This answer is quite good. It quickly sums up what the conversation is about and then gives a good range of examples to show that it is an **informal exchange**. It uses linguistic frameworks, like **grammar**, **lexis** and **phonology**, to describe the text.

The student also gives good examples to support the idea that this is a **cooperative conversation**. If the rest of the essay was in the same sort of style it would get at least **22 marks** out of **30**.

OCR Coursework

What the Exam Board Wants

You have to do **two** coursework tasks for OCR:

	Type of writing	Description
Task 1	Text Study	Analyse two texts, one that is only in **written** mode, and one that is **multimodal**.
Task 2	Adaptive Writing (plus commentary)	Adapt one of the texts from **task 1** into a **new** text with a different audience or purpose (in any mode).

Check the coursework tasks with your teacher — there's a chance they might change.

See Section 6 (written language, purpose, genre and representation, p.76-85).

See Section 2 (terminology and framework for analysis, p.18-35).

Your entire coursework folder should be no more than **3000 words**, including a **commentary** on your **adaptive writing**.

Be Methodical when you Analyse Texts

For your first piece of coursework you need to analyse **two** texts. One text should be in the **written mode**, e.g. a newspaper article or a poem. The other text should be **multimodal**, e.g. a web-based text or a film script. Make sure you **back up** your points with examples.

> ### Text Study
>
> 1) The main thing to concentrate on is **how** the writers convey their **messages** in the two texts.
> 2) You should analyse the texts using the **language frameworks** — lexis, grammar, phonology and morphology.
> 3) These features will also reflect the **audience** and **purpose** of the text (see p.76-79), and the **social** and **cultural contexts** that it was produced in (p.84-85).
> 4) Written modes have unique structures like pages, lines, capitalisation, and some punctuation.
> 5) **Multimodal texts** can include **prosodic features**, such as **tone**, **intonation** and **pitch**.

Adaptive Writing means you Pick the Genre and Target Audience

For this task you can produce a **spoken**, **written** or **multimodal** text. Even though you can adapt the text into something different, you need to make sure that you stick to the **conventions** of the type of text you choose:

> ### Adaptive writing
>
> 1) **Genre** — the **conventions** and **language features** of the type of text you've chosen to write, e.g. if you're turning a short story into a play script, you'll need to incorporate **actions** into the stage directions.
> 2) **Purpose** — what your text is trying to tell the audience and how the text **represents** its **subject** to achieve this.
> 3) **Writer** (or **narrative voice**) — how your text comes across in relation to the **content** and the **reader**, and the ways that the reader is **influenced** by the **lexis**, **grammar**, **formality** and **tone** of your piece.
> 4) **Audience** — the target audience and how your chosen text might **address** them to achieve its aim, e.g. if you're trying to **change** the way the audience **feels** about a character in the original text, think about the kind of language that might **influence** their opinions.

Here's an example of **adaptive writing** — a short story that has been adapted into a play script:

> ### Short story
>
> Joshua was running late again. He just seemed to find it impossible to get himself going at the moment, spending his days in a haze of exhaustion and ill-kept promises to 'go to bed early tonight'. Nina said hello and he managed to mumble a reply before he was gone. She smiled wryly; it was the same every day...

Act Two, Scene One

An office. Very stark and modern. Nina is sitting behind a desk looking bored. Joshua enters stage left in a rush.

NINA: Hi Josh.
JOSHUA: Eh? Oh yes, hi, Nina. *Exits stage right.*
NINA: [*Sighing*] Same every day...

WJEC Exam

*If you're doing **WJEC**, the AS exam is called **Introduction to the Language of Texts**.*

The exam has **Two Sections**

The WJEC paper lasts **two and a half hours** and is split into **two sections**.

Section A focuses on The Language of Texts

1) This section has **one question**. You'll have to **analyse** and **discuss** two or more texts, which will be **linked** by **genre** or **theme**.

2) You'll have to identify the **main purpose** of each text and explain how language is used to **support** this purpose.

3) You'll also need to comment on how language conveys **ideas**, **attitudes** and **opinions**.

4) This section is worth **40 marks**.

Section B is Language Focus

1) There's **one question** in this section.

2) You'll probably only get **one text**.

3) You'll need to write about how speakers and/or writers use language to convey **feelings**, **opinions**, **attitudes** and **prejudices**.

4) There are **20 marks** for this question.

Here's an **Example Question** and **Answer** to give you some tips:

2) Analyse and discuss how the language in the following text conveys the attitude of the writer.

This is an extract from an article from a magazine aimed at young women about to get married.

Deep down, your new husband is a spoilt brat. He might have hidden it well while you were dating — tidying his flat, cooking you dinner, showering... But you'll quickly realise that this was just a crafty ruse to get you to say "I do". Once a boyfriend becomes a husband, something clicks inside him. When it comes to washing up and ironing, we've all fallen for the "Oh but you just do it so much better than me" trick before. It can even seem cute and helpless when you're in the first flush of love. But don't be fooled, this is just his way of telling you that he'll be reverting back to his lazy single ways before you know it.

Anne (28) agrees. She got married to Benjy 8 months ago, and found the honeymoon period doesn't last long. "He's changed so much since we got married," she says. "He spends all his time playing computer games or watching sport on TV, and just grunts if I ask him to help me with something."

So what can you do about it? Well, first of all you need to realise that your new husband isn't *useless*. He's just very good at *acting* like he is. You need to lay down the rules of engagement from day one. *All* chores have to be divided up *equally*. And there's no playtime *until* all jobs have been done, to *your* satisfaction...

Gives a useful overview of content, tone and purpose

This is an entertaining piece of writing that pokes fun at the habits of young married males. Though humorous, the advice it offers has a serious side. The writer is advising young women to make sure that their husbands undertake their fair share of household duties.

The writer addresses the reader directly with the use of the second person pronoun *you* and the possessive adjective *your*. In this way, the writer forms a bond with the reader, as if there is a shared position on the issues that are being discussed.

Comments on how the reader is addressed and the effect this has

Starts to look at how men are represented

Men are portrayed as naturally inclined to idleness and shirking. For example, the adjective *crafty* suggests that they are devious. This is supported by the noun *ruse* which means trick. Similarly the verb phrase *reverting back* (*to his lazy single ways*) suggests that the traditional inclination of men is to think of themselves only.

Uses language frameworks — analyses the grammar

This has a helpful opening paragraph followed by a **systematic approach** to the material. The student starts to explore the **portrayal of men** using **linguistic frameworks**.

The rest of the essay could include further comment on **grammatical features** (such as the use of **modals** and **sentence types**), **phonological features** (use of italics to indicate **stress**, etc.), and **figurative language** (e.g. military term *rules of engagement*, suggesting marriage is like a **war**). If the rest of the essay was in the same sort of style it would get at least **32 marks** out of **40**.

WJEC Coursework

What the **Exam Board Wants**

The **WJEC** AS coursework is made up of two tasks:

See Section 2 (terminology and framework for analysis, p.18-35), and Section 6 (written language, purpose, genre and representation, p.76-85).

Section A — 1000 words plus 500 word commentary	Section B — 1500 words
Original Writing	**Exploring Spoken Language**
Has to be a piece of writing in a fictional, literary mode.	An analysis or comparison of the spoken language of the media.

See Section 4, (specifically p.56-59, language of the media), and Section 5 (spoken language features, p.68-71).

1) The point of the coursework is to make sure you can be creative **and** analytical.

2) You have to be able to **understand language** enough to write in a certain way (a literary, figurative way in this case), and also to **apply** what you know to a text you haven't written yourself.

3) You need to submit a **500 word commentary** alongside your **Original Writing** piece.

Check the coursework tasks with your teacher — there's a chance they might change.

Your **Original Writing** has to be **Literary Fiction**

The board specifically says that your original writing should be like a piece of **literary fiction**. So you **can't** submit a piece of writing that is a **factual** or **informative** article, or **poetry**. This still leaves you with options, though:

- A **short story** (up to 1000 words, obviously).
- An **extract** from a **novel** (e.g. crime, romance, sci-fi, horror, etc.).
- A text that **satirises** or **parodies** another text.
- A **script** (e.g. for radio, play, TV or film).
- A **dramatic monologue**.

You decide the **Genre** and **Target Audience**

In the writing process you should think about the following issues (see p.76-81) and **literary techniques** (p.23, 82-83).

Genre and target audience

1) **Genre** — the **conventions** and **language features** of the type of text you've chosen.

2) **Purpose** — what your text is trying to tell the audience and how it tries to get the message across.

3) **Writer** (or **narrative voice**) — how it's going to come across in relation to the **content** and the **reader**, and the ways that the reader is **influenced** by the **lexis**, **grammar**, **formality** and **tone** of your piece

4) **The Audience** — the target audience and how your chosen text should **address** them to achieve its aim.

To prepare for writing this text, you'll need to have a **thorough knowledge** of the genre you'll be writing in.

Section B is about **Media Language**

This task is quite specific — you have to analyse the **spoken language** of the **media**.

Spoken language in the media can include:

soap opera scripts	sports commentaries	radio phone-ins
chat shows / interviews	voice-overs / trailers	live comedy

You could write about **one form** of spoken media, or you could **compare** the features of **two or more similar texts**.

1) Don't forget the differences between **prepared** and **spontaneous spoken language** (p.70-71) — e.g. the differences between a **live sports commentary** or **interview**, and a **scripted** episode of a soap opera.

2) Think about how the language is **tailored** to suit the **target audience**. It might include **subject-specific lexis**, or more complex or simple **sentences** depending on who the text is aimed at.

Answers to Exam Questions

This answer section gives you some tips about what to include when you have a go at the sample exam questions at the end of sections three to seven. We haven't written entire essays (everyone writes essays differently), but these points are just suggestions for the kinds of things you should think about including in your answers.

Section Three — Varieties of English

Pages 44-45

1 The question asks you to compare and contrast the two extracts in terms of the varieties of English used. Here are some points you could make in your answer:

Text A — transcript of a conversation between three teenagers

Text B — extract from *Lady Windermere's Fan*

- In text A the speakers are a group of teenagers who are friends, so their sociolect is made up of informal, familiar language. This is shown by speaker A's use of the address term *mate*. Their language also includes a lot of slang words, like *minging*, *chucked* and *snogging*, and elision in words like *wanna* and *dunno*.

- Text B is an extract from a play script, so the language is more structured and contains fewer non-fluency features than the spontaneous speech in text A. In contrast to the speakers in text A, the characters in this extract use mostly Standard English, e.g. *It is an awfully dangerous thing*. The writer could have used this as a literary device to suggest that the characters are well-educated or upper-class. This is supported by the fact that some of the characters have titles, for example *Lord Augustus*.

- All the speakers in text A are clearly comfortable using non-standard varieties of English in the conversation, which suggests that it's taking place in a very informal context.

- You can tell that Text B is also supposed to be an informal conversation between friends because of the use of informal address terms like *my dear boy* and affectionate nicknames like *Tuppy* and *Dumby*.

- In text B, words like *hallo*, and modifiers like *awfully* and *perfectly* would have been considered informal at the time the play was written, although they seem quite formal to readers today.

- Text A contains dialect words like *nowt* and *mardy*, which suggest that the teenagers are speaking a regional dialect.

- It also contains non-standard grammar, which is a feature of regional dialects (*she didn't do nowt wrong*, *that don't even make sense*).

- Text B also contains some non-standard slang words like *demmed* and *monstrous*.

- The speakers in text A miss out the definite article *the* in constructions like *she was supposed to meet him at pub*. These two grammatical features are quite specific to the Yorkshire dialect, so this is probably where the speakers are from.

- Their language contains informal fillers, which are common in teenagers' language — e.g. *innit though right* and *like*.

- In text A, Speaker B's idiolect is evident in their use of *well* as an intensifier (*he's well fit*, *he can be well horrid*).

- Lord Augustus's idiolect in text B is evident in his use of ellipsis — he misses out the third person pronoun *she* in these clauses: *knows perfectly well what a demmed fool I am — knows it as well as I do myself*.

Section Four — Language in Social Contexts

Pages 64-67

1 **Conversation between a manager and two trainees**
The question asks you to analyse a spoken discourse between three people — a manager, a male trainee and a female trainee, in relation to the significance of gender in the interaction. Below are a list of language and gender issues that you should aim to cover in your answer:

- The function of the conversation is referential. The manager provides information and guidelines to the two trainees.

- The context is one where language reveals the power relations between the three speakers involved. The manager speaks the most, followed by the male trainee, then the female trainee. This shows that the manager is the dominant speaker in the conversation, and holds most of the power.

- The manager assumes control by virtue of their knowledge of how the shop operates and what is expected of the trainees. They use emphasis and repetition to reinforce this (*and I mean eight-thirty*). The manager also uses politeness strategies (*I'd like you to work*), in which the use of *I* personalises the manager's request, and probably makes it more likely to be respected by the trainees. The manager's speech also contains filled pauses like *erm* but this is more about creating time to think rather than being nervous.

- The male trainee is the more self-assured. He uses informal terms and slang (words like *cool*) and affirmatives like *sure* and *fine* to look for covert prestige. He asks questions and offers answers without being prompted. His informal language affects the amount of power the manager can assert.

- The male trainee also interrupts the manager at one point to talk about his work experience. This assumes control over the manager in the conversation, and suggests that he's a lot more confident than the female trainee. He offers the female trainee a lift to work, assuming a responsible / controlling role.

- In contrast, the female trainee is less self-assured. She hesitates and aims for overt prestige by using fillers like *yes* rather than *yeh*. Her filled pauses show that she is nervous. Her responses are more submissive, with back-channel noises like *mm*. When she attempts to explain her travel issues she is interrupted by the male trainee.

- Of the two trainees, the male is more dominant than the female. This seems to support Lakoff's deficit model.

- The role of the manager doesn't follow any traditional stereotypes, but their language use displays a lot of sexism, e.g. *growing lad like you*, *don't worry sweetheart*, and *little miss efficient*. This is patronising to the female trainee in particular.

- The lexical field relates to the service industry (*tills*) and working routines (*breaktimes*, *lunch time* and *eight-thirty*).

2 **Transcript of a Chemistry lesson**
This question asks you to look at power relationships. Here are some points you could include in your answer:

- The text takes place in a school classroom, so the environment is immediately more formal than that of a conversation between friends. The context means that there is an acknowledged leader of the interactions, the teacher, who you would expect to be the dominant speaker.

- The power relationships in this extract are most apparent in the address terms used by the speakers. The pupils address the teacher as *sir*, a sign of respect, while the teacher addresses them using their first names (*James, Tash*). This shows that he is the authority figure.

- The teacher also shows his authority by using imperatives (*settle down, keep ties on*). As a politeness strategy, some orders are given as questions, but in the context of the school lesson the pupils understand that they're not supposed to respond and they don't have a choice, for example *can we turn to what we were doing last week*.

- The teacher uses direct questions (*what is it that happens to atoms*) to elicit a response from the pupils. He also uses the first person plural pronoun *we* to include them, and as an invitation that any of them can respond to his questions. This is common in educational sociolect. When no-one volunteers to answer, he directs questions at individuals to force them to respond (*what do they form (3.0) James*).

- In contrast the pupils use indirect questions to show respect (*sorry but erm (.) it's really hot in here sir (.) please may I*). This apologetic request to open the window involves lots of hedging, fillers, and false starts, which show that the pupil is uncomfortable about having to ask. The teacher's power is evident in his response — he uses the brief imperative *well open the window*.

- Power structures between the pupils are evident in their interaction. They try to act as a powerful group against the teacher — when one interrupts they all join in to disrupt the conversation as much as possible.

- However, it seems like pupil B is more disruptive than the other speakers, as he or she waits until someone else speaks before interrupting in to add an expression like *yeah*, or a non-standard phrase like *no one remembers nothing about this*.

- Pupils A and D seem more hesitant, although A is quite assertive at first when he or she interrupts the teacher to say *page ten*. However pupil A stumbles over language, e.g. *they don't (.) they don't* when put on the spot. Pupil D appears the least powerful, making a hesitant request to open the window starting with an apology *sorry*.

- The teacher controls the discourse even though the pupils try to assert power by interrupting him and shifting the focus of the conversation. He uses repetition to bring it back to the subject he wants to discuss, e.g. by repeating *what happens to atoms*. Both pupil B and the teacher use tag questions to encourage the other to agree, (*didn't we, does it now*). These are used rhetorically to support their argument and force the other to agree.

3   Chatroom conversation between two friends

This question asks you to think about the impact of technology on the language used by two friends in a chatroom. Here are some points you could include in your answer:

- The function of the chatroom conversation is mostly interactional, but it also has referential elements in which the speakers exchange information.

- As they're friends, and because they're talking in a chatroom, the speakers communicate very informally, using slang like *cool* and *dosh*.

- Technology has had a big impact on the language they use, stemming from a need to communicate quickly e.g. dropping vowels from words like *hw* (how), *havnt*, or *yr* (year) and having relatively limited options on a keyboard compared to spoken language). They use different typefaces from each other so that it will be easier to distinguish one participant in the conversation from the other.

- They use a range of linguistic features: phonetic spelling (*newayz*), non-standard use of punctuation marks, numbers for sounds (*l8tr*), numbers for words (*love 2*), phonetic spelling (*Cud do. Wat time*), emoticons (:'-(),symbols (*be ther @ 8*), upper case (*BRILL*).

- Sentences are often shortened and function words omitted (*hey rosie hw u doin?*).

- The conversation contains many of the features found in spoken interaction: an opening and closing sequence, adjacency pairs, turn-taking, question and answer and topic shifts (boyfriends, college, plans for the evening).

- Chatroom interaction is less spontaneous than regular conversation, e.g. one participant has plenty of time to decide if she wants to accept the other's invitation before replying.

4   Charity website fundraising article

The question asks you how the text influences the reader, so you could structure your response around the list of features on p.58:

- **Lexis** — This advert uses the well-known collocation *Tea Time*. This has connotations of family and friends getting together and relaxing, so it suggests inclusivity and should conjure up a nice image for the reader. An inclusive feeling is also created by the use of phrases like *get together* and *everyone is invited*. The language is quite informal, so the tone is friendly, which adds to this effect: *your best pals and a cracked old tea pot*.

- **Grammar and Pragmatics** — The text includes declaratives, which assume that the audience already agree with a shared truth: *it's hard to beat a nice cup of tea*. It also contains imperatives (*order your free event pack now*) and interrogatives (*what is Tea Time?*) to engage the reader. The use of the second person pronoun *you* (*you can host your Tea Time anywhere you like*) directly addresses the reader, while the first person plural pronoun *we* adds to the inclusive effect.

- **Phonology** — The alliteration in *Tea Time* makes the hook more catchy and memorable. This is added to at the end of the advert in the alliterative phrase *we'll talk Tea Time*.

- **Graphology** — The header *Tea Time* is in large, bold letters to make it stand out to the reader. There is a separate box for the key message that *absolutely everyone is invited*.

- **Graphology** — The links that the reader can click on for more information are separated from the main body of the text by bullet points, which encourages them to follow them.

- **Discourse** — The discourse structure is typical of many adverts — hook (*Tea Time*), further persuasion (*helping people, irrespective of religion, to tackle the problems they face*), instruction (*order your free event pack now*).

- **Discourse** — The main body of the text is structured using discourse markers. These are often interrogatives, which encourage the reader to read on and find out the answer (*what's it all for?*).

Answers to Exam Questions

5   **Conversation between two mechanics and a customer**
The question focuses on the use of language in occupational groups, so your answer should concentrate on the language used by A and B (the mechanics) as they interact. You should also focus on how their language excludes the customer. Here are some points you could make in your answer:

- The lexis is informal and colloquial, as expected in spontaneous speech (*we've had a bit of a problem with it really*). A and B use more formal language with the customer than they do with each other, e.g. A uses a less direct request with the customer: *if you'd just like to come through here*, than is used with B: *do you want to take him through to have a look*.

- It is a cooperative interaction, with feedback features and turn-taking. However, there's an obvious hierarchy between the speakers, which is often evident in language of the workplace. A appears to be in authority over B — A addresses him with his first name a lot: *have a look at the v5 Greg*, also using an imperative in this example. A invites B to take control, but then speaks for him, which suggests that A is in charge.

- The lexical field contains references to cars and specific car parts (*two point five diesel*, *MAF*, *rev limiter*). Much of the lexis is context-specific jargon — it's referential and deictic (*that* *coupe*). This is a quick, efficient way for A and B to communicate.

- The problem with A and B's jargon is that the customer is left behind and hardly figures in the conversation, other than when invited to answer questions. It's clear from the customer's use of fillers, hedging and pauses that they don't really understand. Rather than explaining the jargon, A uses this to avoid having to answer the question of when the car will be finished, simply replying *a bit of Forté will do it*.

Section Five — Analysing Spoken Language
Pages 74-75

1   The question asks you to analyse and compare the three source texts. Here are some features of each text that you might want to consider and use to contrast the texts in your essay:

Text A — conversation between a customer and newsagent

- The conversation has a transactional function — one speaker wants to buy a paper and find some odd jobs for his grandson. This can be seen from the fact that most utterances are either suggestions, questions or responses.

- The conversation contains features of informal, spontaneous speech, including dialect expressions (*now then*), slang (*cheers*, *mate*), ellipsis (*bit late delivering*), elision (*gonna*) and non-fluency features (*he's gonna need some er some work you see (.) while he's (.) but he doesn't drive*).

- It also contains deictic expressions that could only be understood in the specific context of the conversation (*I can put it up there with the others on the board over there*).

- The speakers use adjacency pairs and turn-taking rules, but there are also non-fluency features like self-corrections, false starts and hedging, which are common in spontaneous speech, e.g. *anyone in the village who might need (.) need a bit of work done*. They repeat each other a lot, which suggests they are in agreement.

- The speakers are on first name terms and use phatic conversation (*now then*, *comes round quick*) before B changes the subject. The control of the conversation mostly lies with A, as B is asking for information. B's speech contains pauses, fillers and hedging, as if he feels uncomfortable about asking for help, and so it might be a politeness strategy.

- In contrast, speaker A appears more confident, e.g. using the imperatives *write his name* and the phrase *tell you what*.

Text B — extract from a job interview

- The interviewer is overtly in charge straight away, opening the conversation with a rhetorical question and then an imperative (*come in, have a seat*). Taking control immediately sets the interviewer apart from the candidate who false starts straight away (*that's ri- (2.0) oh right*). This unequal power relationship continues throughout the interview as the interviewer regularly interrupts the candidate.

- An interview situation is always very formal despite being spontaneous speech — there aren't many contractions and there aren't any colloquialisms or non-standard grammatical features.

- The interviewer does give the candidate feedback and some back-channelling (*mmm-hmm*) to try and put them more at ease. They also let the candidate know when to speak by asking tag questions at the end of their utterances (*did you?*).

- There isn't much informal language in this extract. The language is standard English. There are some non-fluency features on the part of the candidate as they try to process the question and then answer it after being 'put on the spot' by the interviewer.

Text C — speech by a company director to company employees

- This is an official prepared speech, so it uses standard language and grammar throughout and is mostly very formal. The speaker has immediate prestige.

- The main content of the speech — the redundancy payments — is framed between two emotive apologies. This discourse structure shows that the speaker is delivering news that will directly affect the audience and has obviously been pre-planned with the delivery worked out in advance.

- Despite this, there is the occasional non-fluency feature and repetition of *I* and *can*. Most likely this is due to the awkward content of the speech, rather than any informality on the speaker's behalf.

- The speaker tries to appear as personable as possible by using collective addresses such as *you* and *hold our place*. This is also evident in the emotive language, such as *hurts* and *valued*, and the apologies that are repeated.

- The content is also emphasised by prosodic features as the underlined words like *no way* and *can't avoid* would be stressed in the actual delivery of the speech.

Section Six — Analysing Written Language
Pages 86-87

1   The question asks you to give various ways that texts A to E can be grouped. The texts are listed below with some of the linguistic features that you should try and focus on when comparing the texts and grouping them together.

Text A — Novel Extract — *The Way of All Flesh*

- **Purpose** — to entertain.

- **Audience** — readers of 19th century literature, and later students of English literature.

- **Genre** — literature, novel.

- **Register** — formal.

- **Lexis** — example of 19th century vocabulary, e.g. *disposition, confinement, Nemesis*.

Answers to Exam Questions

- **Lexis** — references to context by use of *1750, George... reigning majesty.*
- **Grammar** — complex sentences throughout.
- **Grammar** — use of parentheses and semicolons (also complex).
- **Tone** — serious yet with humorous undertones e.g. *who though she loved no one else in the world except her husband (and him only after a fashion).*
- **Narrator** — third person who interjects own personal views, e.g. *to the best of my belief* into narrative.
- **Representation** — depicts a strong woman (abusing the doctor and ignoring advice), though this also makes her seem ignorant when she is in fact pregnant.
- **Representation** — Her apparent inability to have children was considered a *hopeless case,* which reflects the domestic roles of women (i.e. producing children) at the time Butler was writing.

Text B — Film Review — *Sex and the City*

- **Purpose** — to inform / entertain
- **Audience** — predominantly female (*girlish excitement*), those familiar with the TV series as the characters are mentioned by their first names.
- **Genre** — journalism, newspaper, review / critique
- **Register** —mostly standard English but the inclusive first person plural pronoun *we* adds to the chattiness / informality.
- **Lexis** — plenty of figurative language and lots of alliteration, e.g. *clique's curse, walk-in wardrobe, labels and love.*
- **Lexis** — field specific to the fashion industry, e.g. *Vogue, Louis Vuitton, Vivienne Westwood.*
- **Grammar** — mainly compound sentences, lots of punctuation to break up statements and make text less complex. Short paragraphs spread the content out over the page.
- **Narrator** — very subjective, giving opinions and displaying attitudes that the reader is expected to share, e.g. *just as we hoped.*
- **Representation** — represents film audience as females who might be attracted by the fashion labels mentioned (e.g. *coos of admiration*). Females in general are the focus of the review. This gives a certain representation of men as outside the text, and male characters in the film are only mentioned as props to the central characters' relationships.
- The cultural context is also represented by the author making the point that despite capitalism being very prevalent in the film it doesn't necessarily make the characters' lives better when they get what they want materially.

Text C — A web page for an educational childrens' club

- **Purpose** — to persuade.
- **Audience** — parents of young children.
- **Genre** — advertising.
- **Register** — formal.
- **Graphology** — lots of information in a small space, links to different parts of the website in frame and borders, separated by headings and bullet points. Stand-out link to *Join now.*
- **Graphology** — pictures to support information and act as persuasive images for parents / potential customers.
- **Graphology** — Logo for name of company indicates professionalism.
- **Lexis** — emphasises achievement and success, e.g. *learning skills, confidence, respect, invaluable experience.*

- **Grammar** — imperatives: *Realise your child's potential — Join in now.*

Source D — Entry form for a caption competition

- **Purpose** — to instruct.
- **Audience** — prospective competition entrants.
- **Genre** — entry form.
- **Graphology** — businesslike, with brief, essential text. Bold headings for sections that need to be filled in.
- **Grammar** — imperative sentences, e.g. *See over for Terms and Conditions*, *Send your entries to*.
- **Lexis** — no figurative or rhetorical language, only standard vocabulary and grammar.

Text E — self-diagnosis booklet

- **Purpose** — to inform and instruct.
- **Audience** — adults concerned about health, specifically insomnia sufferers.
- **Genre** — medical, self-help.
- **Register** — formal.
- **Graphology** — headings to highlight subjects being discussed, e.g. *Transient Insomnia.*
- **Graphology** — short sentences and short paragraphs, so as not to overload the audience with information.
- **Lexis** — specialist medical terminology e.g. *chronic, symptom, depression.*
- **Tone** — reassuring, explains symptoms and treatment so the reader feels they have nothing to worry about.
- **Grammar** — use of second person *you* e.g. *you can take some measures*, to include the reader.

Section Seven — Language Development
Pages 102-103

OCR style question.

1   These are some of the features your answer could include:

- The baby-sitter encourages Reuben to engage in the activity by using questions. At first she frames this as a shared activity with the use of the first person plural pronoun *we*. But this changes to the second person pronoun *you* as she transfers responsibility for the activity to Reuben.
- The use of a tag question (*you're very good, aren't you?*) and gentle instructions (*let's try this one*) help to encourage Reuben to interact as well as giving him positive feedback. Positive feedback is also shown through exaggerated stress, such as on the adjective *GREAT*.
- The stress and repetition used by the baby-sitter to engage Reuben are typical of child-directed speech, e.g. *you're very GOOD aren't you.*
- Reuben responds to questions and offers explanations without having to be corrected, showing that he has some grasp of participating in conversations in a more adult manner.
- Reuben's speech sometimes seems like an inner monologue. This ties in with Vygotsky's socio-cultural theory. Reuben is displaying signs of private speech, showing that his mental development is still progressing (*it's gonna be finished when granma's here*).
- Reuben displays phonological features typical of a three-year-old, for example, substituting consonants in the pronunciation of *picgi* (piggy), *dat* (that), and *tickie* (dickie), and also assimilation in *waw* (wall).

Answers to Exam Questions

- Reuben is experimenting with the use of demonstrative pronouns (*these / those*), is able to form compound sentences (*you do dat and then you dat*) but sometimes words are omitted, or word combinations are inverted, e.g. *is it too hard* rather than *it is too hard*.

AQA A style question.

1 a) Your answer should try to pick out and expand upon 5 features across the following areas:

- **Pragmatics** — Annie's grandfather engages her by using interrogatives, tag questions and imperatives e.g. *they're nice wellies, aren't they*.
- **Grammar** — Annie leaves out function words, making two word and telegraphic utterances (*like walk, nice welli, they naugh'y*). At one point she over-generalises when she creates a new adjective *barky* based on the way that *noisy* is formed.
- **Lexis** — Annie uses a range of adjectives (*nice, noisy, naugh'y*) and key verbs such as *like*.
- **Phonology** — Annie substitutes consonants (e.g. *wed* into *red*), omits consonants (*naugh'y* instead of *naughty*) and reduces difficult consonant clusters (e.g. *Co'a* for *Costa*).

b) The question asks you to assess the strengths and weaknesses of the imitation theory. You should aim to cover the following points, giving linguistic examples.

- Imitation theory was suggested by Skinner (1957).
- The main idea is that children repeat what they hear, caregivers reward them with praise and correct mistakes, and this is how children learn language.
- Behaviourism suggests that children also learn complex pronunciations and grammatical rules by imitating those around them.
- Children gradually build up the complexity of their language through this system of imitation, repetition and feedback.
- Child-directed speech would appear to be a part of the imitation theory. Caregivers repeat certain features to extend a child's linguistic development, such as questions and imperatives.
- Caregivers also expand on a child's utterances and re-cast what they've said to continue the interaction in a different way.

Once you've explained the theory in relation to language acquisition, you should also discuss some of the problems:

- Over-generalisations suggest that children experiment with using grammatical rules and sometimes get things wrong. This couldn't happen if imitation was solely responsible for language acquisition as children wouldn't hear these kinds of incorrect statements from adults.
- Berko's (1958) Wug Test suggests the same thing by proving that children internalise grammatical rules.
- Berko and Brown's (1960) discussion of the *fis* phenomenon also creates problems for the imitation theory, as children can understand more sounds and words than they can imitate.
- Katamba (1996) found little connection between frequency of inflections being used (from Brown 1973) and the order in which they're acquired. If imitation were the only way of acquiring language, it's likely the most frequently used would be acquired earliest.
- Children can construct sentences that they've never heard before, and they don't memorise thousands of sentences.
- Child-directed speech has not been proven to have any effect on language development, as parents in some cultures don't use it at all.

You could finish by suggesting that language acquisition may be the result of a mixture of different processes — including imitation — but also Chomsky's innateness theory, Piaget's cognitive theory, Bruner and the LASS, Lenneberg's Critical Period Hypothesis and Vygotsky's zone of proximal development. Whilst imitation probably plays some part in language acquisition, it's not the only thing involved.

2 a) You might comment on the following features (you need to pick 5 to talk about):

- **Spelling** — intrusion of letters as the child is getting to grips with spelling patterns (*whanted, aloan*), omission of letters, especially double letters (*sudenly, realy*), some letters are back to front in the original text.
- **Phonological spelling** — e.g. *tole, russling, nufin, makin, behine, wuz*.
- **Graphology** — lack of spacing between words (*Iwas, inthe*) and non-standard capitalisation (*Bushes, Home*).
- **Grammar** — omission of preposition *in* (*was russling [in] the bushes*). Indirect speech (*He said it wuz him in the bushes*).
- **Lexis** — use of adjectives like *scary* and *darc* to create atmosphere. Repetition of *ran* for dramatic effect.
- **Discourse** — narrative continuity helped by the use of the adverb *sudenly* and the subordinate clause *When I got Home* positioned at the beginning of the sentence.

b) The question asks you to look at the stages a child goes through as they develop the skills they need to be able to write. It's probably best to work through the stages in order, so your answer should be organised something like this:

- At pre-school age, children begin to develop the physical skills needed for writing through drawing — this normally consists of scribbling on paper and gaining some initial coordination with a pen or pencil.
- At first they create pseudo-letters, in no particular pattern. Teachers and caregivers encourage their experimentation, by getting children to draw lines and shapes to build up their coordination even more.
- Children can imitate writing e.g. they can copy their own name if it's written out by a teacher or caregiver first.
- They start to write consonants to represent entire word (usually the letter that the word starts with), then combine consonants that sound like whole words (like *sm* for *some*).
- Eventually children begin to combine vowels and consonants in more recognisable ways, and then develop the ability to organise words and letters so that they represent the correct number of syllables (e.g. *sleping*, or *sudenly*). The last step is the process of getting to grips with English spelling patterns.
- The length of time this takes depends on the individual child. In general, aged around 5-6, they can create some letters and words accurately and are encouraged to experiment with different writing activities, in school and at home, like writing a shopping list.
- At age 6-7, they start to develop punctuation in their written English, and are encouraged to write about things of personal interests like their family, or what they did at the weekend.
- Aged 7-8, children begin to write for different purposes and audiences, and experiment with producing different kinds of texts in a range of different styles.

Glossary

abstract noun A **noun** that refers to a concept, state, quality or emotion.

accent The distinctive way a speaker from a particular region pronounces words.

acronym A new word made from the initial letters of all the words in a name or **phrase**, e.g. NASA.

active voice When the **subject** of the sentence is directly performing the **verb** e.g. *Steve burst the bubble.*

adjective A class of words that can appear before (attributive) or after (predicative) a **noun** to describe it.

adverb A class of words that modify **verbs** according to time, place, manner, frequency, duration or degree. They can sometimes modify nouns and adjectives too.

affixation The process of adding an affix before (**prefix**) or after (**suffix**) an existing word to change either its meaning or grammatical function.

alliteration When two or more words close to each other in a **phrase** begin with the same sound, e.g. *down in the dumps.*

anaphoric reference When a word, usually a pronoun, refers back to something or someone that has already been mentioned, e.g. *Barrie can't come because he's ill.*

antithesis Type of **rhetorical language** where contrasting ideas or words are balanced against each other, e.g. *it's just too good from Green, and just too bad for the goalkeeper.*

antonyms Words with opposite meanings.

article A kind of **determiner** that shows if the reference to a **noun** is general (*a / an*) or specific (*the*).

aspect A **verb's** aspect shows whether the action it refers to is already completed, or if it is still taking place.

assimilation When sounds next to each other in a spoken word or **sentence** are pronounced in a different way to normal to make them easier to say.

assonance When the main vowel sounds of two or more words that are close together in a text are similar or the same, e.g. *low smoky holes.*

audience A person or group of people that read, view or listen to a text. A writer or speaker can aim to reach a certain type of audience by using specific literary techniques and language choices.

auxiliary verbs Verbs used before the **main verb** in a sentence to give extra information about it, e.g. *I have seen him.*

babbling The production of short vowel / consonant combinations by a baby acquiring language.

back-channelling A kind of **feedback** in spoken language that supports the person speaking and shows that what is being said is understood.

behaviourism A theory of language acquisition that suggests children learn language through a process of imitation and reinforcement.

blending When parts of two words are combined to make a new one, e.g. *netizen.*

buzz words Words that are fashionable in a particular occupational group.

cataphora A reference in a text to something that follows in later **phrases** or **sentences**, e.g. *These are the directions...*

characterisation The way that a writer conveys information about a character relating to their appearance, speech, etc.

child-directed speech (CDS) The way that caregivers talk to children — usually in simplified and / or exaggerated language.

clause The simplest meaningful unit of a **sentence**.

cliché An expression that has lost its novelty value due to being overused.

clipping When a shortened version of a word becomes a word in its own right, e.g. *demo, phone.*

cognitive theory A theory of language acquisition that suggests children need to have acquired certain mental abilities before they can acquire language.

cohesion The linking of ideas in texts to ensure the text makes sense.

coining The general term for creating new words.

collective noun A **noun** that refers to a group of people, animals or things, e.g. *team.*

collocation Words that commonly appear together in order, in specific lexical units, e.g. *done and dusted.*

common noun A **noun** that refers to a class of things or a concept. Every noun is a common noun except those that refer to unique things, e.g. the names of particular people or places.

comparative An **adjective** that makes a degree of comparison, normally by adding an *-er* **suffix**, e.g. *faster.*

complement A word or **phrase** that gives more information about the **subject** or **object** in a sentence, e.g. *the boy is actually a cow.*

compound A new word created by combining two or more existing words, e.g. *a skyscraper.*

concrete noun A **noun** that refers to things you can physically touch or see, e.g. *chair.*

conjunction A linking word that connects **phrases** and **clauses** to each other to form **sentences**, e.g. *but.*

connotation The associations that are made with a particular word.

context The circumstances that surround a word, **phrase** or text, e.g. time and place produced, intended audience.

conversion When a word becomes part of a different **word class** in addition to its original sense (e.g. *text* is now both a **noun** and a **verb**).

cooing The earliest sounds children are able to make as they experiment with moving their lips and tongue.

coordinate clause An independent **clause** that's linked to another independent **clause** in the same **sentence**.

count noun Nouns that can be preceded by a number and counted, e.g. *one book, two books* etc.

critical period hypothesis A theory popularised by Lenneberg (1967), which states that if a child does not have any linguistic interaction before the ages of 5-6, their linguistic development will be severely limited.

declarative sentence A **sentence** that makes a statement to give information, e.g. *she enjoyed her scampi.*

deixis A reference to something outside of the text or conversation (e.g. location, time) that can't be understood unless you know the **context**.

demonstratives Words that refer to specific objects that only those involved in the discourse can see. They can be **pronouns**, e.g. *I like this*, or **adjectives**, e.g. *I like this bike.*

denotation The literal meaning of a word.

determiner A word that goes before a **noun** to give information about it, e.g. to show possession or number (*his, two*).

dialect The distinctive **lexis**, **grammar** and pronunciation of a person's spoken English, usually affected by the region they're from and their social background.

dialogue Any exchange between two or more characters or speakers.

Glossary

difference model Tannen's (1990) theory about gender and conversation which states that men and women have different objectives when they interact.

discourse An extended piece of written or spoken language.

dominance model Zimmerman and West's (1975) theory that gender differences in conversations are due to male dominance in society.

double negative When negatives are used twice in a phrase, e.g. *I didn't do nothing*.

egocentric The early mental state of a child in which they can only understand things existing in relation to themselves, i.e. things they can see or touch, etc.

elision When sounds or **syllables** are slurred together in speech to make pronunciation easier and quicker.

ellipsis When part of a grammatical structure is left out of the **sentence** without affecting the meaning.

Estuary English An **accent** that was originally from the Thames Estuary area in London but is now heard outside the area and may be replacing RP as the country's most widespread form.

euphemism A word or phrase that is used as a substitute for harsher or more unpleasant sounding words or concepts.

exclamative A **sentence** that has an expressive function and ends with an exclamation mark.

exophoric reference Referring to something outside a text, e.g. *that* tree over *there*.

feedback Verbal and **non-verbal** signs that a person is listening to a speaker.

figurative language Language that is used in a non-literal way to create images and form comparisons, e.g. metaphor.

filler A sound produced by speakers to keep a conversation going and avoid silence, e.g. *mm*.

genre A group of texts with a particular form or purpose, e.g. letters, poems, adverts.

grammar The system of rules that govern how **words**, **clauses** and **sentences** are put together.

grapheme The smallest unit of writing that can create contrasts in meaning, e.g. individual letters or symbols.

graphology The study of the appearance of a text, how it looks on the page and how the layout helps get the meaning across.

head word A word that has the same grammatical function as the **phrase** that has been built around it, e.g. in a noun phrase, the head word is a **noun**.

hedging Word choices that show uncertainty in conversations, e.g. *probably, maybe*.

holophrases In language acquisition, single words that express a complete idea, e.g. *ball*, which could mean the child wants it, or has found it, etc. Caregivers need contextual clues to interpret them.

hyperbole When exaggeration is used for effect.

hypernym A general word that is a term for many **hyponyms**, e.g. *vehicle* is a hypernym of *car, bus, lorry*, etc.

hyponym A word that refers to a specific type of a **hypernym**, e.g. *car, bus, lorry* are hyponyms of *vehicle*.

ideology A set of ideas and beliefs.

idiolect An individual's **accent** and **dialect** features, which are a result of their personal upbringing and experiences.

imagery Describing something in a way that creates a picture of it in the audience's mind.

imperative A **sentence** that gives orders, advice or directions. It starts with a **main verb** and doesn't have a **subject**.

implication When a meaning is suggested, rather than explicitly described.

infinitive The base form of a **verb**, preceded by *to*.

inflection An **affix** that is attached to a base word and gives extra information about it, e.g. its tense or person.

internalisation When a child learning language starts to apply one of the language's rules consistently, even to words they've never seen before.

interrogative A sentence or utterance that asks a question.

intertextuality When a text makes reference to another existing text for effect.

intonation The pitch of a speaker's voice, e.g. rising intonation shows it's a question.

jargon Specialist words that are used by a particular social or occupational group that may not be understood by a non-member.

juxtaposition Positioning words, ideas or images next to each other in a text to create certain effects.

language acquisition device (LAD) The innate ability of children acquiring language to take in and use the grammatical rules of the language they hear where they live, according to Chomsky (1965).

language acquisition support system (LASS) The system of support from caregivers to children that helps them to acquire language and become sociable, according to Bruner (1983).

lexical field A group of words that relate to the same topic, e.g. *hotel* and *destination* are in the lexical field of travel.

lexis A general term for the words of a language.

liaison When a consonant is pronounced between words or **syllables** to make them run together.

loan words Words that are taken from other languages.

main verbs Words that identify the action of a **sentence**.

management speak A way of communicating in the workplace designed to sound up-to-date and formal, but usually overly complex.

mass noun A **Noun** that can't be counted and doesn't have a plural, e.g. *information*.

metaphor Words or phrases that describe something as if it actually was something else, e.g. *the heart of the matter*.

metonymy Using a part of something, or one of its attributes, to describe the whole thing, e.g. *the press* to refer to journalists and the news industry.

modal auxiliary verbs Verbs that give more information about the **main verb**, but can't occur as main verbs themselves, e.g. *can, will*.

mode A way of classifying texts (e.g. written or spoken or a combination of different media).

monologue The utterances of one speaker or performer to an audience.

monosyllabic Words with only one **syllable**.

morpheme The individual meaningful units that make up words (although they don't always make sense on their own).

morphology The study of the internal structure of words.

multimodal text A text that involves elements of different **modes**, e.g. text messages are a mixture of written and spoken language.

Glossary

narrative voice The point of view a text is written from, e.g. a first person narrator tells the story from their personal point of view.

neologisms New words that enter a language.

non-verbal communication Using gestures, expressions and body language to communicate instead of or as well as words.

noun A word used as the name of a person, place, thing or concept.

object The part of the **sentence** that the **verb** acts upon, e.g. in *I broke a plate*, the plate is the object and ends up *broken*.

onomatopoeia A word that sounds like the noise it's describing.

overextension When a child acquiring language uses a word too generally to refer to different but related things, e.g. calling everything with four legs a *dog*.

oxymoron A phrase that brings two conflicting ideas together, e.g. *bittersweet*.

parallelism The repetition of structural features in a sentence or throughout a text, e.g. repeated use of the past tense in a sentence — *he came home, ran upstairs and jumped in the bath*.

parody Subverting traditional expectations of a text's features to produce humour or satire.

passive voice When the **object** of the verb is described first, rather than the **subject** (e.g. *the bubble was burst by Steve*).

personification When an object, concept or situation is given human qualities.

phatic language Expressions that have a sociable function rather than expressing serious meaning, e.g. *hello*.

phoneme The smallest unit of sound that can create a contrast in meaning.

phonology The study of the sound systems of languages, in particular the patterns of sounds.

phrase A meaningful unit of language built around a **head word**.

polysyllabic Words with more than one **syllable**.

post-modifier Words that come after the **head word** in a **phrase**, that tell you something about it.

pragmatics The study of how language functions in social situations.

pre-modifier Words used before the head word of a **phrase** (often **determiner** + **adjective**) that tell you something about it.

prefix An **affix** that comes before the base form, e.g. *unfortunate*.

preposition A word that defines the relationship between words in terms of time, space or direction, e.g. *the toy was in the box*, *he's behind you*.

primary auxiliary verbs **Auxiliary verbs** that can also occur as **main verbs** (*do*, *be* and *have*).

pronoun A word that can take the place of a **noun**, e.g. *he, she, it*.

proper noun A **noun** that is the name of a specific person, place or brand.

prosody **Non-verbal** aspects of speech like pace, stress, pitch, intonation, volume and pauses.

proto-word A combination of sounds that a child uses that actually contains meaning, rather than just being a random utterance like **cooing** or **babbling**.

pun Replacing a word or phrase with one that sounds the same or similar for creative or humorous effect.

Received Pronunciation An **accent** traditionally associated with educated people and the upper class. It's characterised by lots of long vowels and the pronunciation of /h/ and /t/ in words where people with regional accents might leave them out.

referential language Spoken language that gives information by referring to objects or concepts. It usually only makes sense if the listener understands the **context**, e.g. *the vase is over there*.

register A type of language that's appropriate for a particular audience or situation, e.g. formal language is appropriate for a political speech.

rhetorical language Language with phonological or structural features used to provide extra effects or meanings.

semantics The study of how the meanings of words are created and interpreted.

sentence An independent grammatical unit made up of one or more **clauses**.

similes Comparisons that use the words *like* or *as*.

simplification When a child learning to speak drops consonants or consonant clusters to make words easier to pronounce, or swaps the consonants for others that are easier to pronounce.

slang Informal, non-standard vocabulary usually used in casual speech.

sociolect A variety of language used by a particular social group.

Standard English A **dialect** of English considered 'correct' and 'normal', because it has distinctive and standardised features of spelling, vocabulary and **syntax**. It's the form of English usually used in formal writing.

sub-genre A group of similar texts that create a complete **genre**, e.g. tragedy and comedy are types of drama.

subject The focus of a **sentence** — the person or thing that performs the action described by the **verb**, e.g. *Billy ate a sandwich*.

subordinate clause A **clause** that gives extra information about the main clause, but can't stand alone and still make sense.

subtext The implied meaning behind what's actually being said or described.

suffix An **affix** that comes after the base form, e.g. *sadness*.

superlative An **adjective** that states the **noun** it's describing is beyond comparison, usually by adding *-est*, e.g. *fastest*.

syllables A word's individual units of pronunciation.

symbolism When a word or phrase represents something other than its literal meaning.

synonyms Words that have similar meanings.

syntax The order and structure of sentences.

tag question A question added to the end of a statement to encourage a response, e.g. *don't you think so?*

telegraphic stage The stage of language acquisition at which children begin to create three- or four-word utterances containing mainly subjects, verbs, objects and complements.

tense Grammatical **inflections** on verbs that show the time an action took place, e.g. in the past or present.

transactional language Spoken exchanges aimed at making some sort of deal.

turn-taking A feature of orderly conversations when the chance to speak switches back and forth between participants.

underextension When a child uses words in a very restricted way, e.g. using one word like *hat* to refer only to the one the child is wearing.

verb A class of words that describe the action or state that a **sentence** refers to.

word classes How words are categorised according to the function they can perform in a **sentence**.

Index

A

abbreviations 19
accent 36-37, 39
acronyms 54-55
adjectives 4, 7
  attributive 7
  comparative 7
  demonstrative 10
  possessive 10
  predicative 7
  superlative 5, 7, 58
adverbs 4, 9
adverts 58-59
affixation 16-17, 55
  derivational 16-17
  inflectional 17
Aitchison (1987) 92
alliteration 25, 58, 60, 83
ambiguity 20, 85
anaphoric references 28
antithesis 56, 83
antonyms 21
AQA A
  coursework 107
  exam 106
  sample question 106
AQA B
  coursework 109
  exam 108
  sample question 108
articles 5, 10
articulation 24
ascenders 32
aspect 9
assimilation 25
assonance 25
audience 2, 14, 30, 34, 58-59,
  70, 79

B

babbling 88
back-channelling 71
Beattie (1982) 47
Berko (1958) 94
  and Brown (1960) 90
bias 56, 84-85
blending 55
body language 27
broadsheets 14, 19, 57
Brown (1973) 94
Bruner (1983) 97
buzz words 63

C

Cameron (2007) 46-47
cataphoric references 28
characterisation 83
Cheshire (1982) 46
child-directed speech (CDS) 100
Chomsky (1965) 96
clauses 12-13
  combining 13
  conditional 61
  coordinate 13-14
  independent 13-14
  main 13-14
  subordinate 13-14, 50, 56-57
cliché 22
clipping 55
cognitive theory 96
cohesion 3, 28-29
cohesive device 11
coining 17
collocation 29
commentaries 77, 105
comparatives 58
complements 12-13
compound words 18, 58
compounding 55
conjunctions 4, 11-12, 28, 56
  coordinating 11, 14
  subordinating 11, 14
connotation 20, 57
consonants 6, 24-25, 88, 90, 99
context 23, 27, 30, 34, 48-51, 55,
  68, 71, 77, 84
continuum classification 35
conversation 72-73, 79
conversational strategies 51
conversion 18, 55
cooing 88
critical period hypothesis 97
Cruttenden (1979) 94
  (1985) 90

D

DeCasper and Spence (1986) 88
declaratives 58
deictic expressions 71, 101
denotation 20, 57
descenders 32
determiners 4, 6, 10, 28
dialect 19, 36-38, 40, 79
dialogue 54, 82-83
difference model 47
discourse 2-3, 5, 11, 34, 58, 61, 70,
  79

dissonance 25
dominance model 47
double meanings 23
double negatives 70

E

echoing 27
Edexcel
  coursework 111
  exam 110
  sample question 110
education 38, 50, 85
egocentricity 96
elision 71
ellipsis 71
emoticons 54
entertainment texts 77
Estuary English 39
euphemisms 62
exam advice (general) 104
exclamation marks 56
exclamatives 58
exophoric reference 28
expressive language 69
extended metaphor 22
eye contact 27

F

facial expression 27, 52, 54
feedback 72-73
field 34, 81
figurative language 22, 50, 59, 82
fillers 41, 71
first words 89, 92
fis phenomenon 90
Fitzpatrick (2002) 88
fonts 32, 58

G

gender 41, 46-49, 79
genre 2, 32, 80-81
gestures 27, 52, 54
grammar 2, 4-5, 34, 36, 38, 48,
  56, 58, 70
grammatical structure 29
graphemes 33
graphological cohesion 29
graphology 2, 32-33, 58

Index

H

Halliday (1975) 91
head words 6, 12, 60
hedging 71
hiatus 25
Holmes (1984) 46
holophrases 93
hyperbole 23, 50
hypernyms 21
hyponyms 21

I

ideology 84-85
idiolect 36, 41
imagery 82
imitation 96
imperatives 50-51, 58
implication 20
implicit meaning 84
infinitives 8
inflections 5, 8, 94
influence 85
informative texts 76
innateness 96
instructional texts 76
insults 48
intensifiers 46
interaction 91
interactional language 69
internalisation 94
internet 55, 62
interpretation 27, 30, 85
interrogatives 58
interruption 47, 51, 71-72, 79
intertextuality 59
intonation 15, 26, 30, 36, 52, 54

J

jargon 22, 52, 58, 62
juxtaposition 32

K

Katamba (1996) 94

L

language acquisition device (LAD) 96
language acquisition support system (LASS) 97
Lakoff (1975) 46
leading 32
legal language 62
Lenneberg (1967) 97

lexical

asymmetry 48
cohesion 29
fields 20
gap 48
phrases 18
lexicon 50
lexis 2, 18-20, 34, 56, 58, 60, 70, 78
field-specific 81
liaison 25
literary texts 37, 82-83
loan words 18

M

management speak 63
manipulation 84
manner 34
media 56-59, 84-85, 101
Mehler et al (1988) 88
metaphors 22, 82
metonymy 22
mobile phones 54
mode 2, 34-35
monologue 68, 82
monosyllabic words 19, 24
morphemes 16-17
morphology 4, 16-17
multi-modal texts 35
multiculturalism 42

N

narrative voice 82
narratives 84
negatives, development of 95
Nelson (1973) 92
neologisms 18
netiquette 55
non-standard language 46
non-verbal communication 26-27, 35, 52, 54
noun phrases 6, 12
nouns 4, 6
numerals 10

O

O'Barr and Atkins (1980) 46
object 12-13
object permanence 96
occupational language 60-61, 63
OCR
coursework 113
exam 112
sample question 112
Old English 18-19

omniscient narrator 82
onomatopoeia 25, 58, 83
overextension 92
over-representation 48
oxymoron 22

P

pace 26, 30, 52
paralinguistic features 70
parallelism 83
parody 59
parts of speech 4, 18
pauses 26
personification 22, 82
persuasive texts 76
Petitto and Holowka (2002) 88
phatic language 35, 69, 71, 73
phonemes 24, 54
contraction 89
expansion 89
phonological development 90
phonology 2, 24-25, 34, 58
phrases 12
pitch 26, 30, 52
Plain English Campaign 52, 63
plays 82
plurals 4
poetry 25, 82
politeness 31, 50
political correctness 49, 53
polysyllabic words 19, 24, 56
post-modifiers 6, 12-13
posture 27, 52
power 50-53
pragmatics 2, 30-31, 58
preconceptions 85
prefix 16-17
prejudice 56, 84
pre-modifiers 6, 12-13, 60
prepared speech 70
prepositions 4, 11
prestige 46, 52, 70
pre-verbal 88
pronouns 4, 10, 15, 48, 63
demonstrative 10, 28
interrogative 10
reflexive 63
pronunciation 26, 34, 36
prose 82
prosody 2, 26, 30, 35, 70
proto-words 89, 91
punctuation 35, 56, 70
puns 57, 59
purpose 34, 76-77

Index

Q

quantifiers 10
questions 50, 95

R

radio 54
readership 79
reading (learning to) 98-99, 101
received pronunciation 39-40, 46, 52
reference 28
referential language 69
register 2, 34
religion 41, 85
repetition 23, 29, 47, 50, 60, 83
representation 84-85
Rescorla (1980) 92
rhetorical
    devices 23, 50
    language 83
    questions 23
rhyme 25, 58, 60, 83
rhythm 25-26

S

scripted performance 68
semantic fields 20
semantic function 16
semantics 2, 20-23, 48
sentence structure 14
sentences 14-15
    complex 14
    compound 14
    declarative 15, 60
    discursive 58
    disjunctive 58
    exclamative 15
    imperative 15
    interrogative 15
serifs 32
Sex Discrimination Act 49
sexism 48-49
similes 22, 82
simplification 90
Skinner (1957) 96
slang 19, 40, 42-43, 55, 56
social taboos 42
socio-cultural theory 97
sociolect 36, 40, 42, 60
sound symbolism 25
speech 70-71
spelling 38
spoken language 68-69
spontaneous speech 68, 70

Standard English 19, 35, 37-40,
    42-43, 52, 55
stereotypes 37, 59, 84
stress 26, 52, 54
sub-genre 81
subject 12-13
subtext 30
suffix 16-18, 48-49
syllables 24-25
symbolism 82
synonyms 18, 21, 29
syntax 2, 4, 38, 48, 58, 60, 63, 93

T

tabloids 14, 57
tag questions 15, 46
Tannen (1990) 47
technology 54-55
telegraphic stage 93
telephone 54
television 54
tense 5, 8, 61, 70
three-part list 23, 50, 60
tone 14, 78
transactional language 69
transcripts 37
Trudgill (1983) 46
turn-taking 72-73
typefaces 29, 32-33
typology 35

U

underextension 92
unresponsiveness 51

V

verb phrases 12
verbs 4, 8-9, 12-13
    auxiliary 8, 12
    main 8
    modal auxiliary 8
    prepositional 60
    primary auxiliary 8
visual representations 33
vocabulary 2, 36, 38, 92
voice 9
volume 26
vowels 24
Vygotsky (1978) 97

W

WJEC
    coursework 115
    exam 114
    sample question 114
word classes 4, 18, 60
Workman (2008) 37
writing 98
    development stages 99
'Wug' Test 94

Z

Zimmerman and West (1975) 47
zone of proximal development (ZPD)
    97